GOING GLOBAL ON A SHOESTRING

GOING GLOBAL ON A SHOESTRING

GLOBAL EXPANSION IN THE SOFTWARE INDUSTRY ON A SMALL BUDGET

BY

HANS PETER BECH

The use of the Business Model Generation framework and illustrations are courtesy of the Strategyzer® (The Business Model Foundry GmbH) Kalkbreitestrasse 71, 8003 Zürich, Switzerland,

www.businessmodelgeneration.com

TBK Publishing® (an activity of TBK Consult ApS)
Leerbjerg Lod 11
DK-3400 Hilleröd
Denmark
CVR: DK27402917
www.tbkconsult.com/publishing
hpb@tbkconsult.com

ISBN 978-87-93116-28-3 (printed version)

TABLE OF CONTENTS:

TABLE OF CONTENTS ____ 5
FOREWORD BY MARYLOU TYLER _____________________________________ 9
PREFACE ____ 12
IN THE MIDDLE OF A PANDEMIC ____________________________________ 12
SMALL CAN BE BEAUTIFUL ____ 12
IS SOFTWARE AN INDUSTRY? _______________________________________ 14
WHY USE A SHOESTRING IN THE FIRST PLACE ________________________ 16

CHAPTER ONE - INTRODUCTION ____________________________________ 19
ABOUT THIS CHAPTER ____ 19
HOW LONG IS A SHOESTRING? ______________________________________ 20
BUSINESS DEVELOPMENT ____ 21
MARKETING AND SALES ____ 21
PHYSICAL VERSUS VIRTUAL ____ 23
THE VIRTUAL COMPANY ____ 24
THE PHYSICAL COMPANY ____ 26
THE METHODICAL FRAMEWORK _____________________________________ 26
ABBREVIATIONS AND DEFINITIONS __________________________________ 27
OVERVIEW ____ 31
SOFTWARE-AS-A-SERVICE ____ 33

CHAPTER TWO - TALES FROM THE TRENCHES _______________________ 35
ABOUT THIS CHAPTER ____ 35
THE PROJECT IN SAUDI ARABIA _____________________________________ 35
DATACO ____ 37
MERCANTE ____ 38
A MATTER OF LIFE AND DEATH _____________________________________ 39
SETTING YOUR AIMS HIGH ____ 40
WHEN THE TIMING TURNS PROBLEMATIC ___________________________ 41
TAKING IT TO GLOBAL MARKET LEADERSHIP ________________________ 41
TAKE-AWAYS FROM THIS CHAPTER __________________________________ 42

CHAPTER THREE - METHODOLOGICAL FRAMEWORKS ________________ 45
CAN YOU LEARN FROM THE SUCCESSES OF OTHERS? __________________ 45
DIFFUSION OF INNOVATIONS ____ 47
THE BUSINESS MODEL FRAMEWORK _________________________________ 53
ADJUSTING THE BUSINESS MODEL FOR A FOREIGN MARKET ___________ 61
TAKE-AWAYS FROM THE CHAPTER __________________________________ 64

CHAPTER FOUR - THE VIRTUAL COMPANY ___________________________ 66
INTRODUCTION ____ 66
DEFINITION ____ 66
THE FOUR TYPES OF VIRTUAL BUSINESSES ___________________________ 67
VERY SIMPLE ____ 68

SIMPLE 69
COMPLEX 70
VERY COMPLEX 71
LANGUAGE 76
BASECAMP 78
XINK 79
GROWING A VIRTUAL BUSINESS 80
TAKE-AWAYS FROM THIS CHAPTER 82

CHAPTER FIVE - THE PHYSICAL COMPANY 84
INTRODUCTION 84
THE MISTAKES YOU WILL WANT TO AVOID 86
THE SHOESTRING ROLE MODEL 87
THE SEVEN APPROACHES 87
THE TRADITIONAL APPROACH 89
DOMESTIC MARKETS ARE DIFFERENT 91
THE INDIRECT MODEL 91
THE UNEXPECTED OPPORTUNITY 99
THE NARROW GORGE 106
THE TROJAN HORSE 111
THE NAVISION MODEL 114
USING EXTERNAL RESOURCES 118
MERGERS AND ACQUISITIONS 123
TAKE-AWAYS FROM THE CHAPTER 125

CHAPTER SIX - BUSINESS MODEL CONSIDERATIONS 127
INTRODUCTION 127
BUSINESS MODEL ENVIRONMENT 128
MARKET CONDITIONS 137
INDUSTRY CONDITIONS 139
MACRO-ECONOMIC CONDITIONS 141
TAKE-AWAYS FROM THIS CHAPTER 143

CHAPTER SEVEN - INTERNATIONALISATION AND LOCALISATION 144
INTRODUCTION 144
LOCALISATION MATTERS 145
SEVEN MEAGRE YEARS 145
FIRST THE CONTRACT THEN THE LOCALISATION 146
FIRST LOCALISATION THEN SALES 147
EDLUND AND NORWAY 148
TAKE-AWAYS FROM THIS CHAPTER 149

CHAPTER EIGHT - BECOMING A THOUGHT LEADER - GENERATING INBOUND LEADS ON A SHOESTRING BUDGET____150
   INTRODUCTION____150
   STEP 1: KNOW YOUR TARGET AUDIENCE AND HOW THEY BUY____151
   STEP 2: CONTENT CREATION____153
   STEP 3: BUILD A BLOG____156
   STEP 4: PICK YOUR SOCIAL MEDIA PLATFORMS____159
   STEP 5: REVISE AND ENRICH YOUR LINKEDIN PROFILE____159
   STEP 6: POST AND ENGAGE REGULARLY____160
   STEP 7: FOLLOW YOUR CUSTOMERS____161
   STEP 8: INCREASING YOUR 1ST LEVEL NETWORK____162
   STEP 9: INTERACTING____164
   STEP 10: TAKING THE CONVERSATION OFFLINE____165
   ORGANIC DISTRIBUTION____165
   TAKE-AWAYS FROM THIS CHAPTER____166

CHAPTER NINE - ESTABLISHING PRODUCTIVE PARTNERSHIPS____168
   INTRODUCTION____168
   THE BUSINESS MODEL IN YOUR BUSINESS MODEL____168
   STRATEGIC OR TACTICAL PARTNERSHIPS____169
   EM AND WHITE LABEL____172
   STRATEGIC ALLIANCES____173
   GREAT START, TROUBLESOME ENDING____174
   TAKE-AWAYS FROM THIS CHAPTER____175

CHAPTER TEN - PICKING THE NEXT MARKET____177
   INTRODUCTION____177
   MARKET ANALYSIS____177
   GOVERNMENT INCENTIVES____179
   LANGUAGE____183
   SOCIAL PHYSICS____184
   MARKET SIZE____185
   HYPE____186
   THE UNEXPECTED OPPORTUNITY____187
   TAKE-AWAYS FROM THIS CHAPTER____191

CHAPTER ELEVEN - THE HUMAN DIMENSION____192
   INTRODUCTION____192
   FROM GOOD TO GREAT____193
   THE FOUR INGREDIENTS____195
   FINDING THE MEMBERS FOR THE BUSINESS DEVELOPMENT TEAM____199
   MAKE YOURSELF ATTRACTIVE____202

GO FOR THE BROAD SKILL SETS — 204
AVOID THE NAPOLEONS — 206
BECOME A GREAT PLACE TO WORK — 207
TAKE-AWAYS FROM THIS CHAPTER — 208

CHAPTER TWELVE – CASES — 209
OVERVIEW — 209
AGILLIC – FACILITATING THE BUYER'S JOURNEY — 210
DAINTEL – A MATTER OF LIFE OR DEATH — 214
EDLUND A/S - IT-SYSTEMS FOR A VERY EXCLUSIVE MARKET — 218
EPIC - A GENUINE SHOESTRING APPROACH — 222
EUROMAX - A COMPLETE MANAGEMENT SOLUTION FOR NEWSPAPERS — 231
FIRST AGENDA - SOFTWARE FOR BETTER AND MORE EFFECTIVE MEETINGS — 240
FORECAST – A SOLUTION FOR PROJECT-DRIVEN COMPANIES — 243
FOTOWARE - DIGITAL ASSET MANAGEMENT (DAM) – MADE IN NORWAY — 247
IT MINDS – WHERE YOUNG BRAINS ARE NEEDED — 252
MAPSPEOPLE – SHOWING THE WAY TO THE GLOBAL MARKETS — 255
MERCANTE — 259
MONITOR ERP SYSTEM - OPTIMISATION UNDER CONSTRAINTS — 268
NAVISION — 271
NETDIALOG – WHEN IT-PERFORMANCE MATTERS — 284
NORRIQ – AN INTERNATIONAL MICROSOFT DYNAMICS VAR AND ISV — 288
PENNEO - CLOUD-BASED DIGITAL SIGNATURES — 292
PROMANAGE — 295
PRONESTOR – WHEN PHYSICAL MEETINGS ARE A PART OF YOUR VALUE PROPOSITION — 300
RAMBASE - CLOUD-BASED ERP FROM NORWAY — 304
SALES FORCE EUROPE - REVENUE GENERATION AS AS SERVICE — 309
SCANDINAVIAN DATACO — 316
SOFT4 - FROM LITHUANIA TO THE REST OF THE WORLD — 327
SOFTSCAN — 330
SOLVOYO – SUPPLY CHAIN OPTIMISATION — 345
TEMPLAFY — 349
TIA TECHNOLOGY – AN INDUSTRY IN DISRUPTION AND GROWTH — 354
TIMEXTENDER — 361
TRUSTPILOT – THE OPEN PLATFORM FOR MANAGING CUSTOMER REVIEWS — 364
UNICONTA – ERP FOR THE SMB IN THE CLOUD — 370
XINK – AN INBOUND SUCCESS STORY — 374
XOLO - SUPPORTING THE GIG-ECONOMY — 380

APPENDIX 1 — 387

ACKNOWLEDGEMENTS — 390

ABOUT THE AUTHOR — 392

FOREWORD BY MARYLOU TYLER

THE software industry is fascinating. It's young, and the time and money required to turn a new and innovative idea into a product keep shrinking. The cloud platforms provided by the big players, that enables delivering software as a service everywhere, have removed many of the technical obstacles that previously restricted software installation and use. In contrast, all we need today to install and use software is an Internet browser or a simple download of an app.

In line with Marc Andreessen's renown Op-ed published on August 20, 2011, in the Wall Street Journal, titled *Why Software Is Eating the World[1]*, software has crept into all walks of life. There is hardly a business process in any company that doesn't need, or least can benefit materially from running on a software platform.

Where software sales professionals in the past were referred to the busy and unapproachable CIO, today that is no longer the case. Conversely, line managers with a budget can drive a software buying journey, and the subscription format has made purchasing decisions less complicated. The bar for acquiring software-based products has been significantly lowered.

1. https://www.wsj.com/articles/SB10001424053111903480904576512250915629460

2. Kim, W. C., & Mauborgne, R. (2004). Blue ocean strategy: competing in overcrowded industries is no way to sustain high performance. The real opportunity is to create blue oceans of uncontested market space. Boston, MA.

In addition to easy access and download of software, the Internet has tied together all businesses across the globe. Enter your keywords in a search engine, and milliseconds later you get a list of sources ordered according to relevance. It is even very likely that you can find your potential customers by name on social platforms like LinkedIn, send them a message, and start a conversation.

With more sales opportunities, easier access and more transparency, what's not to like if you are a freshly minted tech-company with a great product?

With the growing market and the shrinking barriers of entry, the supply of software products has exploded. In parallel, the proliferation of the Internet and social media have together created a massive wall of noise that stands between you and your potential customer. Add to this challenge the fact that many innovative software solutions set sail in a blue ocean and therefore don't fall into an existing category with established terminology.

It requires more time and effort to educate your target audience in understanding and appreciating what your novel product does and how it helps them. And even if your innovative and extraordinary product delivers measurable results, your target audience has to be aware of it, recognise their need for it, and know how to search for and research how it benefits them.

What do you do then, when you have a great product, but no real budgets to buy the attention of your potential customers?

Lucky for you, that's the subject of this book written by my colleague, Hans Peter Bech. Over the last forty years, Hans Peter has been successful in deploying the principles taught in this book and teaching professionals and companies to do the same. Because the windows of opportunity in the software industry can be narrow, Hans Peter's book applies a global perspective to revenue generation.

The objective for most software companies is no longer limited to only winning customers domestically. Instead, demonstrating that you can grow across national borders immediately increases the value of any software company, even yours. It gives you access to the broadest possible market and paves the road for taking your company in any direction you want.

If you're intrigued and want to learn a process for opening doors to global markets, I believe you'll find Hans Peter's book a worthwhile read.

Enjoy!

Marylou Tyler
Des Moines, Iowa, USA

Marylou Tyler is the author of *Predictable Revenue: Turn Your Business Into a Sales Machine with the $100 Million Best Practices of Salesforce.com* with Aaron Ross[3] and *Predictable Prospecting: How to Radically Increase Your B2B Sales Pipeline* with Jeremey Donovan.[4]

---

3. Aaron Ross, Marylou Tyler (2011). Predictable Revenue: Turn Your Business Into a Sales Machine with the $100 Million Best Practices of Salesforce.com. PebbleStorm.
4. Tyler, M., Donovan, J. (2016). Predictable Prospecting: How to Radically Increase Your B2B Sales Pipeline.

PREFACE

IN THE MIDDLE OF A PANDEMIC

I have written this book to help small B2B software companies (with a staff of between 20 and 200 people) find ways to adjust and make their business model work in foreign markets. Because entering foreign markets is the path to long term prosperity.

By March 2020, I was well underway with the manuscript when a pandemic suddenly hit us. We have had pandemics before, but a comparable one, such as the Spanish Flu, was more than a hundred years ago. The Swine Flu that started in North America in 2009 didn't seem to be the benchmark.

How do you go global on a shoestring when borders close, airlines stop operating, global supply chains break down, the economy falls like a stone, and you need to wear a face mask when going out?

Indeed, some activities have temporarily been rendered impossible, but others have changed for the better. In the chapter describing the virtual business scenario, I explain how the Covid-19 pandemic has moved the thresholds in your favour. Suddenly you can accomplish much more without meeting people in person. Some of these thresholds have moved permanently, while others will swing back when we have the virus behind us.

The recession caused by Covid-19 will not last forever and it will not fundamentally change how we do business in the software industry, but it may have an impact here and there. I do refer to Covid-19 now and then, but this is not a book about how to overcome or take advantage of a pandemic. A book on that subject would certainly be relevant, but it would be short-lived. It would also be hard to write because the Covid-19 pandemic affects businesses very differently.

A company, where I sit on the advisory board, experienced a forty per cent reduction in revenue. Because they are reasonably consolidated, they decided to reorganise and invest in additional sales resources.

Suffering from the recession, customers suddenly had more time to talk about what should change on the other side of the pandemic. The company managed to book virtual meetings with potential customers that previously were too busy, and they will come out of the recession with a very strong pipeline.

SMALL CAN BE BEAUTIFUL

I come from Denmark. We are a small country with a little over five million people. We speak Danish, but most of us speak reasonable English also, and some of us even speak three or more foreign languages such as German, French or Spanish.

Denmark represents less than 0.5 per cent of global demand for anything. This is probably the reason why most Danish software companies enter foreign markets very early in their lifecycle and at stages where most of them only have limited investment capabilities. They get attracted by the promise of the 99.5 per cent of the global market that is elsewhere, they can get a long way with English, German, French and Spanish as their second or third language, but need to find inexpensive hacks[5] to win customers and business partners.

They want and need to go global on a shoestring.

A great example are the products behind Microsoft's Dynamics 365, where the ERP (Enterprise Resource Planning) components originate from the Danish company Navision. You can find the details of how that happened in my book, *5,460 Miles from Silicon Valley - The In-depth Case Study of What Became Microsoft's First Billion Dollar Acquisition Outside the USA.*[6]

---

5. https://tbkconsult.com/why-growth-hacking-can-never-be-common-practice/

6. Bech, H. P. (2018). 5,460 Miles from Silicon Valley - The In-depth Case Study of What Became Microsoft's First Billion Dollar Acquisition Outside the USA (S. Quirke Køngerskov, Trans. A. Hagel Ed.). Copenhagen: TBK Publishing®.

While getting access to international markets is extremely attractive and will multiply the value of any software company that succeeds, this is probably also the most difficult step you can take. As difficult as getting the business started in the first place. Especially if you are on a tight budget.

In this book, I will share my experience and what I believe are fundamental principles that can be used by any small software company that has a great product, but only limited funds. My ambition has been to make this the handbook for how to enter foreign markets without betting the farm and failing fatally on the first attempt.

Calling it a handbook doesn't imply that there is a single and linear approach that will lead to success for anyone anywhere. Such an approach doesn't exist. Instead, it implies that you will find practical examples and down to earth discussions relevant to the subject. You can take away and try out those ideas that you find applicable to your business case.

It is on purpose that I mainly use case stories from companies that you probably don't know. Because no one knows you either. That's the main characteristic of your challenge. How to get business in a new market when you are a complete unknown and only have limited resources available.

IS SOFTWARE AN INDUSTRY?

I claim that this book is for people in the software industry working with getting the first revenue flowing from foreign markets. But is the software industry really an industry? Does Epic, a company developing highly sophisticated software for managing the care of patients in hospitals, have anything in common with XINK, a company developing software for the central management of e-mail signatures? Where Epic has to work with individual, formal, comprehensive and public request for proposals (RFPs) and must entertain complicated and elongated purchase processes followed by massive implementation and integration projects, XINK will experience customers downloading a trial and later purchasing a subscription with their credit card. Do they really have anything in common?

Yes, and more than what you see at first glance.

All software companies face the challenges associated with lack of observability (a phenomenon that I describe in more detail in chapter three). B2B software is invisible, which makes it hard for customers to quickly understand what it is, what it does, how it works and how fast it can be implemented and deliver the value it promises.

Further, the value of B2B software depends on how it gets implemented and used. The benefit of using business software is always situational depending on the user's ability to climb the learning curve and get familiar with the facilities. The same software can improve one person's or organisation's productivity while it appears as a nightmare for another even when they perform similar jobs and functions.

When you are not an established brand, and potential customers do not know what you do, then you have a hard time getting your messages across because a picture or two will not tell the story. It takes genuine creativity to explain your position and your value proposition.

When I started working with XING in the mid-2000s most customers thought that the company was providing digital signatures. Probably because only a few customers knew that managing e-mail signatures was an issue about which they should care. Customers focused on the word "signatures" and instinctively replaced "e-mail" with "digital." XINK needed to explain their category first before they could talk about the product.

The best way to overcome the observability challenge is to become a globally recognised brand. Today, all the customers asking Epic to submit an RFP know very well what their software does. Not necessarily because they have ever worked with it, but because Epic has become a well-known brand in the market for managing electronic health records. Anyone anywhere in the world working with IT in healthcare will know who Epic is and have a good feeling for what they do. It wasn't always so, and Epic chose to work the domestic market for 28 years before they landed their first international project outside North America.

Almost all business software companies share the lack of observability challenge, which gives them common difficulties when expanding internationally.

WHY USE A SHOESTRING IN THE FIRST PLACE

Epic represents the traditional approach to expanding internationally. You concentrate on your domestic market first and become the market leader there. With the support of your leading position and the funds you have accumulated, you then expand internationally.

Today only a few companies will take that route.

Why?

When the owners are afraid of missing out.

Markets for software-solutions tend to be global with seemingly low barriers for entry. If you don't grow globally, your competitors will. They will then grow faster than you, make it more difficult for you to come next and eventually even turn up at your doorstep and challenge your comfortable position at home. In scenarios with externalities and network effects, this risk is even more profound. Take a look at Trustpilot, which is such a case, although not precisely a shoestring role model.

When the domestic market is too small.

Take Tia Technology and Edlund that develop solutions for the insurance industry and RamBase, Monitor and Uniconta that develop ERP systems for selected industries. Even if they managed to get past the 20 per cent market share domestically, it would not be enough to uphold the development activities required for the software to keep up with its international competitors. Because of the global transparency in today's markets, you cannot price your solutions very differently from your competitors, and you cannot afford a substantial gap in features and functionality. Even when there are considerable barriers for entry in the national markets, the customers will begin to consider other alternatives.

When the owners are looking for an attractive exit.

It is beyond doubt that the valuation you can obtain at a liquidity event will be much more attractive if you can demonstrate international growth compared to just showing domestic activities. If an exit is your primary objective, then global expansion appears urgent.

When it is more exciting selling abroad than at home.

I must admit that I am a victim of this point of view. When, in 1986, I left my well-paid job as a sales manager for Control Data's subsidiary in Denmark to join a freshly minted start-up, I was primarily motivated by the opportunity for doing business development abroad. I had to spend the first twelve months getting a healthy customer base domestically before I could appoint a sales manager and devote myself to international expansion. I loved flying around, finding resellers in other countries, and help them get their business going. Working for a Danish company selling worldwide was so much more fun and satisfying than working for a foreign company selling into Denmark. I know that I am not alone in having this bias, and many internationalisation projects are driven by people who simply just find it more fun and meaningful.

When it's hard getting customers domestically.

I once worked for a company where this was the rationale. We had a solution for a market where there were only a handful of potential customers in Denmark. For various reasons, none of these customers were in the market for a new solution when I came on board. We threw all our resources into international activities and won customers in Belgium, New Zealand and the USA. We could only do so because the company had profitable operations in other industries, which could fund our international business development efforts.

Because it is possible and attractive.

When it comes to establishing international supply chains, the software industry is quite fortunate. You don't need to build factories, warehouses and repair shops. You don't need a fleet of vehicles and technicians to service your customers. In some cases, you need to run on-site pre-sales workshops and implementation work, but mostly you can do it virtually. Getting and serving customers in other countries can often be achieved with minimal additional cost, which makes the gross margin you can generate handsome.

You see, there are different reasons for expanding internationally. I don't think that there are any general guidelines for when you should embark on the international expansion. I used to recommend the traditional approach of building a solid base at home first, but I don't do that anymore. In some situations, that's the way to go, and in other cases, it is not. The best timing is entirely contextual and often based on an opportunity suddenly popping up.

I do think, though, that you have to be very careful in not jeopardising your core business at home. Never bet the farm. Going global will take longer and cost more than you expected. Make sure you can afford it or stop before it threatens what you already have.

Hans Peter Bech

Copenhagen, September 2020

CHAPTER ONE - INTRODUCTION

ABOUT THIS CHAPTER

In this chapter, I will clarify what and how long a shoestring is. I will introduce you to the difference between business development and marketing-sales. Knowing and understanding this difference will save you time and help you avoid the most trivial pitfalls when entering new markets.

When I participate in discussions about international expansion, I often experience that we lack a common vocabulary. Much time is spent clearing up misunderstandings because each of us has a slightly different perception of the words we use. What is the difference between a market and an industry? Are a market and a country the same? What is the difference between a lead, a prospect and a potential customer? When is a lead or a prospect qualified? What is a value proposition? What is a position? Is there a global market? What is a business model, and what is the business model environment? How do you define the ideal customer profile? How do you define a market segment? What is the law of diffusion of innovation? Does it apply to you?

To overcome this dilemma, I will introduce you to the main definitions of business concepts and to the vocabulary you can use when you want to conquer new markets.

Although this book is written specifically for software companies, there is still a big difference in the challenges that you face depending on which type of product and revenue generation process you entertain. I propose, therefore, to introduce you to the two revenue generation approaches that demonstrate the most significant difference in how you can expand internationally: The virtual approach and the physical approach.

After introducing the methodology toolboxes with which I believe you need to be familiar, I will provide you with an overview of the book that may help you decide in which order to read the chapters.

Finally, for the sake of good order, I will discuss how the change from the on-premise prepaid perpetual license format to the cloud-based Software-as-a-Service format has affected the options for international expansion.

HOW LONG IS A SHOESTRING?

As the title of the book suggests, my approach doesn't require massive investments. A shoestring is an aphorism for minimal financial means. Going global on a shoestring means expanding internationally on a small budget.

So how much is that? How small is small?

As with anything else in business, that depends, but let's just say that it is an amount of money that you can afford to lose.

If you are venture-funded, then you can, by definition, lose more than you personally can afford because you can also lose the investors' money. That option is not available if you bootstrap. The venture-funded model is per definition, not a shoestring approach. However, if you bring in external funding to scale a business model that you have proven works abroad, then the first part of the journey could have been done on a shoestring. Venture funded software companies are welcome to read along and take away what they believe also applies to them.

Going Global on a Shoestring is a book about how to get *the first* customers outside your domestic market. We could call it establishing the bridgeheads or the foundation for further growth. Getting the foundation in place and then scaling it to market leadership[7] are two very different tasks. This book is mainly about the first task and not so much about the other.

Building the bridgehead in a foreign country or the foundation for international sales is mostly a *business development* effort.

Growing to market leadership is always a *marketing and sales* effort.

---

7. Market leadership typically requires getting past a market share of 20 per cent.

BUSINESS DEVELOPMENT

Business development is the discipline of finding a fit between your product[8] and a *well-defined* segment in the market, which is not completely saturated by competitors. You can also call this your position. With well-defined, I mean that you can quickly identify potential customers with identical characteristics that will very likely have a compelling need for your product now or in the foreseeable future. Likewise, potential customers can quickly identify with you as a relevant supplier of software that is important to them. During their buying journeys, such customers will look for the same kind of information and require the same sort of proof of value.

The objective of the business development effort is finding a business model that can scale. Getting the position right, that is the match between your product or value proposition and a well-defined and available segment in the market, are the critical elements in the quest for a scalable business model.

The business development process will very likely entail adjustments to the features of your current product, your current position and therefore also to the marketing and sales material and the method that you will need for winning customers abroad.

A business development team does not have a sales target and is not on commission plans. The outcome of a business development effort is either the definition of an attractive position or a decision to abandon the market. Both results are legitimate.

MARKETING AND SALES

Marketing and sales are the tactical front-office activities required to scale the business model from the chosen position. You can only do this effectively if your potential customers have fairly identical needs

---

8. Throughout the book, I use the term "products" for any combination of products and services that you sell to your customers.

and buying journeys[9]. The objective of marketing and sales is *scaling* the revenue generation process. This requires investing in marketing activities that can take the same messages to more potential customers and in people that can help the customers with fairly identical needs to complete their buying journey.

Marketing and sales are the labels for the process of systematically generating revenue with the product in the chosen market from a particular position in the race for market leadership. You can predictably scale the revenue generation process by investing more in marketing activities and by adding more salespeople. You know what it takes to generate more leads, and you know which skills are required for performing the sales portion of the revenue generation process.

Understanding the difference between business development and marketing-sales is the key to success, in foreign markets, too! The number one reason for failure in getting an international business up and running is approaching the opportunity as a tactical marketing and sales task. Sometimes it is, but mostly it is not. It depends on your product and the nature of the new market. If the business model environment is the same as at home, then it is a marketing and sales task. If the business model environment is different, then you need to complete the business development process first.

The reason that we mix up business development and sales is that on the surface they look very much the same. Both sets of activities require getting appointments with customers and having conversations about their needs, requirements, plans and expectations. It is the objective of these conversations that are very different.

As this book is written for software companies looking to get their first international customers, I assume that they are looking to expand

---

9. Lewis, M. R. (2018). How Customers Buy…& Why They Don't: Mapping and Managing the Buying Journey DNA: Radius Book Group.

their current business model into foreign markets. This is not just a semantic nuance. A small company cannot run multiple business models at the same time. For new markets, we may need to adjust a few things in our current business model, but the basic building blocks must remain the same.

PHYSICAL VERSUS VIRTUAL

There are two fundamentally different scenarios when it comes to building an international business:

1. Revenue generation abroad doesn't require that you have people on the ground.

2. Revenue generation abroad requires that you have people on the ground.

In the context of this book, a business is considered virtual when it *can generate customers with no or only an inside salesforce.*

A business is considered physical when *it needs an outside salesforce to meet face-to-face with customers* during their buying journey.

The difference is immense and represents opposed levels of complexity and risk. Moving from a one-location operation to a distributed organisation is a massive step for any company. It increases the complexity of the endeavour substantially. Add to that a second language, one or more time zones and a different culture and the magnitude of the complexity increases further.

Because the differences between the two situations are so fundamental, I have devoted a chapter to each of them. After the general introduction to the methodological frameworks, I first have a chapter on the virtual business and then a chapter on the physical business.

THE VIRTUAL COMPANY

You will find virtual software companies such as Basecamp[10], Automattic[11], the company behind WordPress, and XINK, the latter a case study in this book, that have people spread across numerous geographical locations. These companies don't see any value in having their people working in the same building. Doesn't that contradict my claim that managing people in remote locations adds substantial complexity to an operation?

No.

What I am talking about above is the sales stage of the revenue generation process. Not product development, administration, marketing and support.

Basecamp, Automattic and XINK don't have any salespeople. They run online marketing activities, which can be designed and executed from anywhere. None of them have people in remote locations because their customers require it.

Instead, these and many other companies have found a way to manage people irrespective of where they are located.

However, managing people spread out all over the globe is complex.

Then why deliberately do so?

I believe there are two reasons and that they are somewhat intertwined:

Many software company founders are not particularly interested in people-management and have no appetite for building corporate empires. They understand that without a great team, they cannot make a great product and scale the company. Accepting that people can work from anywhere in the world gives them access to a vast pool

10. Fried, J., & Hansson, D. H. (2013). Remote Office Not Required. Chicago, USA: Ebury Publishing.

11. Berkun, S., John, W., & Sons. (2013). The year without pants: WordPress.com and the future bof work. San Francisco: Jossey-Bass A Wiley Brandg

of talent. From that pool, they can now find and hire (or otherwise engage) those that prefer to work out of their homes, from a café or smaller remote offices.

Automattic is by design a distributed and virtual company with 1,170 people working out of 76 countries speaking 93 different languages of which English is the common denominator. Basecamp has a staff of 50 people spread out across 32 different cities around the world. Their headquarters is in Chicago, but everyone at Basecamp is free to live and work wherever they want. XING is a much smaller company with people in Denmark, Spain, USA and the Philippines. Most of the XING people are freelancers.

Recruiting and managing people that do not need or want an office, are delighted by working alone and require little supervision match ideally with many software company founders' idea of running a business. Doing so is perfect for product development, support, administration and marketing of a product that is culture and sales agnostic.

Although the virtual business is a growing phenomenon, it is beyond the scope of this book to discuss all the operational aspects. However, several trends are converging and will make this business model more frequent. The gig-economy, the increasing number of digital nomads, the emergence and sophistication of virtual collaboration platforms, the cloud-based software-as-a-service delivery format and the impact of the Covid-19 social-distancing measures will together push the borders for what you can accomplish without people having to meet physically in the same building every day. The Covid-19 pandemic coupled with the effort to reduce CO_2 emissions has moved the thresholds for which types of products are acceptable to buy without at physical face-to-face meeting between customer and supplier and have pushed the limits for which type of collaborative activities you can accommodate virtually. Even explorative workshops have been facilitated virtually as the travel and meeting restrictions were in place.

These trends are good news for the software industry and will make global market penetration so much easier for many.

THE PHYSICAL COMPANY

The definition of the physical company is one that cannot win customers unless they meet with them face-to-face during their buying journeys. To accommodate this need, they must have an outside salesforce.

The most frequent reason for why physical companies fails when trying to break into new markets is that revenue comes much later and requires much more marketing and sales effort than initially expected. Building up a fixed cost base without a predictable revenue generation approach is a toxic cocktail for any small company.

The longer you can postpone having satellite offices with people on the payroll, the lower the risk of over-stretching your investment capacity. *Going global on a shoestring essentially means finding ways to enter new markets without having to set up a subsidiary and put people on the payroll.* You may not be able to avoid taking this step forever, but the longer you can postpone it, the less exposed you are.

THE METHODICAL FRAMEWORK

Although this book is not an academic thesis aiming at proving global rules that apply to everyone (good luck with that!), it does have a methodological foundation. It consists of Everett M. Rodger's principles around Diffusion of Innovations[12] and The Alexander Osterwalder Business Model Framework. If you are not familiar with The *Law of Diffusion of Innovations*, you should read Geoffrey Moore's book *Crossing the Chasm*[13] in which he explains how the law applies to the tech industry. For an introduction to the business model canvass and the business model environment, I recommend reading *Business Model Generation*, by Alexander Osterwalder and Yves Pigneur (2010) or for a shorter introduction you can read Appendix B (pp 139-171) in my book *Building Successful Partner Channels*[14]. Throughout the book, I will use the vocabulary introduced with these principles.

---

12. Rodgers, E. M. (1962). Diffusion of Innovations. New York: The Free Press of Glencoe.

13. Moore, G. A. (2014). Crossing the chasm: Marketing and selling disruptive products to

The Alexander Osterwalder business model environment framework divides, what we in general call the market, into two separate categories: The *market* and the *industry*. You could also call them the demand side of the market and the supply side of the market. In short, the market is our customers and their stakeholders, and the industry is our competitors, business partners and other supply chain stakeholders. While I find that these definitions can be beneficial for our discussions, they are difficult to apply consistently. In economics and business science, the term market includes both the demand and the supply side. I use both sets of definitions in the book, and it should be clear from the context whether the term *market* refers to the demand side only or it also includes the supply side.

ABBREVIATIONS AND DEFINITIONS

I use abbreviations. They are always written out entirely when they appear the first time.

In the context of this book, there is no difference between a market and a country. In essence, the term *entering a new market* just means entering a new country or a new geographic area, which may be only a region of a nation.

The book is entirely focused on the challenges associated with bringing your current products into new geographic territories and not with how you diversify into another product category. The terms *global or international markets* just refer to foreign countries in general. It does not imply that there is a homogeneous global or international market for your product. Sometimes there is but mostly there is not. Global and international are synonyms.

When discussing issues related to business development, marketing and sales, you need to carefully distinguish between leads, prospects, qualified leads and prospects, potential customers and current customers. However, using such a granulated language would make

---

14. Bech, H. P. (2019). *World Demand for Information Technology is Still Heading East (The BECH Index 2019)*. Copenhagen, Denmark. TBK Publishing®

this book hard to read and would not add to your understanding of the specific issues related to international expansion. When using the term *customers*, I primarily refer to potential customers. I use the term *current customers* if I need to refer specifically to companies with whom you have an established relationship. The status of the term customer should be evident in the context. For variation purposes, I may use the term *client* and *customer* synonymously.

I may often use the word *product* to cover both the software (also delivered as a service!) and the professional services required to produce a working solution or system. I may also use the terms *solution, system or products* and services depending on the context and the need for variating the language.

A sales or purchase process is called *simple* when a single person makes the final decision. It's called *complex* when more people are involved.

I distinguish between *inside* sales and *outside* sales. Inside sales are performed without a need to travel to the customer's location for meetings. Outside sales travel a lot because meeting with customers is a crucial element in performing their job.

I also distinguish between inbound and outbound activities. Although these terms are used widely in the industry, they are seldom precisely defined and are often the source of much misunderstanding.

Inbound marketing is non-individualised activities that may motivate people to react. Using inbound marketing principles, customers find you. For inbound marketing activities to be productive, you must have a clear definition of your target audience. Still, you do not have each person in the audience listed by name.

Outbound marketing is individualised activities that may motivate people to react. Using outbound marketing principles, you find and reach out to the customers. For outbound marketing, you need a list with contact details for the people with whom you want to get in touch.

Inbound sales mean that you only respond to incoming inquiries. Customers contact you and initiate the dialogue.

Outbound sales mean that you make unsolicited contacts to potential customers. You contact people that haven't asked to be contacted.

For many marketers, outbound sales mean cold calling prospects on the phone and often that is also what is needed. However, sending a personal email or InMail on LinkedIn first and then calling to follow up is also considered an outbound sales approach.

You mostly combine inbound and outbound marketing and sales activities. Only a few companies can generate enough leads exclusively through their inbound activities, and therefore they also run outbound activities.

There has been much hype around the term inbound marketing recently and the company Hubspot, the leading voice of the inbound movement, writes the following on their website[15]:

Inbound marketing is a business methodology that attracts customers by creating valuable content and experiences tailored to them. While outbound marketing interrupts your audience with content they don't want, inbound marketing forms connections they're looking for and solves problems they already have.

Nobody should want to interrupt their audience with content they don't want. Outbound marketing and sales initiatives can be effective when we work hard on optimising our contact lists and craft relevant opening messages and conversations. I agree that there is a lot of deplorable outbound activities going on and that it is annoying being disturbed by someone who doesn't have a clue about what you do. Still, there is also an equal amount of poor inbound marketing.

---

15. https://www.hubspot.com/inbound-marketing

Inbound is not better or more honourable than outbound. The mix required for generating enough leads for you to meet your revenue targets depends on numerous variables. Some companies are capable of generating enough leads through inbound means, and that's great. Some are not and have to refine their outbound activities to fill the pipeline. It all depends on the type of product you offer, your business model environment and the skills you have represented in your organisation.

The objective is to find the formula that gives the lowest possible customer acquisition cost. If you are on a shoestring budget, the ratio to the customer lifetime value (which may be a number that you do not know) should be around 20 per cent. If it is lower than that, then you may want to invest more in lead generation. If it is over 33 per cent, then you are spending too much.

In general, anything outbound and in particular cold calling sales activities, is expensive, associated with pronounced waste, hard to manage and challenging to scale internationally. Companies looking for shoestring approaches to foreign market entry should explore their inbound options carefully before deciding on taking a predominantly outbound route. If you do take the outbound route, then you should carefully consider how you can divide your marketing and sales processes into subprocesses that can be performed by specialised people. Finding people that can complete the entire revenue generation process from lead identification to closing is almost impossible or at least very hard to accomplish.

The channels and platforms for inbound lead generation are changing dramatically, which may make mastering outbound marketing and sales activities more critical. I recommend you read David Heinemeier Hansson's testimony on _Online Platforms and Market Power_[16], which lays out how the playing field is changing.

The term _conversion_ rate is a measure used in marketing and sales to express the performance of an activity in the revenue generation process. You convert downloads of a white-paper to active leads. You convert various marketing activities to seminar attendees. You convert prospects to customers. And so on. Defining conversion-points and collecting data to measure performance is crucial for monitoring and optimising the revenue generation process as you enter a new country.

I distinguish between the customer's buying journey and the purchase process. The buying journey includes all the steps a customer goes through from coming across our brand to concluding the purchase. The purchase process refers to the final and formal part of that journey where the customer organises the project evaluation and the vendor selection.

OVERVIEW

I have decided to let the book jump right into the action. The next chapter called, "Tales from the Trenches" will give you examples of failures and successes. The stories will speak for themselves, and you can reflect on how you would have done things differently. There are more case stories, thirty in total, with more details in the back of the book to which I make references throughout.

I am sure you know no method can engineer and guarantee success. Still, there are principles and analytical frameworks that can help reduce the risk of failure. I describe those that I find most valuable in chapter three.

In chapter four, I elaborate further on the virtual company, where you don't need to meet face-to-face with your customers and discuss how you can grow globally from anywhere in the world.

Chapter five elaborates on the physical company, where you need to meet face-to-face with your customers. I introduce several shortcuts you can use to win customers without having to first set up a subsidiary and have staff on the payroll.

---

16. https://m.signalvnoise.com/testimony-before-the-house-antitrust-subcommittee/

Each country in the world represents a specific business model environment. In chapter six, I discuss how these environments can differ and what impact it has on your go-to-market approach.

Chapter seven is about product localisation. As this subject is well documented elsewhere, I have chosen to use a couple of case stories to illustrate various approaches to the job.

You are probably familiar with the terms content marketing and thought leadership. They represent a way to engage your international audience on a shoestring budget, and in chapter eight I introduce my ten-step process for how to do this.

Using resellers, distributors, system integrators (SIs), strategic alliances, and other indirect representations are popular in the software industry. For a detailed discussion, you should read my book, *Building Successful Partner Channels*[17]. In chapter nine, I provide a summary of the main principles in an international context.

Looking at a map of the world, how do you decide which country to enter next? That's the theme of chapter ten, where I also discuss the export promotion programs as well as investment attraction programs that all governments offer.

Maybe chapter eleven is the most important. Here I discuss the human dimension. People and timing can make good ideas successful, and great ideas fail. People make a huge difference. In this chapter, I discuss how to select the right people for your project.

Chapter twelve is a collection of thirty case stories. They illustrate the diversity of the software industry and also how different companies approach international expansion.

In appendix one, I have a summary of the software I have used to research and write this book. As you may know, I publish through TBK

---

17. Bech, H. P. (2015). *Building Successful Partner Channels: in the software industry*. Copenhagen, Denmark: TBK Publishing®.

Publishing®, which is the publishing arm of TBK Consult. Apart from distribution, we do everything ourselves, and without the software, this wouldn't be possible.

The book closes with the acknowledgement of those who have contributed to the writing process. As with all books, many more people than just the author are involved.

SOFTWARE-AS-A-SERVICE

A book for and about the software industry must include a discussion of the impact of the cloud-based Software-as-a-Service paid-for-as-a-subscription format.

Ten years ago, business software was still primarily sold in the pre-paid perpetual license format with the option of subscribing to updates and support for an annual fee of between 15 and 20 per cent of the purchase price. The software was then installed and operated from the customer's data centre.

That format is still around, especially in the enterprise segment of the market, but the cloud-based Software-as-a-Service paid-for-as-a-subscription format has now taken the lead.

How does that impact on the job of winning customers abroad?

The adoption rate of the SaaS-format varies from country to country. However, it is my experience that despite these variations, the degree of acceptance is high enough everywhere for anyone to find a receptive audience. That acceptance now carries across all market segments. When I say that the enterprise segment still holds on to the pre-paid perpetual license format, then it doesn't mean that they are not using products delivered in the cloud-based SaaS format, too. They are. Increasingly.

For the vendor, the main commercial difference between the two formats is the cashflow profile. For the customer, it means that the expense item moves from the CAPEX (capital expenditure) to the OPEX (operational expenditure) portion of the P&L (profit and loss) statement. In general, it is much easier for a line manager to take on OPEX than CAPEX. There are other differences as well, and they are described in more detail in the book *Consumption Economics*[18]. However, in the context of this book, the difference in cash flow is the most important.

The subscription format makes the decision threshold for customers lower, and the absence of IT-technical issues offered by the cloud delivery format makes the purchase process somewhat shorter, but not to the degree that will compensate for the difference in the initial prices.

It takes longer to make a subscription-based business cash positive compared to the prepaid format. And that also has implications for using an indirect channel of business partners. The initial investments in knowledge transfer and brand building are the same, but the cashflow takes longer to ramp up and get positive.

The markets decide which formats they prefer, and as soon as the scales tip, you have no other option than to go with the flow. For a small company, maintaining two versions of your software is neither technically nor economically feasible.

This book assumes, unless otherwise explicitly mentioned, that you offer your software as a cloud-based service and that you charge a recurring subscription fee.

---

18. Wood, J. B. H., Todd; Lah, Thomas E. (2011). *Consumption Economics*: The New Rules of Tech. California: Point B Inc.

Chapter Two - Tales from the Trenches

INTRODUCTION

Before digging into the methodologies and international business development principles, I will share some stories from the trenches. I will introduce you to how I came to work within international business development. Then I will highlight a couple of cases that went south and one that went north.

As you read the cases, you can consider what they have in common.

THE PROJECT IN SAUDI ARABIA

My first flirt with international business happened in July 1979 when I, by chance, joined a consortium that was invited to bid for building and running hospital kitchens in At Taif in Saudi Arabia. Together with two other experts (I was by no means an expert, but no one other than me knew that) I spent a week on location in Jeddah and At Taif, Saudi Arabia, doing the research. Back in Copenhagen, my job was to coordinate the design of the conceptual solution and to write the formal proposal that was picked up by a courier a week later.

We didn't win the project, but we didn't have any out-of-pocket expenses either. The local consortium partner covered the costs associated with travelling to and staying in Saudi Arabia. Although the customer chose another supplier, our partner was so pleased with our work, that he invited us to bid for other projects. By then, I had moved on to the software industry, but it had taught me some valuable lessons.

The value the customer or business partner is looking for may not be what you think at first glance and coincidences play a crucial role in everything. Opportunities present themselves all the time. Picking the winning ones is difficult, but if you go for those that are fun to do, then it doesn't matter so much if you should fail.

The project was long before the Internet made the world transparent. In this case, our Saudi Arabian partner found us through the Saudi Arabian Embassy in Copenhagen.

A Saudi Arabian contractor (our partner) suddenly lost their foreign supplier for a project for which they were prequalified. They urgently needed a new partner to deliver products and knowhow and had asked the Saudi Ministry of Foreign Affairs to help identify candidates. Someone at their Copenhagen Embassy recommended talking to my brother, and then he, in turn, called me. I knew nothing about building or running hospital kitchens, but I could speak decent English and I knew how to write. We then found a company that were experts in the subject matter.

When the representatives from the Saudi Arabian company came to Copenhagen a week later, our team of experts was in place.

The value we could provide was not our expertise in building hospital kitchens. I am sure all the bidding vendors could prove they had done that before. The value was our swift response, that we were prepared to go to Saudi Arabia on short notice and our ability to produce a proposal within two weeks. That was what our local partner needed.

Back in 1979, my dream was not building and running hospital kitchens in Saudi Arabia. I was working as an economist for the Danish government, and I took two weeks' vacation to help my brother with the project. Had we won the business we could also have delivered, but it was the project adventure that drove us.

I am confident that this project changed the course of my working life. I didn't know then that this was international business development on a shoestring, but I knew that this was what I wanted to do for a living.

DATACO

I left my job with the government in January 1980 and became a sales trainee in the Danish subsidiary of American Control Data Corporation. For six years, I worked selling American made IT in Denmark. As the products from our mother company became less and less competitive, we started to source locally and designed the solutions that the market wanted. This was when I first got involved with business development in the IT industry.

In 1986 I was very fortunate to get engaged with another shoestring opportunity. I left Control Data for a job as VP marketing and sales in a startup. Less than twelve months after launching our first products in Denmark, Scandinavian **Dataco** started recruiting resellers abroad. Six months later, more than fifty per cent of our revenue came from international operations, and I started looking at overseas markets.

Dataco, which is described in more detail in the back of the book, developed local and wide area network products for PCs, IBM-mainframe and minicomputer systems. The product line was based on the ISO/OSI[19] public standard architecture and included support for Novell Netware and had built-in protocol emulation and conversion for IBM-3270 and DEC VT-100 terminals. The products were delivered with the software embedded in proprietary hardware as appliances.

Dataco went global on a very short shoestring. We managed all our international activities from our Copenhagen office and didn't have anyone abroad on the payroll. If I am to highlight the single most critical success factor (there were more than one), then it must be the perfect match between our products and the chosen target market segment; our position. We had a unique value proposition, and we were able to communicate this match with just a few illustrations.

19. International organisation of Standardisation – Open System Interconnection

We recruited and enabled resellers to take our products to the market and their ability to generate and convert leads was phenomenal. We were so convinced of the value we provided that we asked the resellers to make an upfront investment in a starter kit with products and training. They did, and that was what financed our international growth.

MERCANTE

My next startup was Mercante (also described in the case story section in the back of the book), and now we started international market penetration immediately upon launching the first products. Within twelve months, we had resellers in all West European countries and had started activities in Japan and the USA.

Mercante developed and produced a high performance 25 ppm monochrome LED printer with a sheet capacity of 2,000 pages, a ten or twenty bin sorter and sophisticated software for executing print jobs, addressing sorter bins and hosting digital templates.

Mercante also had a perfect match between the product and the target market, but it wasn't exactly a shoestring approach. The company was venture-funded, and we hired many more people than was the case at Dataco. When we encountered severe product issues, it hit us hard. Downsizing the organisation while we fixed the bugs was a difficult choice to make. So, we didn't.

Poor product quality killed Mercante, and that taught me another lesson. Having a unique product with an attractive value proposition for a well-defined market segment is not enough if you want to force your global expansion. The quality or at least your ability to swiftly fix problems must also be first class. It's not so much that your resellers and customers will run away, it's more your ability to fix the problems before you run out of cash.

A MATTER OF LIFE AND DEATH

Daintel almost went bankrupt because of a failed internationalisation project.

The company, that developed software for hospital intensive care and emergency care units, jumped on an opportunity to enter the Brazilian market. It was during the era of the BRIC hype, where investment gurus were proclaiming promising growth opportunities in Brazil, Russia, India and China. The export arm of the Danish Ministry of Foreign Affairs also urged companies to look at the opportunities in these markets, to which they organised trade missions often headed by government dignitaries.

After spending heavily on travelling back and forth for demonstrations and on having a representative stationed in the country to establish relationships with leading clinicians, the company hit a formal Brazilian compliance and approval process, which it could not afford.

Should they have known that in advance?

Of course, they should, but no one raised a red flag warning that software for health care management that interfaces with and receives data from medical equipment is considered medical equipment too and thus liable to a compliance and approval procedure that takes years. Maybe a joint venture with a Brazilian company could have accelerated and smoothed the approval process, but Daintel was, at that stage, in no position to continue the spending. They had to stop the Brazilian activity and cut company budgets to a minimum.

It took Daintel several years to recover from the Brazilian adventure. Just recently the company was acquired by Swedish Cambio.

In total Daintel invested north of one million Euros in the Brazilian project and that was very close to more than they could afford. When they realised that any revenue was two to four years out, they had to stop the project and downsize the entire company to recover the losses.

SETTING YOUR AIMS HIGH

Another example of a failed internationalisation venture is Swedish **Intentia's** attempt to enter the US market in the mid-1990s. Intentia, founded in 1984, was a very successful provider of ERP software for the IBM AS/400 and S/390 platforms in Europe.

In the mid-1990s, they embarked on an aggressive internationalisation journey, decided to rewrite their product in Java and switched from an indirect to a direct go-to-market approach. To finance the change in product and distribution strategies the company did an IPO (Initial Public Offering) in 1996. Making so many changes at the same time was in itself very risky, but it was the effort associated with trying to get the business established in the US that killed the company.

When hard times hit the ERP market after the millennium, Intentia suffered from declining revenue and increasing losses. So severe were the issues that you could almost calculate the date for the company's final break down. In 2005 Intentia announced that it would merge with Lawson Software, a U.S.-based ERP company that also suffered from a troubled internationalisation track record. The merger process dragged out, but in April 2006 Lawson took over Intentia for a meagre $480 million, compared to Microsoft's acquisition of the much smaller Navision in 2002 for $1.45 billion. The Lawson takeover ended Intentia's ten years of failed effort trying to build a sales and services organisation USA. I do not know how much Intentia invested in its attempt to enter the U.S.-market but it was nowhere near on a shoestring, as it was much more than they could afford. The accumulated losses for the last three years leading up to the merger was SEK 658 million ($68M/€62M). Infor acquired Lawson in 2011.

Intentia's project was by no means on a shoestring budget, and it serves to demonstrate that generous funding is not necessarily the solution.

WHEN THE TIMING TURNS PROBLEMATIC

Scandinavian IT-security company SoftScan decided to enter the German market, established a subsidiary in Munich, posted one of their senior executives as the country manager and hired a team of ten tele-salespeople. After twelve months and having spent well over one million Euros, they stopped the activity and closed down the office. Interviewing the owners about what went wrong, they mentioned that the main reasons were:

1. We expected the business to be cash-positive within twelve months. When that didn't happen, we got nervous.

2. We underestimated the amount of management support required to help the German subsidiary execute our business model and reach break-even.

3. We missed the difference in labour market legislation and had a hard time replacing people that didn't perform.

4. Our business at home dived, and we couldn't continue investing in Germany.

The company knew very well that finding out how to execute the business model in Germany would require substantial experimentation. Still, they were too hung up with activities in their domestic markets to spend enough time with the German country manager and his organisation. When they finally recognised the problem, they faced a recession at home that prevented them from doing anything about it. They then decided to wrap up the activity and close the Munich office.

Symantec later acquired the company.

TAKING IT TO GLOBAL MARKET LEADERSHIP

When Microsoft acquired Navision for 1.45 billion dollars in 2002, the latter operated an ecosystem of more than 2,000 resellers serving over 100,000 customers through 30 subsidiaries or distributors. By then, more than 80 per cent of Navision's revenue came from international activities with customers in more than 90 countries. Although the international activities were accelerated after the IPOs in 1999, the foundation for Navision's international success was based on shoestring approaches.

Navision's international success is remarkable because their products, ERP-systems, do not travel easily across national borders and because they used a two-tier indirect go-to-market model, which is known to take a long time to become productive. You can find the details about the Navision success story in the case story section in the back of the book. You will notice that there were many bumps on the road and that fortunate timing played a crucial role[20].

TAKE-AWAYS FROM THIS CHAPTER

So, what did the cases described have in common?

Not much, right?

I didn't pick the cases to support a fancy theory, because there is none. At least not one where you can claim that if you do A and B, then you will undoubtedly get C. However, there are some rules of thumb.

What you should take away from this chapter is:

1. Don't jump on the first and the best opportunity. Although failing fast is a sound principle, it doesn't mean that you shouldn't think first. Planning is cheap; execution is expensive. Do more research, more thinking and more planning than you would normally do.

2. International activities require substantial management attention. Monitor progress carefully and adjust as needed.

---

20. Bech, H. P. (2018). 5,460 Miles from Silicon Valley - The In-depth Case Study of What Became Microsoft's First Billion Dollar Acquisition Outside the USA (S. Quirke Køngerskov, Trans. A. Hagel Ed.). Copenhagen: TBK Publishing®.

3. You need superior value propositions where it is easy to understand why you are so much better than the alternatives.

4. The timing is crucial. Consider why you think the timing is in your favour and list the factors that support your assumption?

Considering the changes to the business model required for extending your operation to foreign markets, I have found that the need for new management skills and additional leadership capacity is mostly underestimated.

You are so focused on what is required for finding and managing customers abroad that you overlook the need for management resources and competence to set up, monitor, support and adjust the organisation responsible for the activities.

As you get going in a new country and the revenue doesn't flow as fast as you expected you will soon ask yourself if you have misjudged the market or if you have the right people executing the strategy? Is the difference between your plan and the results a people problem or a market problem? Unless you are very close to the team executing the plan and have significant transparency built into your business development processes - including marketing, sales and customer experience - you will not know.

I am not advocating micro-management here, but entering new countries are business development activities which require close monitoring and frequent and in-depth discussions. What is the feedback you receive from the customers, and how are you going to react to it?

The traditional operational management model where you identify the gaps between budget and results and then ask your subordinates to come up with the corrective actions required to get you back on track is not sufficient. You need to employ a cooperative management mindset where you sit on the same side of the table, jointly analyse the information and decide what to do next. When you review the outcome of your most recent moves and conclude that that didn't work either, then you repeat the analysis/action exercise until you find the combination that works. Only then do you scale.

CHAPTER THREE - METHODOLOGICAL FRAMEWORKS

INTRODUCTION

In this chapter, I cover the methods and vocabulary you can use when you want your company to find and apply shoestring approaches to international expansion.

When I use the term "method", you may get the impression that there is a formula for becoming successful. Such as if you do A, B, C, D, E and F then you get H. Unfortunately, that is not the case.

Nevertheless, business books often follow this straightforward formula:

Identify successful companies or people and find out what they have in common. If you do what they did, then you will become successful too.[21]

This approach has a significant scientific flaw called bias. Verifying that certain activities and behaviour always leads to success requires that you have a control group which didn't do the same and then failed. Having picked a few successful companies, your control group has to be all other comparable companies. Hardly any business book that uses successful persons or companies as the basis for recommendations has a serious control group! Their conclusions and recommendations are, therefore, invalid. That's not the same as saying that they cannot inspire, but doing as successful companies and people did will most likely not make you successful. The dilemma is well described in Phil Rosenzweig's book *The Halo Effect*[22].

---

21. Collins, J. (2001). Good to Great : Why Some Companies Make the Leap... and Others Don't: Random House.

22. Rosenzweig, P. (2014). The Halo Effect: . . . and the Eight Other Business Delusions That Deceive Managers: Free Press.

If you hold a pen in your hand and loosen your grip, it will fall to the floor. Each time - it never fails. The natural sciences describe the phenomenon, and the force in play is called the law of gravity. Using the insight provided by the natural sciences, we are capable of predicting and foreseeing the consequences of numerous actions. As long as we can control the environment in which our activities take place, then the predictions can become highly accurate.

The laws of the social sciences govern most aspects of running a business. Are the social sciences just like natural sciences?

Not quite.

Even when we do control the environment (in experiments), the outcome is never the same each time. We have to operate with probabilities and likelihoods. When you expose people to even basic tasks, they will come up with different solutions and responses because people are different.

Claiming that you can become successful by doing what successful people or companies did ignores the fact that the circumstances have to be completely identical, and they never are. NEVER![23]

(Economists use the term ceteris paribus meaning "all other things equal." Without this unrealistic assumption economics could not claim to be science at all.)

Analysing what makes companies or people fail and then learning from their mistakes, is probably the better approach. We know for a fact that there is a much higher ratio of companies and people that do not achieve the results they hoped for and that success is mostly the outcome of correcting mistakes. The main challenge though is that people are not happy talking about their failures and mistakes. Therefore, such an approach leaves us typically with a limited data

---

23. https://www.linkedin.com/pulse/why-you-cannot-learn-success-from-successful-people-companies-bech/

set. Another issue is that what didn't work for me may work for you. Again, because the circumstances were not identical and because you did some minor things differently.

This book uses a mix of the two approaches. I can freely share my own mistakes and failures, but I have also succeeded in making other companies share theirs as well. In some cases, I have had to make the material anonymous, but that should not make the insight less valuable.

Nowhere does this book claim that what worked for one or more companies will also work for yours. Nor do I claim that what failed for some will also fail for you. I will discuss the specific circumstances around the different approaches enabling you to consider if replication could apply to you or not.

DIFFUSION OF INNOVATIONS

Everett Rogers (born 1931) was a farmer's boy from Carroll, Iowa in the midwestern USA. His father loved electromechanical farm innovations but was highly sceptical towards biological–chemical innovations, so he didn't use the new hybrid seed corn, despite its promise of 25% more crop and resistance to drought. During a drought in 1936, where the hybrid seed corn stood tall on the neighbour's farm, the plants on the Rogers' farm wilted. After that, Rogers' father finally gave in, but his change of attitude and behaviour came at a steep price.

Rogers, then an assistant professor of rural sociology at Ohio State University, published his first edition of Diffusion of Innovations in 1962[24].

His theory[25] is quite simple.

---

24. Rodgers, E. M. (1962). Diffusion of Innovations. New York: The Free Press of Glencoe.

25. https://en.wikipedia.org/wiki/Diffusion_of_innovations

The Law of Diffusion of Innovation

In general, people don't embrace change readily. Even when those benefits are obvious and well documented. Adoption of a new idea, behaviour, or product (collectively called an innovation) is a process where some people are more willing to accept the new approach than others. Adoption means that a person does something differently to what they have done previously, such as purchase and use a new product or acquire and perform a new behaviour.

Rodgers found that people who adopt an innovation early have different characteristics than people who adopt it later. When promoting an innovation to a target population, you must understand these characteristics as they will help you accelerate the adoption.

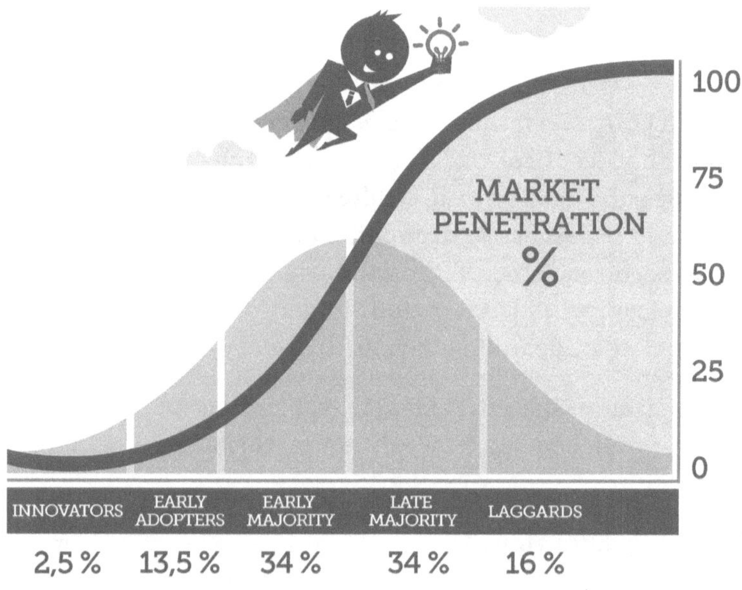

Figure 1: The law of diffusion of innovation.

There are five adopter categories:

The illustration shows an innovation's S-curve and the categories you need to work through to get to the steep section and full adoption.

Beware that many new and brilliant ideas never make it beyond Innovators and Early Adopters!

Innovators - These are people who actively search for innovations on a global scale. If something is genuinely new and offers a substantial productivity improvement, they will find it and check it out. Innovators have global networks and look beyond the borders of their local community for new ideas.

Early Adopters - These are innovators with a local foundation. They embrace new ideas and accept dealing with the risk and uncertainty associated with new and innovative products. However, they do not actively search for inspiration outside their local community.

Early Majority - These people are rarely thought leaders, but they do adopt new ideas before the average person. That said, they typically need to see substantial evidence that the innovation works before they are willing to consider it. The Early Majority prefer to buy from established and recognised market leaders.

Late Majority - These people are sceptical of change and will only adopt an innovation until after the Early Majority has accepted it. The Late Majority prefer to buy after the product or solution has been somewhat commoditised.

Laggards - These people are bound by tradition and are very conservative. They are highly sceptical of change and are the hardest group to bring on board. When Laggards finally are forced to change, they prefer to buy from established market leaders and only after the product or solution has been fully commoditised.

The speed of diffusion

In the B2B environment, only a few have challenged the principles of the law of diffusion of innovation. All innovations will have to travel through Innovators and Early Adopters before they can reach the mainstream market segments.

Everett Rogers lists five characteristics that influence how fast an innovation will diffuse.

Relative Advantage: How much better is your solution compared with the alternatives currently available?

The more significant the difference, the faster the diffusion will be.

Variables giving you relative advantage can be higher productivity, lower price (or lower cost of ownership), better fit for purpose, faster implementation, ease of use (no or little training required to use it) and better support.

Compatibility: How compatible is your solution with current practise, culture and with the environments in which they are to operate?

The more compatible, the faster the adoption will be.

Being compatible means extending the benefits of what the customers already have. It lowers the implementation and switching cost and helps customers understand which problems you are trying to solve.

Complexity: How complex is your solution?

The simpler the innovation is, the faster the speed of diffusion will be.

The complexity issue relates to how difficult it is to understand what the service does, what benefits it gives, how difficult it is to implement and how high the price is. The more complex, the more difficult it will be to win new customers in any new market where you enjoy no brand recognition.

Trialability: How easy is it to try your solution?

The easier it is to try your solution, the faster the adoption will be.

There are two main aspects of trying out software. The first aspect is getting access to the software. The second aspect is trying out how it feels, behaves and performs in the customer's environment and with her data.

Observability: How tangible is your solution and especially the outcome it produces?

The more tangible results your solution provides, the faster the adoption will be. The entire software industry has a hard time with this attribute. Software is, in essence, invisible and the value depends heavily on how the user implements and embrace the functionality it provides.

The five factors listed above have been found to determine between 49 and 87 per cent of the variance of adoption rates. The remaining determinants are the type of innovation-decision (simple versus complex decision), the kind of communication channels available for diffusing the innovation, the nature of the social system in which the innovation is spreading and the extent of the change agents' promotion efforts in diffusing it.

Innovation and internationalisation

Companies with innovative products face Rodgers' five factors each time they are to enter a new geography. In your efforts to differentiate combined with your lack of an installed base of clients and brand recognition, you match perfectly what most potential customers do not want.

Your best bet is to appeal to the Innovators (2.5 per cent) and Early Adopters (13.5 per cent) which gives you access to around 16 per cent of the market. These two segments are always on the outlook for something that can improve their productivity and competitiveness. They get attracted by products and value propositions that represent a new approach to pressing problems.

Following this approach, you have two prime challenges:

1. You have to find the Innovators and the Early Adopters, or you need them to find you.

2. You need to work on the five factors to accelerate the diffusion.

Crossing the Chasm

Rodger's principles were applied in Geoffrey A. Moore's seminal book *Crossing the Chasm: Marketing and selling disruptive products to mainstream customers*[26]. Moore wanted to explain why companies with disruptive technologies had difficulties growing beyond the 10-15 per cent market share. He used the law of diffusion of innovation to illustrate that there is a chasm between the early markets and the mainstream markets. A chasm that companies have a difficult time crossing. His observation was also that companies have to get past *the twenty per cent market share* before they can enjoy the benefits of the word-of-mouth recommendations that lead to the declining cost-of-sales and improved margins that the steep portion of the diffusion curve offers.

Geoffrey Moore doesn't mention the challenges associated with internationalisation, nor did he spend much time on the speed of diffusion. However, I suggest that his observations also apply in this context. If that is the case, then we can easily be lulled into a comfortable misconception when we manage to win the first customers or resellers in a new market.

What we win are often early market innovators with whom the mainstream market segments do not identify.

The real test is if we can make it from a few customers or resellers and past a twenty per cent market share. For most software companies facing international expansion, considerations for how to get past twenty per cent market share in each country is not even on the agenda. Getting a bridgehead established is the first priority. Crossing the chasm is a bridge to be taken later.

---

26. Moore, G. A. (2014). Crossing the chasm: Marketing and selling disruptive products to mainstream customers (Third edition ed.). New York, NY: HarperBusiness, an imprint of HarperCollins Publishers.

However, I think it is fair to ask if you want to invest all that effort if you don't have the ambition of becoming the market leader? The stretch from zero to five per cent market share may be far more complicated than taking it to twenty per cent and beyond. Also, what is the purpose of having a small market share in many countries, if it's not the path to global market leadership? Two per cent market share in ten countries doesn't add up to twenty per cent market share anywhere.

I do understand that it may seem unreasonable spending time considering how to get past twenty per cent market share when you are yet to win the first deals, but I can assure you that it pays off to have the longer perspective in mind. I have often been asked to help clients that are in a catch 22-situation, because of short-sighted decisions made early in the internationalisation process. It is frequently about fixing a setup that provided a few customers, resellers and some initial revenue but then refused to scale. Your early efforts getting that bridgehead established fast may lay the foundation for substantial difficulties later.

In many cases, product localisation and on-going maintenance alone may require some business volume. Ending up with small market shares in many countries may be an expensive and low productivity situation that will deteriorate your competitive position everywhere.

THE BUSINESS MODEL FRAMEWORK

The job of entering a new market can be expressed as figuring out how you can make your business model work and scale in a new and maybe different environment considering the way innovations diffuse.

How different is the new geography from your domestic environment and which changes, if any, do you need to make to your business model? In some cases, you don't need to make any changes at all. In most cases, however, you need to make substantial changes.

The business model

The term *business model* was introduced in the late 1990s, but it wasn't until Alexander Osterwalder et al. in 2010 published their book *Business Model Generation*[27] that we arrived at a common terminology that helps our discussions stay on the same page. A business model describes *the rationale of how an organisation creates, delivers and captures value*. Using the Alexander Osterwalder business model framework, you will notice that all the building blocks on the canvas are (almost) within your full control.

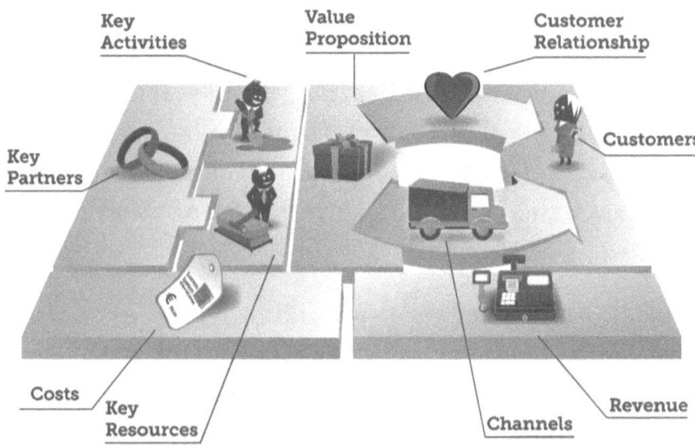

Figure 2: The Alexander Osterwalder business model canvas.

You select your target customer segments. You design your value propositions to serve these customer segments best. You set the

---

27. Osterwalder, A., Pigneur, Y., & Clark, T. (2010). Business Model Generation: A handbook for visionaries, game changers, and challengers. Hoboken, New Jersey: Wiley.

prices that you charge for your products and services. You choose which types of relationships you will have with your customers. You decide which channels you will use to find, nurture, mature, activate, develop, win, make, keep and grow your happy customers. We call this part of the business model the front office. Your front office activities will generate customers and revenue (which are the outcome of your efforts and not something that you fully control).

In the back office of your business model, you need to employ specific key resources that perform certain key activities delivering your value propositions to your customers. The back office may build relationships with key supply-chain partners, as well as generating cost.

The business model environment

You make all the decisions concerning how to design and run your business model yourself. However, when you take a close look at the business model canvas, you will notice the absence of some significant areas impacting your business.

Where do you deal with the competition, the key influencers, the shortages of skilled staff, the technology trends, the availability of business partners, the differences and changes in customer needs and behaviour, the demographic changes, the legal and environmental issues, culture, the global economy, etc.? No business model lives in a vacuum, and the toughest part of any business endeavour is dealing with the issues that you cannot control.

You have to make it to page 200 in Osterwalder & Pigneur's book *Business Model Generation* before you are exposed to what they call *the business model environment*.

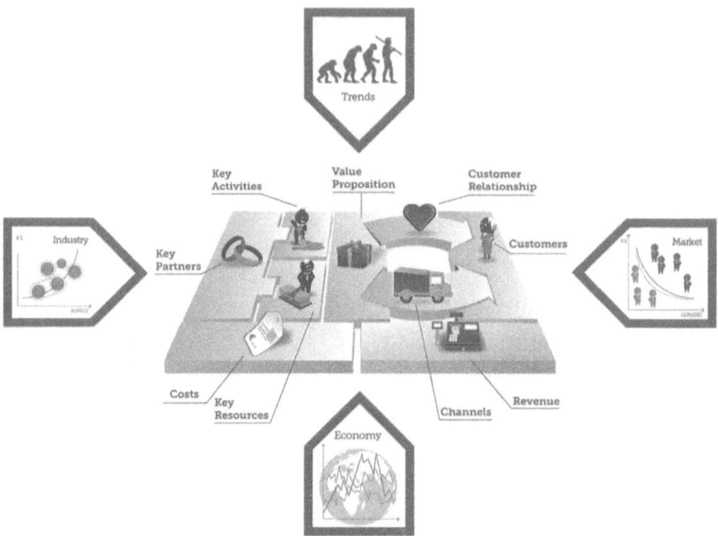

Figure 3: The Alexander Osterwalder business model canvas with the four environment categories.

Separating what you can control, *The Business Model*, from what you cannot control, *The Business Model Environment*, is an excellent way of structuring your strategy development process when you are planning to move into foreign markets. There are two fundamental questions that you need to clarify:

1. Which differences in the business model environment in the new geography dictate changes to your business model?

2. Which other portions of the business model must be modified to work effectively and scale your business in the new geography?

Let me re-emphasise that the key to successful international expansion is replicating your current or at least the same business model in other countries. The complexity associated with running multiple business models is for large companies only. If you find that entering a new country requires changing your business model, then you should consider skipping this market or adjusting your business model accordingly for all your markets.

The Four Business Model Environment "Forces"

To help you make a structured and systematic analysis, Alexander Osterwalder has divided the business model environment into four areas:

1. Key Trends
2. Market Forces
3. Industry Forces
4. Macro-Economic Forces

Osterwalder names these areas forces, which in my opinion may confuse them with Porter's "Five Forces" to which there is some overlap. However, Osterwalder's four business model environment categories are sufficiently comprehensive and complete and will work well for most software companies.

Key Trends

The Key Trends include:

- Technology Trends
- Regulatory Trends
- Societal & Cultural Trends
- Socioeconomic Trends

No two countries are alike, and the big countries may even have substantial regional differences. The questions you could ask concerning the Key Trends part of the business model environment are:

- Is the technology infrastructure for your business model in place?
- Are there legal issues that require changes to your products and services?
- Are there legal issues that require changes to your revenue generation process?
- How will differences in language impact your business model?

- How will "the distance to the market" impact your business model?

- Do employees, customers, business partners and other stakeholders have different behavioural patterns that may impact the performance of your revenue generation process?

Market Forces

The Market Forces include:

- Market Issues
- Market Segments
- Needs & Demands
- Switching Cost
- Revenue Attractiveness

The Market Forces include all issues associated with the size and nature of the demand for your type of product and service. Experience proves that assuming that customers in a new market have the same characteristics as the customers in your domestic market can lead to expensive mistakes, lost investments and lost opportunities. You will, therefore, need to assume that there are differences in the market forces in each new geography you decide to enter.

Key issues to consider when moving into a new market are:

- How big is the market for your products and services?

- Is this market growing, flat or shrinking?

- Is what you offer considered more or less critical to customers in the new market compared with your domestic market?

- What may prevent potential customers from buying your solution?

- What are the switching costs for customers who may be attracted to your value proposition?

- Where do your potential customers go for information about the type of issues you address and who do they listen to for recommendations?

- Are there specific market requirements that you must be able to cover in your product and services?

- Are there specific ways the market buys products and services like yours that require changes to your revenue generation process?

Industry Forces

The Industry Forces include:

- Competitors (incumbents)
- New Entrants (insurgents)
- Substitute Products & Services
- Stakeholders
- Suppliers & Other Value Chain Actors

The Industry Forces include all issues associated with the supply of product and services similar to yours. All your potential customers in a new geography are currently running their businesses without your product and service, which makes it fair to assume that you will have competitors or at least that your potential customers have substitution alternatives.

Stakeholders are people in organisations that influence your business model without being customers. Stakeholders are typically your new staff, labour unions, shareholders, industry associations, the government, lobbyists, consultants, analysts and the media.

The industry forces also include the channels through which the customers are served, the influencers, the organisations and the media dealing with domain matters.

Key issues to consider when moving into a new market are:

- Who are the leading direct competitors in the segments that you plan to address?

- What are the strengths and weaknesses of these competitors?

- Do their weaknesses leave enough room for your value proposition to be sufficiently attractive to the market?

- Do you need to narrow your market focus to remain sufficiently competitive?

- Are there any other new entrants pushing the same value propositions as yours? If so, can you leverage their efforts?

- Who are the main influencers, organisations and media dealing with your domain?

- Can you find "friends" among the influencers, organisations and media that will promote your value proposition?

- Who are the channel players in your domain?

- Can you find channel players that can profit from the success of your value proposition and approach?

Macro-Economic Forces

The Macro-economic forces include:

- Global Market Conditions
- Capital Markets
- Commodities and Other Resources
- Economic Infrastructure

Macro-economic forces are highly unpredictable and may change quickly. For example Covid-19. The Macro-economic forces should, therefore, seldom have any significant importance for your considerations concerning entering new markets. Achieving any significant position in a new market is typically at least a three to a five-year project. Within such a time frame, the macro-economic forces may have changed completely.

Big consulting companies may make predictions on the development of specific countries and regions and may appoint these regions as future growth centres. Such predictions were established in 2001 for Brazil, Russia, India and China under the label BRIC, and in 2014 the MINT countries (Mexico, Indonesia, Nigeria and Turkey) were named the new growth countries. None of the predictions have been reliable. The economic climate and the political situation can change the projections with very short notice.

The Covid-19 pandemic will make companies revisit their international supply chains and consider how they can make them more resilient to regional interruptions. Some governments, especially the current US-administration, may also revisit their international trade agreements. However, I am not convinced that these initiatives will have any substantial impact on the audience for which this book is written.

If you run a virtual revenue generation approach, then you can ignore the generic advice provided by the big consulting companies. Small software companies with little international experience, limited capital resources and a shortage of management and leadership capacity should first focus on developed and stable markets that are not too far away from their home turf or consider a virtual approach.

ADJUSTING THE BUSINESS MODEL FOR A FOREIGN MARKET

Identifying significant differences in the business model environment will call for adjustments or even changes to your business model compared to how you operate it in your domestic market.

These changes can best be defined by reviewing each element of the business model separately.

Value proposition and market segments

Your value proposition and the target market segment(s) you decide to approach are very closely related. As customer requirements and the competitive situation may be different from country to country, you often have to make adjustments here.

You can ask if the differences in the business model environment:

- Will require any adjustments to your value propositions?

- Will require any adjustments to your target market segments?

Channels

The channels are employed to find, nurture, mature, activate, develop and win happy customers.

You can ask if the differences in the business model environment:

- Will require any adjustments to how you facilitate the customers' buying journeys?

Customer relationships

Your Customer Relationships are designed to make, keep and grow happy customers.

You can ask if the differences in the business model environment:

- Will require any adjustments to how you keep and grow happy customers?

Revenue

The revenue is a function of your ability to facilitate the customers' buying journey and the prices you can charge.

You can ask if the differences in the business model environment:

- Will affect the prices you can charge?
- Will impact how you charge or invoice customers?
- Will impact debtor days and payment collection?

Key activities

Running the business model front office, including defining and making changes to the products and services behind the value propositions, adjusting the target market segments, refining the process to find, nurture, mature, activate, develop, win, make, keep and grow happy customers and finding the right pricing level, may require different and additional activities.

Managing staff or business partners in other locations, speaking different languages and understanding different cultures will undoubtedly add a layer of complexity that you need to master.

You can ask if the differences in the business model environment:

- Will call for new activities to be undertaken?

    - What are these activities?

    - Which of these activities can be undertaken at the headquarters level and which must be conducted in each region or country?

Key resources

Running activities requires employing and engaging resources. In the discussion so far, we have stressed that becoming successful in a new country may (most likely will) require tweaking everything in your front office. You perform not only more activities, but also different activities, which again implies that you need not only additional resources but also new types of resources.

You can ask if the differences in the business model environment:

- Will require additional resources and if so, which and how much?

    - How will you recruit these resources?

    - How will you onboard these resources?

    - How will you organise these resources?

    - How will you manage and measure the performance of these resources?

    - Which resources do you need at the headquarters level and which do you need at the country or regional level?

    - How will you keep the information flow running smoothly in the new organisational setup?

Key partnerships

Key partners are vendors and strategic alliances in your supply chain that form a critical part of your value creation. If they fail to deliver, then you cannot deliver. If you cannot integrate with them, then customers may not be interested in your product. Today, where the general market is moving towards solutions made up of best-of-breed components, strategic alliances become increasingly important. Such partnerships may differ substantially from country to country.

You can ask if the differences in the business model environment:

- Has any impact on your key partnerships?
- If some key partnerships are critical for market acceptance?
- If new key partnerships in the country could improve your value proposition and competitive position?

Please observe that, in the Osterwalder business model terminology, potential distributors and resellers are part of your channel and are not considered strategic alliances!

Cost

Entering foreign markets require investments and recurring operational costs. Knowing how fast you can win the first lighthouse customers and form a bridgehead from where you can scale the business is extremely hard to predict. Not even big companies that set up their own operations, hire their own staff and invest massively in building market awareness can predict if and how soon they will reach break-even.

As planning is cheap and execution is expensive, it makes good sense to run several planning sessions and gather market intelligence before committing resources to engage with partners and customers to whom you will have obligations if you fail to establish a sustainable business in that country.

TAKE-AWAYS FROM THE CHAPTER

There is no shortage of business strategy concepts; however, none of them is specially developed to help smaller software companies enter foreign markets. Even the two frameworks that I have described in this chapter do not in their original documentation include the international dimension or the fact that different countries may represent different circumstances.

In this chapter, I have briefly described the law of diffusion of innovation as it is applied in Geoffrey G. Moore's *Crossing the Chasm* and the business model framework as described in Alexander Osterwalder's book *Business Model Generation*. Getting familiar with the principles laid out in these two books will give you and your team a vocabulary that you can use in your discussions as you design your international expansion strategy. The summary provided in this chapter may be all you need but reading the books is also be recommended.

As I write in the chapter, *planning is cheaper than execution*. In general, you should spend more time planning, meaning that you use more time discussing, researching and documenting your assumptions before you execute. Your plan (the mix of objectives and activities) will never survive the meeting with reality, but only by having your assumptions well documented will you have an idea of what needs to be fixed or adjusted for the next round.

Figure 4: My seven-step learning model

CHAPTER FOUR - THE VIRTUAL COMPANY

INTRODUCTION

Before the Covid-19 related social distancing measures and restrictions on travel, the option for running a virtual operation was mainly reserved for inexpensive, easy to understand and non-mission-critical applications. My prediction is that the threshold has been moved considerably. More customers are now prepared to make more investments and vendor selections without the need for face-to-face meetings. That also applies when you are not the market leader and not an already established brand.

However, even when you can win customers without the need for face-to-face meetings, there is still the question can they find you or can you find them?

In this chapter, I will discuss the situation where you do not need to meet face-to-face with your customers at any time before or after they decide to use your product. When getting your first customers abroad, this represents a significant advantage. It means that you can win customers without having people on the ground. You may even be able to win customers without employing salespeople at all, or at least you can operate with an inside salesforce only.

DEFINITION

A virtual company is usually the term used for businesses that do not have a physical presence. You can buy from them and sell to them, but you cannot ask for a meeting at their offices because they don't have one.

Numerous software and e-commerce companies operate in a virtual mode with people scattered all over the globe and with their web presence as the only customer-facing manifestation[28]. Basecamp and

---

[28] https://github.com/yanirs/established-remote

Automattic (the company behind WordPress) are some of the more prominent examples of virtual companies. XINK, one of the case stories in this book, is also an entirely virtual company.

With the rapidly declining cost of voice and data communication through the Internet and with the availability of business management and collaboration software offered as a service from the cloud, setting up and running a virtual business has never been easier and financially more attractive.

There are now also dedicated platforms available for setting up and supporting virtual companies. An example is XOLO that takes advantage of Estonian e-citizenship. XOLO allows you to set up a company in Estonia and run your business from there, although you physically remain in your home office in Sankt Georgen in Schwarzwald or Leavenworth in the state of Washington (just two examples of places that are quite remote but also extremely picturesque) or you are a digital nomad on the road exploring the world. XOLO then provides banking (through Transferwise), invoicing, bookkeeping and tax reporting services. Applications such as Basecamp, Atlassian, Google Apps, Microsoft Teams, Slack and others are designed to help people work together while physically apart. Skype, WebEx, Zoom, TeamViewer, FreeConferenceCall, Google Meet and similar platforms enable online meetings and demos.

The cost advantage of not having to have offices is easy to understand. Just the possibility of working without the need to commute saves people hours every day. The benefits of not having to meet physically with customers are also easy to grasp. You can have many more customer meetings per day if you do not have to travel. You can have coaches listening in or record your conversations and analyse them afterwards. An option that is not feasible with physical meetings.

The challenge is how you can innovate, work effectively together, learn from each other and perform consistently when your people are not physically together. That subject is beyond the scope of this book but reading the literature[29] it seems that entrepreneurs that decide to take this path also find out how to make it work.

The people behind XINK did not set out to create a virtual company, but as the business grew, they realised their distaste for management, and especially for sales management. They also felt the pressure of having to feed people on the payroll. The solution was to operate as a virtual company where everybody, including the founders, is a freelancer. They have even found a way to engage new team members without having to meet with them face-to-face first.

By employing or engaging people that prefer working remotely instead of going to an office every day, it seems as though companies can also reduce management overheads. People management accounts for 10-20 per cent of total OPEX in most companies. That's a significant expense line in the P&L. The COVID-19 situation that, as I write this book, is reaching its peak will expose millions of people to working virtually. As we come out of the crisis, some of that experience will support the creation of new virtual teams, more remote working and more virtual companies.

In the context of this book, I use the term virtual company for a business model and especially a value proposition, where enough customers will buy and use your product irrespective of where you are located and without the need for any physical face-to-face interaction. All pre- and post-sales communication can be done electronically, and your customers either don't care about where you are physically located, or they see no major disadvantage associated with your remoteness. As a virtual business, you do not need an outside salesforce.

Whether or not you operate the back-office of your business model physically or virtually is not the main criteria here. If your customers couldn't care less about where you are located and how you operate your front- and back-office, then you can run as a virtual company.

---

29 Fried, J., & Hansson, D. H. (2013). Remote: Office Not Required. Chicago, USA: Ebury Publishing. and Berkun, S., John, W., & Sons. (2013). The year without pants : WordPress.com and the future bof work. San Francisco: Jossey-Bass A Wiley Brand.

With a virtual business model, you do not need to meet physically, face-to-face with your leads, prospects and customers.

If your customers don't care where you are located, and you don't need to show up in person to complete the sale and provide support, then you also have the opportunity of serving customers in foreign countries without the need for a local presence. That is an enormous advantage if you want to go global on a shoestring.

THE FOUR TYPES OF VIRTUAL BUSINESSES

Virtual businesses can be sorted into four main categories using two dimensions. One dimension defines the need for individual conversations with your potential customers. In figure 5, below, the dimension is *low* when there is no need for such conversations, or on *high* when there is. The other dimension defines what type of marketing activities are required to generate enough leads. Such activities may be primarily inbound or primarily outbound.

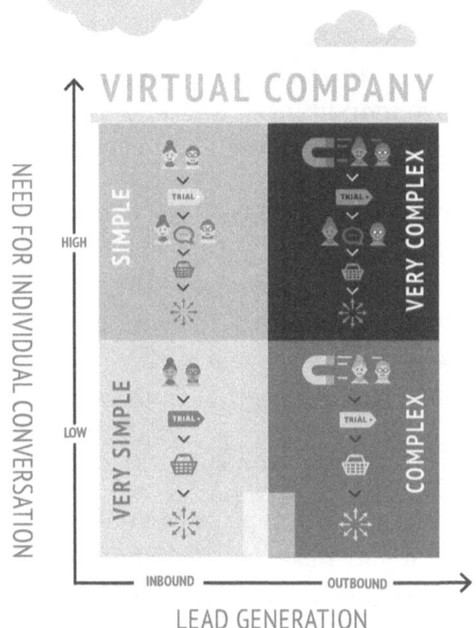

Figure 5: The four types of virtual businesses

A very simple virtual business is characterised by the ability to create a reliable inbound lead generation process with no or little need for individual conversations with customers. They find you, check out your value proposition, sign up for a trial, buy and expand. For this approach, you do not need a salesforce.

A simple virtual business is characterised by inbound lead generation and a need for individual conversations with customers. They find you, check out your value proposition, sign up for a trial, but they don't buy anything without having a conversation with you first. For this approach, you need an inside salesforce that can handle incoming calls.

A complex virtual business is characterised by a requirement for outbound lead generation, and a limited need for one-on-one conversations with customers. You need to find and get in touch with them, expose them to your value proposition. Then they sign up for a trial, buy and expand.

A very complex virtual business is characterised by a requirement for outbound lead generation, and a need for individual conversations. You must find and get in touch with them, expose them to your value proposition and have individual conversations before they buy. For this approach, you need an inside salesforce that can handle outbound calls.

By using the term "simple", I am not referring to what it takes to make a beautiful and valuable product that thousands of customers want to use and are prepared to pay for once they have found you. Neither am I referring to what it takes to find and implement the marketing activities that make customers know that you exist nor to what it takes to design the sales process that makes them buy and expand.

None of that is by any means simple.

The term *simple* refers to the type of back-office required to run your business model once you have verified that customers will find you and will buy your product without seeing you physically. If you need salespeople to do outbound lead generation and close sales, then your go-to-market approach is by definition *complex*.

Very simple

Since the introduction of the PC and especially with the proliferation of the Internet and cloud-based Software-as-a-Service offerings, the very simple virtual business format has been an attractive option for many software entrepreneurs. Most of the software I use to run my shop come from companies using this approach. In appendix one, you will find a list of the software I have used to write this book.

Many software entrepreneurs deliberately design businesses that are intended to be very simple. They do so because they can be operated with very little OPEX and be scaled with limited people management effort.

Based on data from your website and the communication channels that you use, you can refine the inbound streams of leads and the process of converting them to customers. SEO (Search Engine Optimisation), SEM (Search Engine Marketing) and SMM (Social Media Marketing) become key activities in your business model back-office which requires employing what we could call *marketing engineers*. That's people who know the mechanics of the web and social media, can analyse data and run the optimisation process.

As there is no need for individual real-time, synchronous interactions with customers, you don't need staff to attend to such one-on-one conversations, and you are not immediately affected by time zones. From anywhere in the world, physically or virtually, you can serve customers in all markets.

Many talented entrepreneurs enjoy the freedom and independence of running their own business but have no ambition of building a vast corporate empire. Only very few entrepreneurs have the ambition of becoming the next Bill Gates or Steve Jobs. They may like making money, but they have no appetite for the management side of the endeavour. For such people, the very simple virtual business format will work well.

Simple

In the simple virtual business scenario, you need staff to undertake individual conversations with customers. However, as these interactions are requested and initiated by the customers, you can concentrate on providing the communication channels and the human resources needed for responding. Over time you can develop tools for customer self-service and minimise the staff required for the individual interactions or reserve such support for the bigger deals.

Customers have different preferences for how to communicate, and you can increase your conversion rates by offering a multitude of channels: Chat, email, phone and a searchable FAQ. The material in text format, as well as videos and podcasts, will satisfy some of the information requirement, bringing down the need for individual one-on-one conversations.

If you are successful and can attract international customers, then you will soon be faced with a time zone issue. Customers may want to chat or talk with you, and mostly the response time and the quality of the answers you provide are decisive for the conversion rates.

Indeed, you can have staff working in three shifts to cover all time zones, but that often turns out to be unpractical and is under all circumstances, not a healthy lifestyle for anyone.

As long as we are talking about conversations initiated by the customers, then it is relatively simple to organise such activities from either remote support centres or outsource them to external business partners. You can record conversations and coach your staff and partners to improve quality and performance.

Complex

The virtual business approach may also work even when you need outbound activities to generate leads. However, there is a fundamental difference between customers contacting you and you contacting them. The difference is so substantial that it justifies the term *complex.*

I haven't come across many companies that fall into the complex virtual scenario in the southeastern area of the illustration above, figure 5. When generating leads requires outbound activities, developing and closing them normally also requires substantial individual dialogues.

If there is no active search for what you do, then building an inbound lead generation machine will probably require too much customer acquisition cost. You are better off identifying potential leads according to your ideal customer profile and then start reaching out to them. When potential customers cannot find you, and you, therefore, need to find them, then it usually takes considerable effort to win their business.

The details of the difference between the inbound and outbound approach are well documented in Mark Roberge's book *The Sales Acceleration Formula: Using Data, Technology, and Inbound Selling to go from $0 to $100 Million*[30]. In brief, inbound leads are active, but unqualified, while outbound leads are qualified but inactive.

The outbound approach is described in Marylou Tyler's book, *Predictable Prospecting: How to Radically Increase Your B2B Sales Pipeline*[31].

Most companies that need outbound lead generation activities, therefore, tend to fall into the category *very complex.*

Very complex

The outbound approach involves typically setting up a telesales facility that reaches out to potential customers that are either cold or based on some qualifying activity. With today's telecommunication technology, it is technically quite easy to set up a central operation that calls customers in different countries, making it appear as a local call.

---

[30] Roberge, M. (2015). *The Sales Acceleration Formula: Using Data, Technology, and Inbound Selling to go from $0 to $100 Million.* Hoboken, new Jersey: John Wiley & Sons, Inc.

[31] Tyler, M. D., Jeremey. (2016). Predictable Prospecting: How to Radically Increase Your B2B Sales Pipeline.

The challenge is managing the people operating the outbound call centre.

Finding, recruiting, managing, motivating and retaining outbound telesales-people is difficult and expensive. The performance of an outbound telesales operation is extremely people dependent and requires attention to all the details in the process.

It first and foremost requires a sales manager that knows and genuinely loves this type of work.

Predicting how a person will perform in a specific outbound telesales operation is almost impossible, so you need an ongoing recruitment activity finding and testing new talent. You need to onboard them and coach them.

I cannot stress the people aspect of telesales strongly enough. I have seen so many examples of outbound telesales experiments fail because of unqualified staff, insufficient onboarding, lack of coaching and inadequate management.

It is beyond the scope of this book to elaborate on the minutia of making an outbound marketing and sales operation work efficiently. On that subject, there are plenty of other books[32].

"In the first few years of HubSpot, we targeted marketing professionals. Therefore, my sales training goal was to teach our new sales hires what it was like to be a marketer. New sales hires did not spend their first few weeks in sales training, memorising scripts and discussing objections. Instead, our new sales hires spent their first few weeks at HubSpot developing their own website, writing their own blog, and creating their own social media presence. By the completion of training, our new sales hires would often rank at the top of Google search results for dozens

---

[32] Roberge, M. (2015). *The Sales Acceleration Formula: Using Data, Technology, and Inbound Selling to go from $0 to $100 Million*. Hoboken, new Jersey: John Wiley & Sons, Inc., Tyler, M. D., Jeremey. (2016). Predictable Prospecting: How to Radically Increase Your B2B Sales Pipeline, Aaron Ross, M. T. (2011). Predictable Revenue: Turn Your Business Into a Sales Machine with the *$100 Million Best Practices of Salesforce.com:* PebbleStorm.

of keywords. They built social media followings of hundreds of people for their websites. They published blog articles, set up landing pages, ran A/B tests, segmented leads, created email nurturing campaigns, and analysed the conversion of website visitors to leads to customers, all using the HubSpot software. Sales hires felt the pain of a marketer because they lived through it.[33]"

If cold calling on the phone is part of your outbound lead generation approach, then you need to understand the differences in legislation and culture from country to country. Some countries have a no-name practice meaning that they won't accept a request to connect you to, for instance, the IT- manager unless you know his or her name. I came across this practice in the UK, while it wasn't an issue in the Nordic countries. With the popularity of LinkedIn in most countries, it shouldn't be too difficult to find the names of people responsible for a certain line of business, but it may take a little more time than just asking the receptionist for it when you call a company.

Managing a virtual sales process is much more likely to be successful if the customer's purchase process is simple. That means that the person you are talking to can decide on the purchase. When more people are involved, a purchase process will take longer and be more difficult, although not impossible, to facilitate. A purchase process that is simple in one country may be complex in another. I came across this practice in Germany where IT-managers in SMB-companies had far less delegation than IT-managers in corresponding companies in the Nordic countries. A company selling IT-security solutions was very successful using an outbound approach in the Nordic countries. When they applied the same approach in Germany, the outcome was different.

---

[33] Roberge, M. (2015). The Sales Acceleration Formula: Using Data, Technology, and Inbound Selling to go from $0 to $100 Million. Hoboken, new Jersey: John Wiley & Sons, Inc.

In the Nordics, it took, on average, 6.18 hours of sales time to get an order. Forty-six per cent of the time was used for getting in touch with someone, forty-six per cent on pitching, four per cent on demo and four per cent on closing. Booking one order required calling one hundred leads of which 85 responded, 21 listened to the pitch and 1,5 accepted the demo. It turned out that the number of calls needed to get an order in Germany was about fifty per cent higher, mainly because the final conversion rate was substantially lower. That made the sales process in Germany much more expensive because you had to make many more calls and most of the time (which is equal to cost) was used *before* the final closing phase.

It's worth repeating that outbound lead generation using the phone requires considerable effort calling people that are not available and talking to people that will not buy. In the example mentioned above, 170 minutes were used per won deal just to get the first conversations established. Of the total time of 371 minutes it took to get a deal, ninety per cent of that time was spent talking to potential customers that decided not to buy. Outbound lead generation and sales using the phone is associated with a substantial amount of rejection, which many people have a hard time coping with. That is one of the main reasons that this type of revenue generation approach is considered difficult.

However, difficult is not the same as impossible, and under certain circumstances, it may work and can also be scaled.

Language

Language plays a vital role when you set out to get customers in foreign countries.

Most virtual businesses begin with capturing English speaking customers. With well over *one billion people* in this category, the market is big enough to build and maintain an increasing revenue stream. Although Chinese is the language spoken by most people (1.3 billion), English is the language representing most market potential.

With English, you can get access to about *forty per cent* of the global market. For most small software companies, that is more than enough.

However, the role of language differs substantially depending on the type of product and value proposition that you offer. A rule of thumb is that if your customers expect the product to provide local language user interface (UI) and documentation, then the revenue generation and customer success processes also need to take place in that language. Another rule of thumb is that if your product requires substantial localisation for each country, then it most likely also needs to offer local language UI and documentation.

Products that are used by a broad audience, such as business software, must be available in the local language. Products that are used by IT- or by other very specialised groups of highly educated professionals typically only need to be available in English.

If your domestic market is big and more than ten million people speak your native language, then it will probably make sense to support both English and your local language. However, going from one to two languages is a significant complication of your business. Therefore, stay with one language for as long as possible. Even if your local language is not English you should seriously consider if you are not best served by only operating in that language.

In certain countries, such as the Nordics, The Netherlands, Benelux and Switzerland, where English is not an official second language, the proficiency is very high, and many professionals are prepared to buy and use a product that is only available in that language.

Language is not only a market issue. It also has a fundamental impact on your organisation and partner relationships.

If you operate entirely virtually, then there is no shortage of English-speaking talent (potential employees or business partners). Also, if you operate from a physical location in a major metropole, it should be possible to find the English-speaking staff and partners required.

Basecamp

Basecamp is a project collaboration tool offered in a cloud-based SaaS format.

The company[34] is an excellent example of a virtual and very simple inbound business model. The company was founded in 1999 under the name 37signals. They started with four people and are today a company with a staff of about fifty spread out across 32 different cities around the world. The headquarters is in Chicago, but everyone at Basecamp is free to live and work wherever they want. Over the years, Basecamp has served thousands of customers including some of the world's largest - and smallest - companies. Freelancers, small shops, mid-sized companies, and multinationals all rely on Basecamp.

Basecamp is more than just a project management tool — it's a better way to work. Teams that switch to Basecamp are more productive and better organized. They communicate better and require fewer meetings. And they're far more efficient than before.[35]

The pricing is very simple - $99 per month with 500GB of storage and virtually an unlimited number of users and projects. You can sign up for a 30-day free unlimited trial without leaving credit card details.

Basecamp was previously available in several languages, but from version 3 it is exclusively available in English.

The reasons that Basecamp has been capable of attracting customers from all over the world (initially on a shoestring budget) are:

1. They offer a service for which any company or organisation on the globe has a need: Project collaboration.

2. That need is widely recognised, and customers are actively looking for solutions.

---

[34] https://basecamp.com

[35] Quote from the Basecamp website.

3. Basecamp is a great product. It is powerful yet simple to use. You can try it for free, and the learning curve is short. You don't need any training to use Basecamp. It is so intuitive that you can use it immediately. Most questions are answered through their website where you can find ample documentation on how the service works.

4. It is inexpensive, and you can discontinue at any time. The risk associated with using Basecamp is minimal.

5. They have used content marketing measures very cleverly.

In my opinion, Basecamp is the role model for how to run a global virtual and a very simple inbound business.

XINK

XINK (previously EmailSignature) provides a solution to streamline the signature in your personal work email account according to your organisation's corporate identity guidelines (CID). Although the responsibility for complying with CID mostly resides with the marketing or communications department, it is often the IT-department that is asked to find the technical solution. They then search the Internet and find XINK. With a website in English and German only, XINK has managed to get customers in more than 100 countries.

XINK was born with functionality to use email signatures for marketing campaign purposes, but very few marketers had thought of such an application and the IT-people even less. Therefore, only a few searched for it. Today that has changed, and XINK gets many inbound inquiries from companies that want to use corporate emails as a marketing channel or organisations that need to maintain specific standards in their external communication.

"We started with an outbound lead generation approach in 2003, says Jesper Frier, COO and co-founder of XINK. "It worked, but it was tough to scale. Around 2005, and especially following activities in Germany, we then started experimenting with online marketing activities. The market had matured, and through organic and paid search, we could

generate a substantial flow of website traffic and trial-downloads. Now we just needed to find ways to improve the conversion rates."

Today XINK has customer success resources in Denmark, Germany, the USA and the Philippines and can attend to customer inquiries 24/7.

"We have tried outbound sales activities again and again," says Jesper Frier, "and every time we have failed. We believe that there is a huge potential in the market waiting to be activated, but we still miss the approach to do so with reasonable customer acquisition cost."

The reasons why the virtual business format works for XINK are:

1. XINK is a solution to a recognised problem for which customers are actively looking for an answer.

2. There are a substantial number of searches for specific keywords that XINK can include in their website and to which they can advertise.

3. Mostly it is IT-people that search for a solution on the Internet and they are prepared to download and try out the software.

4. XINK has a customer success team that answers questions and helps with overcoming technical issues.

5. Enough customers are prepared to communicate with XINK in English or German and can accept that the product is only available in those two languages.

6. Enough customers are prepared to make a purchase decision without a face-to-face meeting with XINK and can accept remote support for implementation and maintenance.

GROWING A VIRTUAL BUSINESS

Although this book is primarily about getting the first customers abroad, I will add some closing comments to this chapter about the challenges associated with growing a virtual revenue generation approach.

If you operate physically and prefer having people in the same building then hiring more English speaking staff may not be a challenge, but as you expand into German, French, Spanish, Italian, Dutch, Russian and so on, only the major metropoles will offer enough choice.

For businesses that depend on having conversations with customers, different time zones soon become a headache. Serving a global customer base from just one location requires people working around the clock. Not everyone is prepared to work shifts, and it does not support a healthy lifestyle. Growing such a business will sooner or later need satellite operations to serve customers in different languages and time zones.

I guess we can all appreciate the immense advantages that an entirely virtual setup enjoys when growing a business internationally. Nevertheless, there are three reasons why most companies do not choose this format.

1. They started as a physical business and have no experience with operating virtually. Therefore, migrating to a virtual setup is not considered an option.

2. Management and staff prefer to come together physically.

3. Outbound lead generation and sales are difficult to manage in a virtual format.

Although Covid-19 has exposed most of the software industry to remote working and thereby given everyone practical experience with the tools it requires, there is still a divide between the people that enjoy it and those that hate it.

I don't think that's going to change.

Therefore, if you have ambitions of running an entirely virtual operation, then it has to be an integrated element of your company culture. You believe it can work and you hire and engage people that share this belief. Building a company with people that love working remotely and independently is much easier than trying to force someone down this route. You will seek inspiration from those who went before you, and you will invest time and effort in building the platforms and collaboration formats that can make it work.

For companies with very simple and simple virtual revenue generation models, I believe that the full operation quite easily can be made virtual too, especially when that is the model from the very start.

If you rely on inside resources to do outbound lead generation and sales, then that part of your organisation is hard to operate in an entirely virtual setup. Growing an outbound revenue generation operation requires recruitment, onboarding, training, supervision and coaching. As I explained above, outbound sales is associated with a significant amount of rejection and only by training people well, by monitoring their actual behaviour - which requires monitoring their conversations with customers - and by performing on-the-job coaching, can you help them improve, become and remain successful. I have yet to see someone do this successfully in a virtual setup.

TAKE-AWAYS FROM THIS CHAPTER

The virtual company model is ideal for going global on a shoestring.

It fundamentally requires that customers don't care where you are located and that they don't need to meet with you face-to-face at any stage during and after their buying journey.

If you hire people that have a preference for working from home, then you may operate entirely virtually, which will make going global on a shoestring even easier.

With English as your prime language, you have access to forty per cent of the global market and provided your product doesn't require localisation, then you can view the world as a single market. By not being present on the ground in foreign countries, you can sidestep regulations that may otherwise require you to offer a local language version of your software.

The virtual business model works best if you can fill your pipeline through inbound activities. That means customers can and do find you.

If you need outbound activities where salespeople must call on prospective customers, then there are not so many examples of how this can work well in a virtual setup. Outbound sales are associated with a considerable amount of rejection. It requires ongoing supervision, coaching and management to maintain productivity in an outbound sales department.

Covid-19 may have moved the threshold for when and what customers are prepared to buy and implement without having to meet the suppliers face-to-face during and after completing the buying journey. Therefore, we may see many more virtual businesses in the future.

Chapter Five - The Physical Company

INTRODUCTION

I call a business physical when the revenue generation process requires meeting face-to-face with customers. In this context, I am only referring to the customer-facing activities and how you can meet this need with the lowest possible budget.

Having subsidiaries in foreign countries staffed with local people is a standard procedure for running an international or multinational operation. As you grow your business, you may have to take that route, too. The challenge is that setting up the first subsidiaries and hiring local management and staff, and especially building an outside sales team, represents a substantial risk for any small company.

Why is that so?

Because there is not a wide selection of talent that can develop a business from scratch, because it can be tough to predict how fast your revenue will start flowing in a new country, how soon you will be cash positive and when you will reach breakeven. It may take three months, one year, or it may take five years. For how long can you keep funding these activities?

The physical business requires an outside sales capability. In this chapter, I will review several approaches for how you can meet face-to-face with potential customers and win projects in foreign countries without setting up a subsidiary and hiring a team of local people first.

THE MISTAKES YOU WILL WANT TO AVOID

Here are some of the most frequent mistakes companies with physical revenue generation approaches make:

You establish a local marketing and sales organisation and then realise that what you need is a business development team. This happens when a new country turns out to represent a completely different business model environment than the one you are operating in domestically. To get traction, you will need to revisit your value proposition, your market segmentation, your position, and maybe even reconsider your go-to-market approach. Doing so is a business development and not a marketing and sales effort.

You hire the wrong people, but as you do not have the resources to manage and coach them effectively, it takes too long before you find out. The combination of your lack of management experience and bandwidth at the headquarters level and getting the wrong people on board is toxic. Admitting to your lack of experience is hard but assessing why your subsidiary doesn't deliver on its budget is even harder. Did you misread the market? Are you investing too little? Is the budget unrealistic? Do you get honest feedback from your people? They claim that their market is different, but is it?

You may end up in a situation where you bleed more than you can afford, and you don't know how to fix it.

For the reasons mentioned, the shoestring approach is to explore alternative options for getting face-to-face with customers. Find out if they are responsive to your value proposition and if your go-to-market approach will work. If it does, then you can build enough revenue to financially justify setting up that local operation which deeper market penetration calls for, or which makes sense because you are approaching or have achieved critical mass.

There are situations where setting up the subsidiary and building the local organisation is the only route to get sufficient market penetration. Trustpilot (the online customer review platform) is a good example. However, Trustpilot's business model is highly affected by network effects, which means that reaching market leadership as fast as possible is crucial. Therefore, Trustpilot doesn't apply a shoestring approach. The company has raised a total of 192.8 million dollars in funding over seven rounds[36]. So, although Trustpilot, according to the definitions of this book, is a virtual business that doesn't require meeting face-to-face

---

[36] https://www.cnbc.com/2019/03/05/reviews-site-trustpilot-raises-55-million-series-e-funding-round.html

with customers for revenue generation purposes, the dependence on network effects makes it unsuitable for a shoestring approach.

THE SHOESTRING ROLE MODEL

Epic, on the other hand, with a revenue of three billion dollars and 10,000 people on the payroll has and continues to apply a shoestring approach to its international expansion.

"We have never considered the world organised into country-markets that we could proactively decide to approach," says Mercedes McCoy, VP of international business development at Epic. "For us, the market is where customers are active, share our vision for an integrated system, have requirements that match our products and prefer our implementation approach. We are one hundred per cent customer-driven and not market-driven."

With customers in fourteen countries, Epic is a role model for how to go global on a shoestring when your revenue generation process requires substantial interaction with your customers. Providing EHR (Electronic Health Record) platforms for large hospitals, Epic's solutions are multimillion-dollar deals. They are acquired through a public procurement process, the product and support documentation must be made available in the local language, and the implementation requires integration to new subsystems. And in most cases, there are already established local competitors.

In general, such market conditions makes penetration from the outside difficult, but Epic does it again and again. The recipe is quite simple to understand, although not so simple to execute.

Founded in 1979 Epic won its first international customer outside North America in 2007 in the Netherlands. Epic was invited to bid for the project. So, what happened in the previous 28 years?[37]

It took Epic six years to hit the one-million-dollar revenue mark. In 1990 they employed 29 people, and in 1992 they released the industry's first Windows-based EHR system, EpicCare. In 1997 EpicWeb, a suite

---

37 https://isthmus.com/news/cover-story/epic-systems-an-epic-timeline/

of Web-based healthcare IT-programs, was introduced. By 2000 Epic had 400 employees and reported revenue of fifty million dollars.

In 2003, Kaiser Permanente, the largest managed care organisation in the United States, chose Epic as the platform for its new company-wide EHR-system. Over the next seven years, Kaiser Permanente would invest a total of 4 billion dollars in development and implementation, which funded the training of their staff, hardware purchases, the software from Epic, and more. Within the innovation diffusion terminology, Kaiser Permanente was an innovator and early adopter, and with that project under its belt, Epic crossed the chasm in one single jump. Kaiser Permanente became a global showcase, and healthcare professionals from all over the world made pilgrimages to Kaiser's locations in California and across the United States to see and hear what was going on.

By 2006 the company reported revenue of well over 400 million dollars and had more than 2,000 people on the payroll.

Epic's strategy for international expansion has been and remains reactive. They don't do traditional marketing or paid advertising and don't cold-call prospective clients. They only respond when potential customers invite them to participate in an RFP (request for proposal) and then only when the requirement specifications are close to what they can offer and that they agree on the implementation approach.

Today Epic has subsidiaries in several countries, and they were all opened after they had landed the first projects. They are a role model because they have a razor-sharp focus that allowed them to take full advantage of the Kaiser Permanente showcase, which they managed to win in 2003.

THE SEVEN APPROACHES

The methods for winning customers in foreign countries without a local representation and a big budget are closely related to the type of product you offer and your competitive position.

The general rules of thumb are that your chances for success are far better if there are only a limited number of local competitors, and if the customers perceive your value proposition as superior. The potential customers do not necessarily need to call you. When they get acquainted with you, then they should consider your value proposition extremely attractive and the risk, associated with choosing you as a vendor, manageable.

With this in mind, we can now explore the various shoestring options for finding and winning customers in foreign countries.

1. Win your domestic market first. I'll call this scenario *The Traditional Approach*.

2. You can find distributors or resellers that are prepared to develop the market for you. I'll call this scenario *The Indirect Model*.

3. An opportunity materialises out of the blue in a market where you haven't planned to have any activities. I'll call this scenario *The Unexpected Opportunity*.

4. Your product and the market segment that you serve is so special that there is only minimal competition. Customers cannot find a solution locally and are prepared to engage with you despite your lack of local presence. I'll call this scenario *The Narrow Gorge*.

5. Customers in your domestic market use, or want to use, your product in their international operations. Without you having to do much, you get customers in foreign countries. I'll call this scenario *The Trojan Horse*.

6. You can find joint venture partners that are prepared to develop the market without you having a local operation. I'll call this scenario *The Navision Model*.

7. *Outsource the job*. With the popularity of the gig-economy and the increasing demand for business development resources, more and more agencies offer to walk the first difficult miles for you.

The seven approaches are not exclusive and can be combined.

THE TRADITIONAL APPROACH

Starting by building a leading position at home first, refining your value proposition and accumulating funds for international expansion later has always been a popular approach. Despite the global visibility and transparency that the Internet and social media has brought along, it still is.

How far you can get with the traditional approach depends heavily on the size of your domestic market. Countries such as the USA, China, India, Japan and Germany, that together account for more than half of the global demand for software-based products and services, each have large domestic markets where companies can enjoy the comfort of proximity, the native language and a common culture. On this base, they can verify their business model, grow and consolidate their position.

Some types of products do benefit from a large domestic market. Developing comprehensive monolithic systems for large customers, such as Epic, Tia Technology, and Edlund do, is difficult in a small local market. Nevertheless, it took Epic 28 years before winning their first customer outside North America. They still generate ninety per cent of revenue in the USA, but income from international projects is expected to grow substantially in the future. Edlund, founded in 1992 in Copenhagen, still have to win their first foreign account.

The preference for the traditional approach also explains why many of the worlds large software brands originate from the USA, and, helped by protective trade policies, now even from China. However, when looking at the software industry in the big countries, a surprisingly large share of the incumbents never manages to get any significant international coverage. Many are quite comfortable with what they can achieve at home. If you have to meet face to face with potential customers, then you will intuitively understand that the size of your domestic market plays a vital role for how much you can grow before having to deal with foreign markets. If the local market is big enough to keep you busy, then why look elsewhere? Also, while having more financial power should, theoretically, increase your chances of breaking into foreign markets, it often leads to making expensive mistakes.

Money in itself is seldom the solution to everything. Instead, small budgets and small domestic markets force you to be innovative and take swift actions when results don't materialise as expected.

A large domestic market should, in theory, be a considerable advantage, but in my experience, it just as often becomes a comfortable pillow. If you do not have a large domestic market and therefore need or want to go global, then you must, and you will pursue other shoestring approaches.

I must admit that I never subscribed to the traditional approach, but maybe it is because I am located in a tiny country. When I joined my first startup, Dataco, in 1986, we immediately understood the potential of the global market but deliberately decided to get a domestic customer base first. In this case, things developed very fast, and within a year we took on most of Europe and became immensely successful.

Joining my second startup, Mercante, in 1988, we had a global perspective from the start. Within twelve months from launching the first product, we had established distribution and channel partners in ten European countries and made an OEM deal with Xerox in the U.S. We also negotiated OEM deals with all major printer manufacturers in Europe, the U.S. and Japan.

DDE (Unix computers and various vertical industry solution), a company I joined in 1992, had focused on the domestic market for years before they considered moving out. That turned out to be very difficult, and the company never managed to make their international activities profitable.

Daintel (Software for intensive care units) had a fifty per cent market share at home before moving out, but that wasn't enough to sponsor the expensive sales process in new countries.

Concentrating on the domestic market first and accumulating the resources required for international expansion can be a sensible approach. However, it can also be a trap. I believe that the difference lies in your ambitions and intentions. Knowing that you will someday do business abroad will help you trim your organisation and processes from the start. You will choose English as the base language for product and marketing communication, and you will ensure that the people you hire have sufficient English language skills. When you do this, then your outlook will be global, and customers abroad can find you.

DOMESTIC MARKETS ARE DIFFERENT

If your domestic market is small, say less than one per cent of the global demand, then your chances of gaining any significant momentum here are slim. In that case, you should apply a global mindset from the start, although you may wait a year or two before investing actively in international activities.

If you wait too long approaching the global opportunity, say more than two years from product launch, then you may end up with an organisation that is hard to internationalise. Unless your native language is English, then the job of translating internal and external documentation becomes a notable effort, and you will most likely have people in key positions that do not speak English well enough.

According to my estimates, only nineteen countries in the world represent more than one per cent of global demand. In Europe that is Germany (3.4%), the UK (2.5%), France (2.4%), Italy (1.9%), Turkey (1.7%) and Spain (1.5%). The remaining 47 countries each represent less than one per cent of global demand and can be considered small markets.

THE INDIRECT MODEL

If your go-to-market approach is indirect in the first place and that model works well in your domestic market, then it also makes perfect sense to continue using this modus operandi abroad.

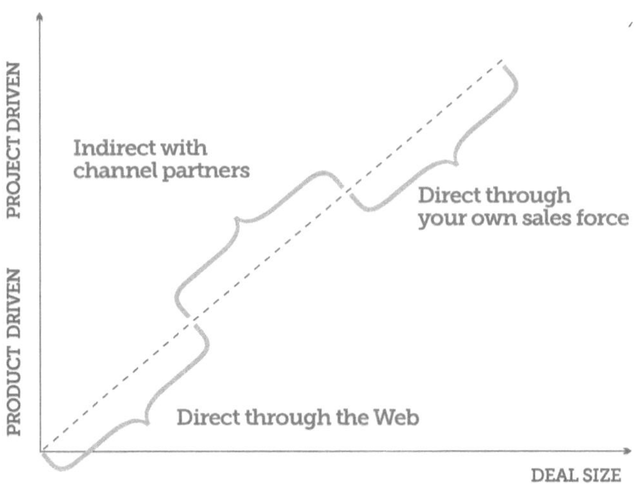

Figure 6: When to go direct and when to go indirect.

[38]When deal sizes are small, and the functionality of the software is easy to understand (product-driven) then running a direct virtual setup may be the fastest route to foreign markets. This approach seldom benefits from using independent channel partners. Companies with such business models are better off applying a direct approach where they can fine-tune the virtual lead generation and conversion processes with full control over resources and activities.

As deal sizes grow so does the complexity of the customers' buying journeys, and your sales activities become project-driven. When the price tag grows, and there is also a need for industry-specific functionality, customisation, integration and implementation services to make your product work, then proximity, intimacy and trust become essential to your customers' decision-making criteria. The purchase process of such solutions often requires an outside sales capability while understanding and responding to specific customer requirements becomes vital in driving the project to successful completion. This is where the indirect approach with VARs (Value Added Reseller) flourishes.

---

[38] This section is from my book Building Successful Partner Channels.

Moving further upmarket, where deals become even more prominent, but few in number, makes the pendulum swing back in favour of the direct approach. With highly complex purchase situations and only a few deals a year, the independent channel partner approach is no longer a feasible option for extending your market reach. The learning curve for new partners becomes prohibitively steep and spreading a few annual deals over several partners spoils the advantages of the economy of scale opportunities for all the partners.

In the latter scenario, you will meet the SIs (System Integrators), who make a living from helping large customers with IT implementation projects. If you are successful, the systems integrators may be interested in the service revenue opportunities associated with your products, and you may choose to work with them, expanding your delivery capacity. Unfortunately, system integrators are often prevented from undertaking direct third-party product sales activities, and it is, therefore, impossible to sign them up as genuine channel partners. They are also driven by extreme customer intimacy value propositions and are seldom geared for developing a market for a product.

Scaling your market reach through independent channel partners is a feasible option where there is a substantial deal flow, where the average sales cycle is no longer than 12 months and where the deals require auxiliary services giving the partner margins from other sources than just your product. The more value-add the channel partners can provide the better, the probabilities for making resellers successful then increases, making them stay loyal and helping scale your market coverage.

Finding distributors and resellers in foreign countries is probably the most used go-to-market approach in the software industry. In my book, *Building Successful Partner Channels*[39], I explain that the indirect channel mainly is a scalability instrument. It is not a model that lends itself well to a shoestring approach.

---

[39] Bech, H. P. (2015). *Building Successful Partner Channels: in the software industry.* Copenhagen, Denmark: TBK Publishing®.

I know this sounds counterintuitive and defies common sense. Why is leaving the cost of developing a market and winning customers to a third party not a shoestring approach?

It takes additional time. First, you need to identify, recruit and onboard the distributor or resellers. Then they need to find and win customers. They do so in their own name and at their own risk, which means that you have little control. You introduce a third-party business model into your business model, as illustrated in figure 7.

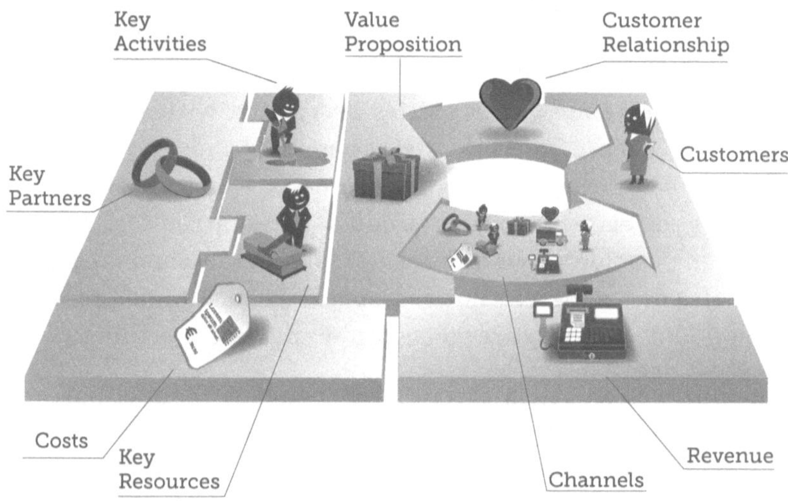

Figure 7: Note that you have a foreign business model in your business model when using an indirect go-to-market approach.

Further, distributors and resellers are predominantly fulfilment driven. They prefer satisfying demand. It means that the majority of distributors and resellers are not motivated to take on market development and investing in winning the first customers for a new product. There are exceptions, such as the ones that I describe below as the Navision Model, but they are rare.

The situation gets even worse if there isn't an established channel for your type of product. Building a new channel for a new product in a new market is not a shoestring type of project.

The change from pre-paid licenses to subscription-based paid SaaS has made building indirect channels even more challenging. The investments required to develop a market have not diminished, but the prolonged cash flow profile of the subscription-based revenue stream makes the endeavour capital intensive. SaaS-based businesses can become very valuable but getting them off the ground and making them profitable takes time.

The shoestring approach requires doing lead generation in parallel with channel recruitment. It is much easier to find and engage distributors and resellers when you bring qualified leads or even revenue to the table.

MapsPeople

Most of MapsPeople's (indoor mapping software) current customers have been sold to and served virtually, and so far, it doesn't seem as though there is a need for meeting physically with the customers. Sales, implementation and project management can be operated remotely using conference calls, web-meeting and other collaboration technologies. However, going forward, MapsPeople would prefer to build an ecosystem of SIs (System Integrators), OEMs (Original Equipment Manufacturers) and VARs (Value Added Resellers).

"We prefer serving the market through SIs, OEMs and VARs, not because we have difficulties finding customers," says Michael Gram. "It's because we need someone to deliver the auxiliary services from a time zone close to the customer and in her local language."

The indirect go-to-market strategy is based on the ambition for achieving global market leadership and is meant to make scaling the global rollout faster. Finding these partners has proven difficult, and so far, most of the customers have been handled directly by MapsPeople.

"We have hired pre-sales staff that master the main languages and that has increased the conversion rates considerably," Michael Gram explains. "We will continue to go down this route and will cover Europe from our office in Copenhagen and North America from our office

in Austin, Texas. As soon as we see solid demand from Asia, we will establish an office most likely in South Korea, Singapore or Japan."

With the investment in outbound lead generation activities, MapsPeople are convinced they can generate the critical mass of projects required to keep partners busy and justify the employment of dedicated resources for indoor navigation projects.

"The Indoor Navigation market is taking off just now," Michael Gram concludes. "We are investing in the commercial infrastructure to take the major share of this growth and are convinced that the SIs, OEMs and VARs will show increased interest and commitment when the project volume picks up."

Soft4

Soft4, a Microsoft Dynamics 365 Business Central ISV based in Lithuania, has resellers in Germany, Albania, Estonia, Latvia, France, the UK, Ireland, Benelux, Norway, Romania, Kenya, Canada, USA, Bahrain, UAE, Cambodia, Laos, Myanmar, Philippines, Singapore, Sri Lanka, Maldives, Thailand, Vietnam, Australia, Hong Kong and Indonesia. International activities generate more than half of Soft4's revenue.

"All our resellers are recruited based on customer opportunities," stresses Ugne Kontare. "We have learnt that it takes 3-4 projects for a reseller to become familiar with the solution, the industry and the revenue generation process. There is no point in recruiting a reseller and then waiting for something to happen. That only leads to disappointment on both sides."

Soft4 invests heavily in global organic and paid inbound lead generation activities and have staff in place to follow up, qualify and develop them into warm prospects. Soft4 does not engage in national marketing and lead generation activities competing with their resellers, but their international activities do generate leads directly. They also close the deals directly if possible before handing them over to the resellers for implementation.

"The world has changed," Ugne Kontare explains. "More and more companies are prepared to reach out to and engage with a supplier abroad. It all depends on the type of solution and the amount of consulting required for implementation and support."

One advantage that Soft4 enjoys is the existing global Microsoft Dynamics 365 channel. Although the Soft4 solutions do represent a learning curve for any new partner, it builds on top of something they already know and where they are already running a business.

Soft4 had expected international activities to generate revenue much faster. Still, they have learnt that it takes time to build the marketing frameworks, the partner program, the support organisation and making the resellers comfortable with selling the products with their own resources.

RamBase

RamBase, a cloud-based ERP system from Norway, has chosen a dedicated indirect go-to-market approach where value-added resellers are responsible for the revenue generation process. The first partners in each country receive substantial support from RamBase, including co-funding of the investments in market development.

"The competitive situation differs from country to country," explains Odd Magne Vea, "but as far as we can see, there are opportunities everywhere. Apart from Sweden, Poland and the UK, where we are currently making heavy investments, the sequence for when to enter which country is very much dependent on the people we can find. It takes an entrepreneurial mindset to start up a country operation, and there are only so many people for which the task and the timing are right."

When entering a new country, RamBase engages a local business development manager to recruit the business and implementation partners and to work closely with them in winning the first deals. The cooperation works like a joint venture where the objective is creating a first bridgehead for the product.

"The partners that help us get established in a new country will enjoy co-investments and dedicated support," Odd Magne Vea continues. "We understand that our partners are breaking the ice for us, and we will help them protect their investments and commitment. Building an ERP-reseller channel has been done before, and we have learnt what it takes to grow the business and keep partners happy at the same time."

Uniconta

Uniconta, a cloud-based ERP system launched in 2016, was designed as a global product and is distributed in Denmark, Norway, Estonia, Iceland, The Netherlands, Germany, Austria, The UK, South Africa and Egypt.

"We have chosen an international go-to-market approach through distributors," says Per Pedersen. "Each distributor has exclusive rights and are committed to building brand awareness and recruiting partners in her territory."

The global rollout has primarily been decided by where there were committed people available.

"Building a market for a SaaS product is a long-term and entrepreneurial effort," says Per Pedersen. "It requires experience, stamina, patience, hard work and deep pockets. Such people are hard to find, and mostly they find us."

The customer acquisition approach is inbound. While all SMB companies are potential customers, it is difficult to apply a segmentation that will narrow down on those prepared to migrate within the next 12 months.

"Outbound lead generation is ineffective in this market," Per Pedersen says. "We charge €27 per user per month, which makes €3,210 per year for a 10-user subscription. An outbound salesperson should on average be able to close one deal a day for that model to work. We can produce a new customer for less using the inbound approach and improve brand awareness at the same time."

Pronestor

Despite operating only out of Copenhagen, Pronestor, a company offering meeting management software, has customers in Norway, Sweden, Belgium, France, the UK, USA, Canada, Australia, Argentina and Brazil.

"Fifty per cent of our revenue is from international accounts," says Karsten Busck. "These are either international customers with worldwide representation or national customers that have found us. Our second-biggest market is the USA."

The global go-to-market approach is currently being refined. Pronestor will apply a direct go-to-market approach in some markets while other markets will use an indirect partner model.

"We have learnt that getting international customers does not require that we have representations abroad," explains Karsten Busck. "However, we need that if we want to undertake deeper market penetration and win considerable market shares. And that is our ambition."

Currently, the product is available in the main languages, but the localisation effort is minimal and having a new language in place is only a two-week effort.

"We have partners in place in some countries, and we consider expanding this model with more partners and to more markets," says Karsten Busck. "For the larger markets, we may need a two-tier approach, ensuring that the general market development and management tasks are performed according to our standards. However, we have not decided if we are to take this role ourselves or subcontract to a value-added partner network."

Most of the current partners have found Pronestor and the most successful have the products as their primary offering.

THE UNEXPECTED OPPORTUNITY

In business, it often happens that an opportunity suddenly presents itself. Pursuing this unexpected opportunity will mostly require that you deviate from your plan and abandon some of the strategic objectives towards which you are currently working. Unexpected opportunities often promise a fast return on your investment, and that's why you are prepared to sacrifice your strategy and plan.

Let's imagine that you have decided to get into the German market, and you are currently executing on the plan to make this happen. Suddenly you are presented with a hot project opportunity in Turkey. With the resources you have available, pursuing this unexpected opportunity in Turkey will require that you accept a delay in your German project.

What should you do?

Euromax

I worked for a software company that offered a complete prepress solution for newspapers. It covered the full editorial and pagination process, the advertisement sales and customer management process as well as having management tools for balancing the newspaper's mix of editorial and commercial content. The software was developed together with a European newspaper group, which, at the time when I joined the company, was also the only customer. The company had an older product, which was used by smaller newspapers and magazines. Still, my employer decided to discontinue supporting the product and did not want to invest in the development of a replacement for small customers. The new product was exclusively for the biggest newspapers in the world with a circulation of over 100.000 copies daily.

When I was brought in to take care of sales, the company had a subsidiary in the UK, where several customers used the old product, and a subsidiary in Belgium, where the new customer was located. The company had also hired an outside salesperson in Germany and one in France.

While reviewing the sales strategy (the current setup was a costly operation for my employer), we received an inquiry from New Zealand. A previous employee had emigrated there some years before and had implemented the old product at the small newspaper where he now worked. The owner of the newspaper was a large media group with several other papers in New Zealand, Australia and on the US west coast. They were very interested in introducing new technology that could help reduce operational costs and provide a better service to their advertising customers. He had told group management of the project we were doing with the European newspaper group, and they were now interested in talking us. Were we prepared to come down to New Zealand and make a presentation?

After a few additional phone calls, the opportunity was confirmed, and it was also confirmed that our lack of local presence wasn't a critical issue that would impact their choice of vendor.

Pursuing this opportunity would require substantial sales, pre-sales and management resources. If we could close the deal, we would have to station some of our most critical support resources in New Zealand for six to nine months. We couldn't fly them back for a day or two to help with pre-sales projects elsewhere. The opportunity cost was very high. Looking through the project pipeline, it was clear that we had no other sales opportunities in Europe that were scheduled to close sooner than the one in New Zealand.

I was not in favour of pursuing the opportunity, but my management decided otherwise, and soon I was on a plane to New Zealand.

We did win the business, and after having signed the contract, I finally had time to revisit the general sales strategy. The New Zealand project convinced me that:

- We had a superior value proposition for newspapers with a complex operation (all large newspapers are complex).

- Customers were not overly concerned about vendor proximity. Mainly because there were only very few vendors in this market and none of them were close.

- The market was not particularly national. Even on a global scale, there are not many newspapers with a circulation of over 100.000

daily copies. (The newspaper in New Zealand didn't print 100.000 copies daily, but we accepted to deviate from this threshold as the deal would give us access to the group's other large newspapers. At least that's what we thought).

The opportunity gave us a crucial independent reference and taught me that we were facing the Narrow Gorge scenario that I describe in more detail later in this chapter.

Navision Software

In 1989 three gentlemen from Jutland (the part of Denmark that sits on top of Germany) approached the small Danish software company PC&C in Copenhagen to suggest that they established distribution of PC&C's Navigator, an ERP-system for the mid-market, in Germany.

After lengthy discussions, a business plan was agreed upon and in 1990 Deltacom GmbH was founded by the three Danes and they started operating out of a small office in Hamburg.

Nothing went according to the business plan, but after three tough years, the company reached break-even. When PC&C changed their name to Navision Software in 1995 and launched Navision Financials certified for Windows95, the business took off like a rocket. Navision Software became the market leader in Germany and contributed substantially to the high valuation the company achieved at its IPO in 1999.

PC&C initially took a 20 per cent stake in Deltacom and provided a generous credit that was extended again and again. Although Deltacom did the German translation and localisation of the software, PC&C also had to devote attention and resources to the activities. People with less patience may have given up, but neither Deltacom nor PC&C did.

No one could have foreseen that Windows95 would outcompete all other operating systems and within just one year become the preferred IT-platform across all industries and all types of organisations. Navision

Financials was the first and for some time also the only ERP system certified for Windows95. As I will explain below, it was like surfing the highest wave in the ocean while all your competitors were elsewhere.

Damgaard Data

With its portfolio of Concorde products, Damgaard was the domestic market leader in ERP systems to the mid-market in Denmark in the 1990s. Despite being successful at home, they had a tough time getting international traction. Several initiatives, including setting up subsidiaries in the UK and Germany, had failed.

In 1993 IBM reached out to Damgaard and suggested a joint venture where IBM was to sell the Concorde products through their global network of subsidiaries. Damgaard was quick to jump on this unexpected opportunity only to learn that IBM couldn't deliver on its promise.

In 1998 the owners of Damgaard bought IBM out of the joint venture and carried on independently. From then on, international business accelerated.

The joint venture coincided with IBM going through a significant turnaround. From 1990 to 1993, IBM lost 16 billion dollars and an external CEO, Lou Gerstner, was brought in to fix the problems. In parallel, IBM fought the war on the operating system for the PC with Microsoft and lost. The successful business IBM Denmark ran selling software and PC systems to the mid-market didn't catch the interest of other IBM subsidiaries to a degree where they were prepared to invest in the Damgaard project. When, in 1997, IBM decided not to be active in application software but instead cooperate with all major software vendors ensuring that their products could run on IBM hardware, the joint venture with Damgaard was doomed.

The details of this case story are described in my book *5,460 Miles from Silicon Valley - The In-depth Case Study of What Became Microsoft's First Billion Dollar Acquisition Outside the USA*[40]. The joint venture

---

[40] Bech, H. P. (2018). 5,460 Miles from Silicon Valley - The In-depth Case Study of What Became Microsoft's First Billion Dollar Acquisition Outside the USA (S. Quirke Køngerskov, Trans. A. Hagel Ed.). Copenhagen: TBK Publishing®.

did get Damgaard a reseller and customer base in Norway (where they outcompeted their own distributor), Sweden, Germany, Austria, Switzerland and the US, but it was small and poorly positioned. In the same years, their main competitor, Navision Software, grew way faster in the international markets.

Damgaard sales rose from 30 to 93 million dollars in the period 1994 to 1999, while Navision Software's increased from 13 to 167 million dollars. During the same period, Damgaard realised a total net profit of 19 million dollars, while Navision Software's corresponding profit totalled 40 million. It is fair to note that Damgaard's export performance in the years 1994 to 1997 is not included. These figures were reported in the joint venture with IBM, Damgaard Data International, and not consolidated with the Damgaard sister company. If revenue from Damgaard Data International was recognised as 50 per cent (not counting the results in Denmark twice), turnover in 1999 would have been 111 million dollars, which is still 57 million short of what Navision Software booked.

All other things being equal (which I know is never the case), Navision Software performed significantly better internationally without IBM than Damgaard did with IBM.

When the two companies were listed in 1999, it seemed as though the difference had disappeared. At the time of listing, their market caps were almost identical. However, facing declining demand after the millennium and difficulties associated with the burst of the dot-com-bubble, Navision Software turned out to be far more robust. When the two companies merged, the Damgaard shareholders were left with 28 per cent of shares, while the Navision Software shareholder took 72 per cent.

People make the difference

So, what can we learn from the case examples above?

I am convinced that an unexpected opportunity is mainly a people thing.

Judging if the people, who approach you with what seems like a good idea, can pull it off or not, is extremely hard. Some companies may give such an unexpected opportunity a chance, but minimise its own investment and support, pushing all the risk to the other party and think, "what the heck, if they fail, we haven't lost anything."

PC&C didn't do that. They took their time, almost a full year, carefully discussing the German business case with the trio and finally took a twenty per cent stake in the project. Through the first three tough years, they supported the venture with extended credits and management support.

My example of selling software in New Zealand was only made possible because a decision-maker at the executive level in the newspaper's holding company had seen the potential in our software. The management at the newspaper, where we did the first implementation, would never have dared to choose a vendor located 17,900 kilometres and twelve time zones away. We invested the sales and pre-sales resources required to convince the newspaper staff to recommend our solution to group management, knowing very well that it would be approved.

Daintel that pursued the Brazilian opportunity was less fortunate. They invested time and money only to find out that the unexpected opportunity was a mirage.

You shouldn't automatically ignore the unexpected opportunity. I have seen so many successes grow out of something that was not a part of a plan. The reason is that people in general very often make a big difference. People that approach you because they have seen the light and are prepared to invest in the project may have more execution power than anyone you can recruit through the traditional procedures.

Entering Germany with a team of dedicated entrepreneurs that know your product very well and that have their skin in the game may be a much better opportunity than entering the German market by opening a subsidiary and hire your own staff. By, "skin in the game", I mean majority equity ownership with a realistic capitalisation event in view.

I do not consider a bonus or a commission on top of a fixed salary or a retainer or a small stock option to be a "skin in the game."

However, don't push the unexpected opportunity to assume all the risk. That's the same as conveying that you don't believe in the project. If that's the case, then don't do it. If you believe in the people behind the business idea, then give them the possibility of presenting their case. If it has merit, then take the next step and let them work on the objectives and a plan. Be constructively critical but committed to the planning process. Planning is cheap, and execution is expensive. If the team cannot put together a solid plan, then they probably cannot do the implementation either.

Damgaard's joint venture with IBM turned out to be very expensive. An unexpected opportunity that went sour, so to say. How could that happen? The short version is that the arrangement sat too low in the IBM organisation. While it was extremely strategic for Damgaard, it never was and never became strategic for IBM. Instead, as time passed, it became anti-strategic. The promises of global distribution that IBM made as they signed the papers had no foundation.

I think the lesson learned from the Damgaard example is that you shouldn't treat an inquiry from a big company differently than inquiries made by any other contact. Big companies are not per definition more professional than smaller companies, and it is still people that make the difference. People at big companies may pretend that they have more clout than they actually have. Take your time, check their motives and get some firm commitments.

THE NARROW GORGE

When a market is characterised by a few, large deals at any point in time, then there is not enough flow in market to support many and local vendors in every country. Then you may have a *Narrow Gorge* situation.

Taking advantage of this shoestring opportunity requires that there are customers with similar sets of needs at the functional level across many countries, which is often the case in the large enterprise segment of the market.

Epic

When US-based Epic won the €135 million EHR project in Denmark in 2014, they did not have any operation there. Two local vendors, CSC Scandihealth and Systematic were also bidding for the business. Still, the Regions of Copenhagen and Zealand, which represents fifty per cent of the Danish market for healthcare systems to hospitals, preferred the Epic solution. The decision was based on many parameters and there were two areas where Epic had a clear lead. They could offer more out of the box functionality, and they had other references with 40,000 users. The Regions of Copenhagen and Zealand wanted to avoid a development project and they wanted to make sure that the system could support the workload from 12,000 concurrent users.

Despite having two vendors with local operations and references, Epic was viewed as the best fit for the requirements and the low-risk choice. Second, came Cerner, another US-based vendor. Systematic, which was a subcontractor of IBM, came third while CSC Scandihealth, the previous market leader in Denmark, didn't even make it through the pre-qualification filter.

However, winning the project in Denmark was not done just by responding to the RFP.

Healthcare is an international industry where knowledge sharing across national borders is extensively practised. Danish health authorities had paid several visits to Epic's Kaiser Permanente reference and were very familiar with the company and its products.

Edlund

The primary source for cost reductions in the insurance industry is the optimisation of business processes, including the automation of payments and the introduction of consumer self-service platforms. Making improvements requires the supporting software to be changed, too. These should, preferably, be with standard systems that are easier and less expensive to implement, change and maintain than their current legacy systems. The industry doesn't consider their internal IT-platform a competitive differentiator, and therefore an international market for software companies offering standard solutions has slowly evolved.

In this space, we find Edlund, a major Danish fintech company looking for ways to expand internationally.

"In the past, we were an IT-consulting company developing software," *says Gert Bendsen, CEO of Edlund. "This we are changing. In the future, there will be a much larger standard core shared by all customers, and the customisation effort will decline correspondingly. The bottom line is a much more attractive value proposition for our customers. They will get more and pay less."*

To deliver effectively, Edlund needs to win customers outside of Denmark.

Tia Technology

Tia Technology is one of a handful of players that delivers standard software to the general global insurance industry. Tia's core platform has been developed in close cooperation with customers and partners over the past 30 years. It is offered both through a serviced cloud option or on-premise.

"Tia was originally implemented in the UK and then spread into Denmark and Norway in the late 90s, so we have had an international outlook from the start," emphasises Anders S. Rosenbeck. "Last year, we generated 74 per cent of our turnover outside of Denmark, but we cannot be everywhere and bid on all projects in the world, so we are considering carefully where to focus our resources when prioritising opportunities."

To concentrate the effort, Tia Technology has divided the global market into four categories:

Core markets

Core markets includes the Nordic countries, the Baltics, Poland and South Africa. In these countries, Tia has a good position with many customers and their own representation. They have invested massively in localisation, i.e. integrations to all relevant platforms and systems necessary to run an insurance business in these markets, which, in countries with a well-developed administrative infrastructure, can be quite demanding. As such, customer project risk is minimised, and therefore the choice of using Tia becomes easy.

Mature markets

Markets, where Tia has years of experience and more than one live installation, is defined as a near-core market. This category includes the UK and Ireland, the Netherlands and Germany. In these markets, Tia also owns part of the country-specific components for localisation facilitating the discussions with potential new customers.

Follow-the-footsteps markets (Trojan Horse)

Opportunities elsewhere in the world are pursued on an opportunistic basis primarily by "following the footsteps" of existing customers. It is well known that selling to people who know you is much cheaper than building reputation and trust from scratch. The markets in focus here are in South America, where Tia is already, in Brazil, Columbia and Ecuador with a large European based insurer, and in Africa based on expansion out of South Africa. In such markets, Tia will always go with an implementation partner, never alone.

No-Go markets

The USA and Asia, which are the world's largest insurance markets, have been designated as no-go territories.

"We might come to them at some point through established relationships, but it's not right now," explains Anders S. Rosenbeck. "We are running at our full capacity in the markets where we are active, and the complexity of those two markets would be a major distraction. We do receive inquiries regularly but politely decline them."

Besides the market dimension, Tia uses profiling when prioritising opportunities to go for or to decline. Together with an international management consultancy, Tia has carefully analysed and profiled the "sweet-spot" insurers that are most likely to choose Tia compared to the competition. Elements used in the profiling include the size of the company, lines of business and technology preferences, among other things.

Euromax

After winning the project in New Zealand, I was curious to learn if there were other potential projects where we stood a reasonable chance despite our lack of local presence. At conferences and exhibitions, I addressed the issues with several newspapers from around the world. Although you should always take customer feedback that is not provided in an actual purchase situation with a grain of salt, my conclusion was that provided you had a superior product, then the lack of a local presence was not a critical issue.

We then closed down the subsidiaries in Belgium and the UK and terminated the salespeople in Germany and France. Our sales force was from then on based in Copenhagen, and from there, we covered the global market. Except for the US, even the big markets were simply too small to support local operations until we could see a clear pattern in demand.

The sales team consisted of two colleagues and me. One covered Asia, one covered EMEA, and I covered North America. We were all stationed in Copenhagen, but each of us travelled more than two hundred days a year attending conferences and visiting customers. As soon as we had identified a qualified opportunity, we flew in a team of pre-salespeople to run demos and workshops for about a week. Using this approach, we systematically grew the project pipeline.

At a newspaper conference in Brussels in the autumn of 1990, we were approached by the head of Gannett Co.'s Advanced Systems Laboratory who asked for a demonstration of our system. I didn't know who Gannett was, but as I was looking for someone to help me with the demo, I learned that they published USA Today and a lot of other newspapers. That opened the door to several other newspaper groups, and soon I spent most of my time in Canada and the USA, presenting our solution and building relationships with potential customers.

In November 1991 I received a tip from my friend at Gannett, and after running demos for a suburban newspaper in Washington DC, we booked our first North American project. It was very close to Christmas and to speed up things I took the Concorde from London to New York for the final negotiations and could return a few days later with the signed contract. We had won a project in the USA without having an office or a single person permanently located there.

However, the Euromax story doesn't have a happy ending. You can find the details in the case story in the back of the book.

THE TROJAN HORSE

Moving internationally with your customers is what I call the Trojan Horse approach. Your domestic customers have international subsidiaries and activities where they want to use your software. They ask you if and how you can support such endeavours.

The benefits of using the same software across their international operations may compensate for some of the disadvantages associated with the initial lack of support for the national language and missing local functionality. Your challenge is to decide if there is enough business volume to justify developing this opportunity further. Ending up in a situation where you have to support a small number of customers across many countries may prove inefficient.

The Trojan Horse only works if you have a sufficient number of international customers, and there is a definite advantage of using your software across their operations. It is not enough that they like your software and recommend it to their subsidiaries. There must be a compelling reason strong enough to compensate for the inconveniences of your missing presence and lack of full product support.

Monitor ERP

Monitor is a Swedish provider of ERP to discrete manufacturing companies in the SMB-segment (Small and Medium Businesses).

"Our customers have spearheaded our international activities," explains Johan Holmsten, sales and marketing manager at Monitor.

"Swedish SMB manufacturing companies started setting up operations abroad in the 1980s and asked us to provide Monitor in local languages and with support for the country-specific requirements. The first main hub was Poland, and after building a solid base of customers there, we opened a subsidiary in 1992."

In 2007 the customer base in the Baltics called for local support and Monitor engaged with local companies to represent them in the region. Later came China and Malaysia.

With customers ready to pay for the software and the support, Monitor's main challenge was to find qualified people and train them in the product. Although finding qualified people that are prepared and suited for working in a small setup is by no means trivial, it is much easier than finding customers that are prepared to be the first users of a foreign ERP-system.

The reasons why the Trojan Horse works for Monitor are:

> 1. Their customer had established international operations and subsidiaries.

> 2. Their customers had substantial benefits from using the same system across their global operations.

> 3. There were enough customers in the new markets to justify building national product and support organisations.

The Trojan Horse approach is common in the market for mission-critical business software where the benefits of using the same software across the organisation compensate for the initial lack of complete localisation.

Uniconta

Uniconta, the cloud-based ERP-platform, has achieved swift acceptance domestically. Starting at the low end of the market, Uniconta has rapidly moved up and is now used by larger companies with international operations.

"One of our customers has an operation in Romania and wanted to implement Uniconta there as well, says Erik Damgaard, CEO and founder of Uniconta. "As we didn't have support for the Romanian language, the customer offered to do the translation if we would then add it to Uniconta. So that's what we did. Uniconta is now available in 25 languages."

Although many of Uniconta's international customers have come through the Trojan Horse approach, they do have plans for a more active penetration of the global markets also.

"International expansion in the ERP-market requires time, money, people and management attention," says Per Pedersen, Executive VP, marketing and sales at Uniconta. "Time and money are not a big issue for us, but finding the right people and giving them adequate support and attention is. We have established independent distributors in some of the key markets and are convinced that this approach (the Navision Model) will help us break the ice, but growing with our customers (The Trojan Horse) is a great way to get started."

So far, the Trojan Horse approach has generated customers for Uniconta in several countries.

Tia Technology

Danish Tia Technology is expanding in South America. Through a European based insurer, they now have customers in Brazil, Columbia and Ecuador. As this customer extends its reach into other countries, Tia follows suit.

The same Trojan Horse strategy is applied in Africa where their customers in South Africa have international ambitions for the continent.

"We ensure that the implementation capacity is in place to support our customers' expansion projects," says Anders S. Rosenbeck, CEO of Tia Technology. "We do that through local partners, and as they get familiar with the system, they also become ambassadors. It will lead to additional projects when the time is right and doesn't require

us investing speculatively in markets where the timing of the project opportunities is hard to predict."

Using the Trojan Horse approach, Tia can win projects in markets where they would otherwise not be represented.

THE NAVISION MODEL

The *Navision Model* means setting up exclusive distributors as joint ventures that perform the same activities as a subsidiary would do and where you have a pull-option for the remaining shares.

From the outside, customers and stakeholders will perceive the operation as yours.

The difference from the traditional distributor model is that:

- The setup has mutual exclusivity. You do not appoint additional distributors, they only represent your product and interests, and they follow your business model.

- You clearly state your intention of acquiring the business at a later stage and you include a formula for calculating the acquisition price.

The distributorship doesn't have to be a joint venture. It just turns out that this format may have some advantages. It gives the vendor a seat on the board, full disclosure to the books, and it feels more like a true partnership with fully aligned interests.

Navision Software initially didn't have a formalised process for acquiring the shares of their distributors. As they came to consider an IPO as a future option, they changed that. It gave the joint venture partners an incentive to grow the business as fast as possible. The quicker they grew, the higher the acquisition price would be. It also provided the vendor with the possibility of rolling up the distributors before the IPO, which had a substantial and positive impact on the valuation.

Exclusive distributors are always concerned about the vendors taking over their activities. Sometimes it can be done amicably, but often it requires legal action that may be costly and time-consuming. No one, other than the lawyers, benefits from such a conflict. With a formalised approach and a formula for calculating the acquisition-price there is a much better chance of a friendly takeover, where the local joint venture partner or partners may continue as the country management team for the subsidiary.

The Navision Software go-to-market approach was indirect through resellers. The joint ventures, therefore, acted as distributors responsible for brand building, lead generation and for recruiting and managing resellers. In this case, they were also responsible for product localisation.

The revenue split in such a setup, where you leave market development to a distributor, is usually 30/70. If the final end-user price is 100, the distributor gets 70 and the vendor 30. The distributor typically passes on 40 to resellers. For cloud-based solutions where the vendor also provides the data-centre portion, there seems to be some variation in the revenue split. Some companies split 40/30/30 while I have seen others split 25/25/50 because they want to motivate distributors and resellers to invest in faster market penetration and compensate for the initial lack of brand recognition.

Exclusivity

For all practical purposes, such arrangements must be exclusive. It's hard to convince someone to invest in market development, direct or indirect, on your behalf if there is a risk that you can appoint someone else at a later stage that will get a free ride on her investments.

Exclusivity is always tied to performance. Certain minimum numbers must be achieved to maintain the exclusivity. Commonly, these numbers are not met, but you retain the exclusivity because you can see that the effort is being made and that the results will eventually materialise. No plan survives the meeting with reality and cooperating on getting the business off the ground is often a better option than terminating the agreement and finding a replacement.

Finding the right partners for the Navision model

An exclusive reseller- or distributorship can be a very profitable business and does represent an appealing opportunity for someone with an entrepreneurial mindset or someone already active in the same or a complementary space. The value of the opportunity, however, increases substantially if you express or even state an intention of buying the business at a later stage. Defining the formula for calculating the acquisition price and the time for triggering the event upfront will help the reseller or distributor drive towards this scenario as fast as possible.

How do you find such potential resellers or distributors?

Initially, it was the distributors that found Navision. Their operations in the US and Germany were the outcome of inbound inquiries. Spain came through their cooperation with, but was not supported by, IBM[41]. IBM-Denmark - that was the distributor for Navision from 1987 to 1994 - did not succeed in convincing their sister companies elsewhere, that Navigator, which was the Navision product at that time, represented a golden opportunity for boosting PC sales. IBM employees in Spain did see the potential and left IBM to pursue the opportunity. The distributors in Austria and Switzerland found Navision at the CeBIT fair in Hannover. The Austrian distributor knew someone in The Czech Republic. Around the time where Navision released Financials for Windows95, the company initiated a distributor recruitment activity focused on the English-speaking markets. However, the UK and the Australian distributors also found Navision. In 1997 they found and established a joint venture with an Italian distributor.

Technically oriented individuals usually drove the new Navision distributors. When things didn't go as fast as expected, Navision pushed them to hire a sales manager. After a year or so, the entrepreneur and the sales director would typically disagree on the strategy, after which Navision bought out the entrepreneur; then hired and promoted the

---

[41] You can find the details in my book 5,460 Miles from Silicon Valley - The In-depth Case Study of What Became Microsoft's First Billion Dollar Acquisition Outside the USA.

sales manager to country manager. This happened in the Netherlands and Sweden in 1997.

Developing a market is typically a three to five-year effort. Finding the people that have the combination of skills, drive and the financial means to do this is not easy. Preferably you will be looking for a team, which makes the recruitment job even more difficult. Looking through the Navision experience, most of their distributors found them. In today's more transparent world being found may be a more fruitful approach than trying to find.

Don't let the perfect solution stand in the way of a good solution

In the ideal world, you would want the distributor or reseller to assume all the cost and risk, but in the real world that is often not an option.

Navision had a mix of ownerships in their distributors. They took a twenty per cent share of the German setup, none in the Austrian and Swiss distributors, 70 per cent of the Italian and after a short while, full ownership of the Dutch. It was a question of doing what was necessary and possible. The higher the initial stake, the lower the future acquisition cost.

The Navision model was born out of necessity, and the first distributor agreements did not include pull options. It was only as the idea of making an IPO entered the board room that the streamlining of the distributor agreements and the ownership model took form. When the IPO was executed in the spring of 1999, Navision had acquired most of its distributors. They didn't establish new distributors following the joint venture model, but continued to acquire those that were still left and invested in their own subsidiaries instead. With the proceeds from the IPO and excellent profits from operations, they could now use brute force to pay their way into new markets.

When Microsoft acquired Navision in 2002, the latter was represented in thirty countries, from where they managed 2,000 resellers and 100,000 customers.

Standardise

We don't see many examples of using the Navision Model for international expansion. The type of people required are difficult to find, and there is some scepticism against the joint venture format. Nevertheless, I believe it should remain an option that you can exercise when the circumstances are right. Having entrepreneurial people onboard with a vested interest in the outcome can produce impressive results. If you are short on funds, then that may be your shortcut to international success.

If you decide to implement this model, I recommend standardising the agreements. It will ease your operation when all distributors follow the same procedures and have the same obligations. The day may come when you need to roll up and acquire your distributors. You will be grateful for having the formula in place for doing so at the same time as you prepare an IPO or some other type of liquidity event.

USING EXTERNAL RESOURCES

For a software company that has only operated domestically, it can appear a daunting task to find your way into a new market. Especially when it concerns a country of which you know very little. Can you find someone that knows the market and can do the initial business development for you?

For most software companies, business development, marketing and sales - demand and revenue generation - are the most challenging business processes to get right. The primary reason is that the founders are mostly technical wizards that do not have much experience with or interest in running the commercial side of the business model. When that is the case, then he or she is also not particularly qualified to find the people who can perform commercial functions.

Another reason that demand and revenue generation is tricky is that it covers a multitude of disciplines and requires a wide variety of skills.

Figure 8: Sample revenue generation process.

Designing and managing a demand and revenue generation process that can run across national borders requires a team of people. As you get started on the journey, you may not be capable of hiring a complete team, and even as you grow not all the functions can justify a full headcount until you reach a certain size.

If you don't have a commercial resource on your executive team, then I recommend you get that first. That person, who will be responsible for demand and revenue generation, should be a partner (shareholder) and should devote his or her full attention to the job. With that person on board, you can now explore options for outsourcing some of the business development activities to a third party.

In most countries, there are individual freelancers and boutique agencies that perform business development activities, including marketing and sales. You can find them all through LinkedIn, where they are usually quite active.

Sales Force Europe

For this book, I have interviewed Rick Pizzoli from Sales Force Europe (SFE). Rick primarily offers business development services in European countries. You can find the full interview in the back of the book, and if you are considering outsourcing, then reading it will be worthwhile.

Senior people, who do business development in the software industry, and do it well, have found out that it pays better and is more fun to work on a project basis rather than being fully and permanently employed by a single company. Most of them are organised in boutique agencies, such as SFE, representing the full array of services required to bootstrap a market while others work as individual freelancers.

Instead of hiring your own resources and dealing with local labour market issues and the associated administrative overheads, you contract with an agency and receive a monthly bill. You agree on the terms and conditions, including the termination options, and don't have to worry about local labour market legislation, which in many cases can be rather complicated.

I include the outsourcing option as a shoestring approach because you can engage a mix of resources without everyone on the team working full time for you. These agencies have an established network and can usually find the resources required at short notice and because they are prepared to work on a negotiated contractual basis.

Formally these agencies or individuals often work as your agents. It means that they represent you in the lead generation, sales and customer success process, and may even carry your business card. Still, the final commercial relationship is between you and the customer.

Let me pre-empt an expectation that I often come across from companies that look to engage an agent. Agents in the software industry seldom offer their services on a commission-only basis. The reason is that developing a market and winning customers for a new product is typically a team effort, that it is hard to predict how long it will take and for which the process requires your support. Therefore, most business development agents and agencies are paid a retainer, are reimbursed for their expenses and may receive a performance bonus or commission on top.

Using an agent is not the cheap option, but it may be the fastest, the most flexible and the least risky option. The only real difference between agents and employees is that you get an invoice from the first and pay a salary to the latter. You can freely agree on the termination options with the agent while the termination of employment contacts is regulated by legislation. However, getting rid of people may not be your most urgent priority.

I don't subscribe to the idea that hiring people and putting them on the payroll will internalise the accumulation of knowledge. People resign for all sorts of reasons and as they leave, they take their heads with them. If none of their knowledge is documented, then it's gone. I could argue that agents are much more loyal. As long as you pay them well and on time, they will stick with you forever. When it comes to finding the talent that can help develop and scale a revenue generation process that works across international borders, the legal minutia of the relationships should be kept as simple as possible.

The reality is that business developers are difficult to find and that you shouldn't be concerned about how you engage with them. The value of the difference between someone who can do the job and someone who cannot can be counted in millions, so have an open mind. For management positions, the agent format will not work, but for most operational jobs it will.

By accepting to use agents, you get access to a vast pool of talent. With the growing gig-economy and the increasing number of digital nomads, there is qualified talent available out there. While you are limited to hiring employees to where you have legal entities, you can use agents from anywhere and if you can organise work to be performed by virtual teams your pool of potential talent is unlimited. The agent format may also allow you to try and test until you find what you are looking for, which could lead to employment or a joint venture.

Livefyre

San Francisco-based Livefyre helps companies engage consumers through a combination of real-time conversation, social curation and social advertising. With Livefyre, brands can integrate real-time, social content into their websites, mobile apps, advertisements and television broadcasts to increase viewer engagement, boost website traffic and drive revenue.

After five years of building the business in the USA, the company engaged SFE to help with bootstrapping the market in Europe. With an account executive based in London, the first lighthouse customer was signed up within ninety days after the launch. The engagement was then expanded to France, Germany, Italy, Spain, and the Nordics. Within the first year, Livefyre had secured revenue of 1.6 million dollars through SFE. In the second year, SFE generated four million dollars in new business and in the third year it grew to ten million dollars.

Based on the successful rollout in Europe, Livefyre asked SFE to expand into Asia and Latin America.

When Adobe acquired Livefyre, they also took over the SFE sales team while the marketing and support people returned to work for other SFE clients.

The SFE team succeeded because of the perfect combination of local networks, tech sales experience and a great product. SFE fully integrated with the Livefyre sales team in the USA, matching their pipeline growth KPIs, close rate and ROI. SFE provided not only local sales executives but also business development, marketing and lead generation services, all with local language and cultural knowledge, overseen by regional management.

"We were tasked to rapidly expand our global footprint in a highly competitive space, and, without the Sales Force Europe territory team, we would not have been able to hit the ground running with relevant local resources nearly as fast had we used the traditional recruitment mode."[42]

NetDialog

NetX is a technical software product that crosses borders very easily. It requires no localisation, and, as it is used exclusively by IT-specialist in primarily international organisations, the English UI (user interface) and documentation are adequate. NetDialog also has had global ambitions from the start and have recruited business

---

[42] Source: Scott Sorochak, SVP Global Sales at Livefyre.

partners that could bring the product to potential customers outside the domestic market in The Netherlands. As eighty per cent of the revenue now comes from abroad and while most of the new business comes from international customers, the time is ripe for considering what the next steps should be.

"I believe we can continue to manage our business in the near time zones from Amsterdam," Olaf Hasker, CEO at NetDialog, explains. "Expanding our market share in Asia and the Americas will require that we establish some kind of local representation."

Olaf Hasker is fully aware that setting up satellite offices adds a layer of complexity to the operation and management of his company. He has seen from others how this step can go very wrong, so he is cautious and considers various approaches where he can adjust quickly if required.

"Outsourcing the initial steps may be a way to minimise the risk," Olaf Hasker concludes. "We want to demonstrate our long-term commitment to the international markets, but we don't want to be caught in a trap. Our business is still very project-driven, and we need the ability to adjust according to the actual deal flow."

MERGERS AND ACQUISITIONS

You can get access to new markets through mergers and acquisitions, but they can hardly be labelled shoestring approaches. They are generally used to consolidate and strengthen positions and are seldom an appropriate tool for a small company trying to gain a bridgehead in a foreign country.

I have been involved in quite a few mergers and acquisitions, and they are high-risk projects that require deep pockets to pay for the advisory and legal fees and a firm management hand aligning organisations and cultures.

The immediate benefit of an operational merger or acquisition between smaller companies is the so-called synergy opportunity. That is the possibility of cutting costs due to overlapping functions. You only need one board of directors, one CEO, one CFO and her G&A department and one HR department. As a means of expanding internationally, you should have the option of moving all the customers to your product, and if that is possible, then you can also save on R&D.

The risk is that both the staff and the customers of the company that you acquire or with whom you merge become hostile and flee. When that happens, you are left with a liability rather than an asset.

I have often been asked to help software companies identify acquisition targets in other countries with competitive but outdated products. The idea is to either convince them to do an OEM deal or acquire them for a low price, preferably with an earn-out option. In both cases, the objective is replacing their products with yours.

It sounds like a great strategy, but in reality, and for several reasons, it usually doesn't work.

First and foremost, unless the target is already actively searching for a replacement, it is highly unlikely that you can activate the desire to do so. In smaller software companies, management and ownership are overlapping, and there are many emotions involved. Accepting that you have an outdated technology doesn't come easy and when it does there is usually an in-house anchored product succession plan in place, or at least a fantasy that this should happen.

Therefore, my advice is: People looking for a technology replacement will find you. Don't waste your time looking for them.

People don't like the idea of being acquired. Maybe the owners can cash in and move on, but the staff becomes insecure, and so do the customers. As you start harvesting the synergy options, the level of uneasiness increases. It takes considerable management effort and very visible signs of good intentions to calm people down and make them return to doing their assignments rather than gossiping around the water-cooler or starting to apply for new jobs. The best people leave first, so unless you make sure they know their worth before the acquisition is announced, then you risk ending up with the people you don't want to keep.

If you make an acquisition abroad to gain access to a market, then make sure that the people you want to retain can see a better future with you than the one they had before you came along. And make sure you have leadership and management in place to make them stay happy and motivated.

A foreign acquisition, as a means to gaining market entry, only makes sense if you can move their customers to your product. With software that's not an easy call. Customers are often emotionally attached to the software they use and don't want to be forced to switch. If you announce the discontinuation of a product, customers may be annoyed and look elsewhere for a replacement. If you make the switch voluntary, then you are stuck with the obligation of supporting a second product line, and you may not know for how long.

You could acquire a consulting company with activities in the same domain where you operate and make them sell your product. Then you don't have the product issue. But you will not get any customers either. You get a consulting company and turning that into a product sales company is not a walk in the park.

I guess you sense that I am not a big fan of using mergers and acquisitions as a means for smaller software companies to get access to a new country. The risk is too high.

There may be a case out there where my concerns do not apply. If so, then I would be happy to learn about it.

TAKE-AWAYS FROM THE CHAPTER

As described, there are plenty, or at least seven, ways to win customers in foreign markets without you having to set up a subsidiary first, and when meeting physically face-to-face with customers is a requirement.

Inbound opportunities mostly drive these shoestring approaches. Making yourself and your value proposition visible and easy to understand will help people find you. Participating in industry events is also a great way to meet international customers and partners.

If your visibility is high and if you attend international events, but you never receive any inquiries, then something is wrong. You should revisit your business model, your market positioning and the way you communicate it. Either you are not communicating clearly, or your value proposition is not strong enough.

Figure 9: Salespeople and customers often speak a different language.

You may have seen the illustration of the king and the salesman before. Given the situation, you would agree that the salesman has a product that could be of great benefit to the king. However, he doesn't know how to communicate it, and the timing may not be perfect either.

If you want inbound inquiries, then you must be very careful with your product marketing.

Using the outsourcing options listed in this chapter doesn't require being found, but I would be reluctant to pursue that path unless I have seen clear signs of market interest first.

Making shoestring approaches successful is very people dependent. Some people can pull it off; others cannot. No matter how attractive a shoestring option may appear, I recommend taking the time to vet it. Remain calm and maintain your common sense and business acumen. When something sounds too good to be true, then it is probably because it is. Test, test and test until you have found a way that works.

Chapter Six - Business model considerations

INTRODUCTION

In this chapter I will discuss some of the typical issues your business model has to address when you move from solely operating in your domestic market to operating internationally. The structure of the discussion will follow the business model and the business model environment framework as described in chapter three.

There are fundamentally two aspects to consider:

1. Issues related to customer and market acceptance - that's your business model *front-office*.

2. Issues related to your internal operation - that's your business model *back-office*.

With *customer and market acceptance* I refer to those aspects of your value proposition, position and other customer and market facing topics and activities that may have to change from country to country including those dictated by local legislation.

With *internal operation* I mean how engaging resources and performing activities may have to differ from country to country including those dictated by local legislation.

When you operate a version of the simple revenue generation approach then you can choose to ignore the differences in the local business model environments. Your potential customers find you, they self-qualify, and you only get those that find your value proposition attractive as it is and can accept your terms and conditions. If your value proposition is exceptionally attractive, then you may get customers from all over the world and you can choose to be indifferent to where they reside geographically. However, it is unlikely that this approach will make you a market leader anywhere.

When you run a physical revenue generation approach, then the differences in the national business model environments may play a significant role from the start. This chapter is primarily relevant for companies that have physical or complex virtual revenue generation processes and for companies with simple virtual revenue generation processes, see figure 5, that want deeper penetration of local markets.

BUSINESS MODEL ENVIRONMENT

When you travelled the world (that was before Covid-19), you could easily get the impression that we were facing global alignment. You saw the same shops everywhere and when you sat in your hotel room, walked the isles of an exhibition and listened to presentations at conferences you could be anywhere. Everything looked the same.

Yes, international trade, investments and travel have increased dramatically over the last fifty years and as we recover from the covid-19 restrictions, these trends will continue. However, when you dig a little deeper you will still find substantial differences between countries.

Alexander Osterwalder has developed a handy tool[43] called *Mapping the Business Model Design Space*. It is a deck of cards that can help facilitate a workshop where you map the business model environment. It is not designed specifically for taking your business model international, but it can be easily adapted to and also works well in this context.

All you need to do is to ask if there are issues in a country, where you wish to become active, that may affect how you support your customers' buying journeys and how they will impact on how you run

---

[43] You can get the card here: https://www.stattys.com/en/methods/business-model-generation/business-model-supporting-tools/bmg-environmental-cards

your back office. The card deck helps structure the discussion around the four areas of the business model environment. With the four areas, 18 subjects and a list of 73 questions, you will cover all the important bases. Some of the questions will not apply to your situation and can be skipped. You can then add the questions I have listed in chapter three and you should be well covered.

As you go through the exercise you will come across questions that are highly relevant, but where you do not have any data or insight. This is a great opportunity to identify sources that can help you get access to the information or list them as issues that you will need to explore as you get in touch with potential customers and stakeholders.

TECHNOLOGY, REGULATORY, SOCIETAL, CULTURAL AND SOCIOECONOMIC ISSUES

This area covers high level issues across all markets and industries within a country.

Technology

A research paper[44] that compared the adoption of cloud-based SaaS solutions in small and medium enterprises in Germany and New Zealand came to the following conclusion:

"While both countries have a similar penetration with present-day technology in general and with the Internet and the Web in particular, their SMBs exhibit many differences, as do the ways in which their SMBs perceive their IT business.

The findings of our study suggest that New Zealand SMBs are different to their German counterparts in two key ways:

> *1. As smaller companies, they [New Zealand] do not have dedicated IT staff and, as a result, are reliant on the advice they receive from so-called cloud computing experts, who would naturally present the technology in a positive light.*

---

[44] https://www.ercis.org/sites/ercis/files/structure/network/research/ercis-working-papers/ercis_wp_19.pdf

2. There have been few, at most, well-publicised security breaches involving cloud services in New Zealand. It is not a significant target of industrial espionage or hacking, and as such, is probably not at the forefront of the minds of New Zealand SMBs.

However, there are also significant commonalities between the results of the two countries."

Most of you reading this book will be engaged in companies that offer a cloud-based SaaS product. For most of the markets, that you will consider, the technical infrastructure in terms of Internet access and bandwidth will be in place to deliver your product. What will differ from country to country is the level of acceptance of SaaS as a viable delivery format. For your particular product you may not have a technology infrastructure issue, but you may have an innovation diffusion issue. I'll get back to that later.

The legal framework

Do you have to add and pay value added (VAT) or sales tax in the countries where your product is sold? How much revenue can you make from a country before you have a tax liability issue? When are you subject to paying withholding tax? Are there trade restrictions that you need to consider? Are there restrictions on the storage of your clients' data and especially of their personal data? Are you obliged to provide certain documentation in the local language? Does your product require certification or approval before you can deliver, and the customer is allowed to use the product[45]?

Offering software as a service from the cloud and charging a monthly or annual subscription fee paid by a credit card technically allows you to sell to anyone anywhere, but that doesn't mean that you do not have to comply with the legislation in the countries where the products are used. And far from all customers are prepared to pay for software with a credit card.

---

[45] https://blog.chartmogul.com/saas-in-china/

Daintel almost went bankrupt because they did not realise that none of the hospitals in Brazil could buy and use their software unless they had achieved an official approval and getting that would take years. Such an approval was not required in Denmark, so they didn't even think about it until they had invested time and effort in demonstrations and pilot projects.

Companies such as Tia Technology, Edlund and Epic, that operate in regulated markets, are highly affected by local legislation and by national, public IT-systems with which they must communicate. ERP systems, such as Uniconta, RamBase and Monitor, are also affected by local legislation, accounting standards, integration requirements and reporting formats.

Even when you can charge by credit card or get prepaid for your products and services is it worthwhile to meticulously check the legal framework before you accept an order in a foreign country. You can probably get a long way ignoring these issues, but the penalty of violating local legislation often follow Murphy's law: *Everything that can go wrong will go wrong - and at the worst possible time.* Such as when you negotiate a funding round and during the due diligence the question about tax liabilities comes up.

Take legal and tax issues seriously. You do not want to come up against a government, which is always a counterpart with no feelings and bottomless pockets.

Language

English is the most used language in the world by number of speakers, and the third most-spoken native language, after Standard Chinese and Spanish. It is the most widely used second language and is either the official language or one of the official languages in almost 60 countries. Around 1.5 billion people master English and for about 360 million people it's their native language.

Focusing on English as your primary second language (assuming that your native language is something else) is a simple way to minimise the complexity of your initial international operation.

It is not difficult to imagine the level of complexity and overheads that you introduce by deciding to add an additional language to your operation. Your website, your marketing and sales literature, your product and associated documentation and your internal and external communication now need to be translated and maintained in an additional language. Going from one to two languages is a big step in terms of cost and operational complexity. This explains why most software companies embarking on a global endeavour decide to operate in English-only first, maybe supplemented by their domestic language.

For some niche and technical products, this approach may represent no major limitation to where you can sell. However, for most products it does. While you may strike lucky and win a handful customers or two with an English approach in e.g. China, Korea, Japan, Germany, France, Italy or Spain you will never get any significant business going there.

An intermediate approach is to make the product and its associated user documentation available in the local language and maintain English as your marketing and operating language. Several of the companies described in the case story section of this book use this approach successfully.

The choice between using resources on adding and maintaining more languages versus improving the English version of your product is not easy, but the latter may be the shoestring option. It may be better to have a superior product in English than having a mediocre product in several language.

Internal communication

The question of whether your product and services should support other languages than English depends on your situation and ambition. One area where I do recommend you insist on only using English is your internal operations. Demand that your staff only use the English version of all software tools. It will help them improve their English skills, it will ease internal IT-support and it will help you avoid compatibility problems. It's an issue that most organisations don't think much about in the beginning, but as they grow their operation it comes back to haunt them. Making your staff change something that they've got used to is not easy.

First Agenda

"Speech recognition technology is a key part of the solution," explains Kasper Lyhr, CEO at First Agenda, "and in this domain, the best-supported language is English. Outside the Nordics, we, therefore, focus all our efforts on the English-speaking markets."

First Agenda, developing software for meeting management, is currently operating in Denmark, Germany (R&D) and the USA. Twenty-five per cent of revenue comes from abroad. Because English speech-recognition technology is more developed, the company is currently concentrating its efforts on the UK and the USA.

"We are up against the law of diffusion of innovation," Kasper Lyhr stresses. "The technology is mature and the return on the investment attractive and well documented. However, we are an early mover in the industry, and with only a few competitors, we are a small voice in the market. I expect demand to increase substantially over the next couple of years and then we are well-positioned to become the market leader."

The company has established a subsidiary in Boston, MA, and relocated their Danish VP of sales to spearhead the build-up in North America.

Innovation adoption

Businesses all over the world operate according to the same basic principles. To survive they need to make a profit. To grow they need product marketing, ongoing product development, leadership, management and to exhibit some degree of operational excellence. You would, therefore, assume that when it comes to culture the main differences are to be found in how you communicate, establish relationships, interact and negotiate. You would expect that business-people irrespective of culture are curious to learn how to increase revenue and decrease operational expenditure and capital requirements.

But that may not be the case.

According to a study published in 2003 by Yvonne M. Van Everdingen and Eric Waarts[46], both from Erasmus University Rotterdam, culture apparently has a major impact on how innovations diffuse. Their study reported considerable variations in how fast ERP-systems were adopted in different countries. They then went on to explain these differences by relating them with Hofstede's then five (now six) cultural dimensions[47] and with Hall's Cultural Classification Schemes[48].

"The results of our study also have important implications for suppliers of innovations who want to launch their product in multiple countries. An essential message is that even within Europe, large cultural differences exist that substantially affect the adoption of innovations. Overall, the Nordic European countries seem to be most receptive to breakthrough innovations (e.g., ERP systems). Countries characterised by a high level of uncertainty avoidance and a low level of long-term orientation (e.g., Mediterranean countries) are less likely to adopt such innovations spontaneously."

The study found the lowest adoption rate in the UK (lower than southern Europe), which came as a surprise to me. The UK is frequently on the top of the list of countries to enter, mainly because it is a big market (#8 according to the BECH Index[49]) and because English is the main language. Everdingen and Waarts' study indicates that the UK may not be such an attractive place to launch an innovative product. Given that many technology-companies flock to the UK first, we seem to have a cocktail of hyper competition and customer conservatism that may not be very attractive for companies on a slim budget.

---

[46] Everdingen, Y. M. V. W., Eric. (2003, January 15, 2003). The Effect of National Culture on the Adoption of Innovations. Marketing Letters, 14(3), 16.

[47] Hofstede, G. (2013). Culture's consequences: Comparing values, behaviors, institutions, and organizations across nations. Thousand Oaks, Calif.: Sage.

[48] Hall, E. T. (1976). Beyond culture / Edward T. Hall. Garden City, N.Y: Anchor Press.

[49] Bech, H. P. (2020). And the Winners Remain China and India (TBK-WIPA-036). Copenhagen, Denmark. TBK Publishing®

You may argue that Everdingen and Waarts' study is outdated, relates to ERP only and cannot be extrapolated to other innovations and markets. That may well be, but that does not mean that different countries may not adopt innovations differently. Hofstede's cultural dimensions may provide us with valid indicators if we experience that our value proposition is received differently in various countries.

Culture

In addition to language, legislation and the potential variance in the receptiveness to innovations, culture may also have a significant impact on how you can win customers in a new country.

Running a very simple or a simple virtual go-to-market approach you may not consider this an issue, but I am sure that you will experience that certain markets are more responsive to your value proposition than others. When your business requires outbound lead generation and face-to-face activities, then culture does play an important role.

Culture determines how you build relationships, communicate and negotiate, and which role relationships work for doing business. However, cultural traits differ from person to person. Therefore, when you look at the Hofstede cultural dimension for a country it doesn't mean that each and every person you come across has exactly the same profile.

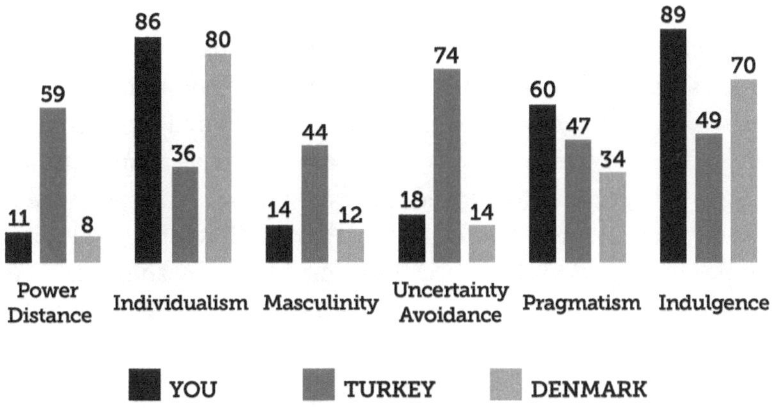

Figure 10: Culture profiles according to the Hofstede dimensions

Some years ago, I was running a series of workshops for The Sabanci University in Istanbul in Turkey. Preparing for the workshops, I bought a Culture Compass Report from Hofstede for the role of a person transferring know-how. The results from the report are summarised in Figure 10 and shows that I differ considerably from the average Turkish person, but that I also differ somewhat from the average Danish person.

The report highlighted a number of issues that I should consider as I prepared and delivered my material. I did pay close attention to these hints and the workshops became a success. Some of the content in this book and in *Building Successful Partner Channels* comes from preparing this knowledge transfer.

While it certainly makes sense to understand cultural differences it is also crucial to understand that people within a certain culture can be very different. Especially in the software industry where most of us are internationally oriented, have travelled abroad and speak several languages. Using shoestring approaches, we often get in touch with innovators and early adopters that are more open minded and less conservative than the mainstream. Therefore, you should remain respectful to other cultures, but also treat people as the individuals they are.

On a personal note, I have learnt that coming from a small country like Denmark can be an advantage. Denmark doesn't play any role in big politics, which means that people in other countries are seldom judgemental. We never expect anyone to speak our language or know our ways. We are well aware that we are the ones who must adapt. Our biggest disadvantage may be that we in general are very informal, direct and lack respect for formal authority (low on power distance and high on individualism). Delivering the workshops in Turkey I wore a dark suit and a tie, which I never do at home. I did so to show my respect for Turkish business culture and to align with their expectations to me as an authority figure.

MARKET CONDITIONS

A few years ago, a software company had conducted a market survey in Germany that indicated that SMBs were reluctant to embrace cloud-based SaaS solutions. Therefore, they had decided to postpone market entry in Germany until the situation had improved. A few months later I talked to another software company that had found the same reluctance but came to the opposite conclusion. The percentage of German SMBs that were prepared to embrace a cloud-based SaaS solution was small, but it still represented a substantial number, qualifying them was straight forward and by moving in early the company could get a position from which they could grow when the acceptance took off.

It reminds me of the old joke about the two salesmen of shoes that were dispatched to a country where no-one wore shoes. One saw no market opportunity and the other saw a huge opportunity. Same market - different perspective. I tend to agree with the first salesman. If we have to convince people to wear shoes first before we can sell any, then we may have a gigantic task in front of us. What happens when we have developed that market and a global brand moves in with big marketing spend and investments setting up shops everywhere? Slack versus Microsoft Teams!

Shortly after I started working for Damgaard (later Navision) in Germany we were hit by what you today would call a shitstorm. The reason was that our ERP product, Concorde XAL, couldn't by default produce a standard German VAT report. It was not a strict legal requirement, and it was something you (the customer or the reseller) could define in the report generator, but the person, who made the news media pick up the story, expected such a report to be included as a default in the standard product.

Concorde XAL was a very successful ERP product and it couldn't produce a standard VAT report in any country. It was a feature that Damgaard expected the resellers to add to the product. The reason it had never been a problem before was that the resellers did add the report to the product as part of the implementation. However, a customer in Germany had managed to buy Concorde XAL without using a reseller for the implementation and now realised that it didn't come with the standard VAT report. All cheaper ERP systems came with this report and thus Concorde XAL was apparently an inferior product.

Why would the media run with a story about a missing VAT report in a foreign ERP product?

Because at the time the story started, IBM was the distributor of Concorde XAL in Germany. They had even named the product IBM Concorde XAL. Therefore, the core of story was that IBM had an inferior ERP product. However, I had moved to Germany to take over the distribution and now it was my problem.

I chose to apologise and made sure the VAT report was made a standard feature. When we launched AXAPTA (today Microsoft Dynamics AX or FO) in Germany two years later, we had it certified by a renowned German chartered accountant firm.

Danish Navision was very successful in the German speaking countries, but we also had to invest more in localisation than we did elsewhere. Resellers and customers simply expected more.

Markets can be very different from country to country, and I am not talking about the competitive landscape, which is the subject of the next section. I am referring to differences in the business demographics, such as size, industry and location, in delegation of authority, in traditions and in mindset. While demographics are tangible and quantifiable, the other parameters are more subtle and, just as culture, they vary from company to company and from person to person.

Mercante

In the 1980s I was the VP of marketing and sales for Mercante, a startup making high-performance printers. You cannot be in the printer industry without sourcing most of the parts in Japan. So, we did. Most of the photo chemical components were provided by Japanese suppliers. We had excellent relationships in Japan (you normally have excellent relationships with people from whom you buy stuff!!).

Someone suggested we should use our connections in Japan to make OEM deals there. I should have vetoed that. I only resisted, then gave in. Big mistake.

We went to Japan twice and we wasted lots of money and precious time, but I did learn something.

Unless you are Apple, Armani or Porsche, Japanese businesses prefer to buy Japanese manufactured products. To penetrate the Japanese printer market, you must do joint ventures. Joint ventures require investment and time. If you want to make it big in Japan you must have someone on the ground, patience and lots of money. It may pay off handsomely someday, but it is not a quick win for a start-up.

We gave up Japan and returned our focus to Europe.

INDUSTRY CONDITIONS

Some years ago, we were approached by a German company that wanted us to help them expand their business into Sweden. After having interviewed about twenty potential customers, some of the competitors and some other players in the market, it became apparent that the value proposition of the German company was identical to what the local competitors already offered. It also became clear that the German company only had less than one per cent market share in Germany, and that their customers were spread across several industries and sizes of companies. Entering the Swedish market would require several years of investment and time-to-break-even would be hard to predict. Wouldn't it make more sense to go for two per cent in Germany rather than trying to bootstrap Sweden? Wouldn't it make more sense to focus on a single market segment in Germany and achieve a 20+ per cent share of this specific segment, before initiating international activities?

This is by no means an unusual situation. The company had had many years to develop their business in Germany and it was very much up to the individual salesperson how they found and won new customers. As a consequence, the company had customers of all sizes and across various industries.

Compared to most other industries, the software industry is young and in many aspects immature. The barriers to entry are generally low and despite the massive coverage of the Internet getting customers abroad remains quite difficult. For most type of products, we therefore find pronounced differences in the competitive landscape from country to country. Even for products that do not require any or only little localisation may we find different sets of suppliers in each country.

Again, if you run a version of the simple virtual approach you may not care too much about such differences, but if you rely on investing in outbound or face-to-face activities, then the competitive landscape plays a crucial role.

You may find that the market segment you serve is already occupied by other vendors with solutions that are identical to yours, or at least not so different that it is worthwhile for enough customers to consider switching. A shoestring approach, where you cannot invest massively in branding and market penetration, requires that you have a customer value proposition that is unique or significantly more attractive than the current alternatives.

Different countries not only have different competitors they also have different industry analysts, media, consultants, systems integrators, resellers, industry associations and other stakeholders that may affect your business. Doing a quick desk-based industry analysis may reveal some of these idiosyncrasies, but talking to potential customers will give you a better picture. Applying a business development approach to the initial market penetration efforts will pick up these characteristics and help you navigate more easily.

Moving into a new country may require that you revisit your customer value proposition and the characteristics of your ideal customer profile, which again may require that you adjust your positioning and product development plans. For any company pursing a shoestring approach, that is a serious decision. It's difficult and expensive to entertain numerous value propositions and it dilutes your brand. Unless the market potential is considerable, you will be better off skipping a country that has a poor match.

Agillic

The market for omnichannel solutions is global, and many of the vendors already have a global presence. Upholding the R&D effort to stay competitive requires an installed base of customers, for which the Danish market is too small. The problems and solutions in the omnichannel domain are identical across borders, and apart from translating the user interface, there are no significant requirements for localisation. Success, however, requires a local presence for delivering the professional services associated with implementation, integration and ongoing support.

Agillic, which has expanded into Norway and has started penetrating the Swedish market, is currently considering which countries to enter next. The UK, DACH and the Benelux countries are the most prominent candidates.

"We have received some inquiries from potential partners in the US, reveals Jesper Valentin Holm, CEO at Agillic. "However, our primary focus just now is to consolidate our position in the Nordics and explore further opportunities in the UK, DACH and Benelux."

The international expansion strategy entails building a network of sales, integration and implementation partners.

"On a global level, IT for marketing-driven B2C companies is a fast-growing market," concludes Jesper Valentin Holm. "However, each country is different in terms of the competitive landscape and service provider infrastructure. We need to identify where the timing for market entry is most optimal. Then we will invest in a presence and set up the organisation to support our partners."

MACRO-ECONOMIC CONDITIONS

I have come across companies that looked at the estimated economic growth as a parameter for market selection. In my opinion that doesn't make any sense.

In the software industry we enjoy a unique advantage. Irrespective of whether the times are good or bad we can always be a part of the solution. You may have to adjust the narrative of your value proposition, but companies in trouble need software to increase productivity and companies in growth mode need software to increase capacity. Both sets of problems can be addressed by using software and both sets of problems ignite causes for change.

You could even argue that companies in an economically tight market have a more compelling reason to do something than companies experiencing unexpected growth.

Large companies are affected by macroeconomic forces, but small companies always have the opportunity to manoeuvre, adjust their narrative and find pockets of demand.

The Covid-19 situation was still young when software companies started editing their marketing messages. Everyone needed to let the world know that they had taken measures to protect their people and the interest of their customers. Wherever possible, Covid-19 was also given a spin to the marketing messages and used as an argument for acting now.

Solvoyo

The dust will settle sooner or later. Now is the time to prepare your supply chain for the future.

Two thirds of supply chain planning across the globe is still done using spreadsheets. The COVID-19 crisis has proven that, now, more than ever, businesses need to speed up digital transformation initiatives.

Now is the time to take advantage of advanced analytics and artificial intelligence to detect and adapt to the changes in your business environment. Automate the daily planning decisions so your teams can focus on strategic issues.

Solvoyo is offering a no-cost opportunity for you to experience our data insights & analytics platform for 2 months.

The text above is from Solvoyo's homepage. They have also added a section with COVID-19 Supply Chain Planning Best Practices.

TAKE-AWAYS FROM THIS CHAPTER

Assume that each country has its own business model environment and that it is very different from that of your domestic market. Perform a business model environment analysis before you make any speculative investments in market penetration.

Big companies pay consulting companies hundreds of thousands of dollars for performing business model environment analysis. They do so because the subsequent investments they make are in the multi-million-dollar league. That's no guarantee for success, but jumping blindfolded into a new market is the perfect career-stopper.

Big companies can afford to spend and loose big money, which you cannot. The shoestring approach, therefore, is to do your own analysis and use the Osterwalder business model environment card deck and the questions I propose in chapter three.

It's an ongoing process and you should maintain the information preferably in a graphical format. Use any opportunity to ask questions and collect intelligence. You will learn that the information you receive is often inconsistent and contradictory. That's because no one has the complete picture. With time your overview may become the most comprehensive and then you have a competitive advantage.

CHAPTER SEVEN - INTERNATIONALISATION AND LOCALISATION

INTRODUCTION

Internationalisation, also called i18n, is the design and development of a product that enables easy localisation for target audiences that vary in culture, region, or language.

Localisation, also called l10n, refers to the adaptation of a product, application or document content to meet the language, cultural and other requirements of a specific target market.

Thus, the job can be divided into two main areas:

1. Prepare your product for localisation - i18n.

2. Localise it for the individual country - l10n.

The first job is generic, and there are plenty of sources and resources available to help you make your software international and localisable. The Unicode[50]-initiative has especially contributed to making operating systems, middleware and applications prepared for supporting different character sets, keyboards, languages, data formats and sorting principles.

The second job requires local domain expertise. Are there legal or market requirements beyond the generic standards covered by the Unicode-initiative? How do you find out what they are and how do you get them specified to a degree where you or someone else can develop the code? What should be the release process for localised components, and how do you organise and provide support?

This chapter is the shortest in the book because internationalisation and localisation have been the subject of considerable standardisation

---

[50] http://unicode.org/main.html

in the software industry and because there are other sources that specialise in precisely that. An excellent overview of issues and solutions on this subject can be found on the Microsoft website.[51]

LOCALISATION MATTERS

Only very few software products can be used without some level of localisation, and no doubt, winning significant market shares in a country requires a fully localised product.

The shoestring question is how much localisation you need to do before you can win the first customers in another country? Can you wait until you have won the first contract(s) before doing the full localisation? It's not only a matter of financing the localisation, though that would be nice too. It is just as much deciding upon which country you should localise first and having customers help you specify the requirements.

The answer is that it depends on the competitive situation. You should check the industry section of your business model environment analysis. How much inconvenience are the customers prepared to accept to get access to your technology?

SEVEN MEAGRE YEARS

A software company had for seven years tried to win projects abroad without any success.

The company was the market leader in their domestic market, they had deep domain competency, and they were well acquainted with the developments in the international marketplace. Customers were predominantly government institutions, and the vendor selection was always the outcome of a public tender process.

A review of their global go-to-market approach indicated that the company failed to have sufficient customer contact before the RFPs were written and therefore couldn't influence the requirement specifications. Customers were very receptive having the company

---

[51] https://docs.microsoft.com/en-us/globalization/

bid for the projects, they always let them pass the prequalification threshold, but they never ended up selecting them.

Two key observations were made:

1. Government institutions are seldom innovators and early adopters. They prefer a vendor matching the requirements specification and representing the lowest risk. A low price doesn't compensate for high risk.

2. Unless you can influence the requirement specification, then someone else will, and your chances of winning become slim.

The conclusion was to stop bidding here, there and everywhere. Instead, the company decided to invest in building a presence in the neighbouring markets and get some smaller deals there. They also chose to invest in localisation and thereby minimise the risk for the customer.

Did they become more successful in pursuing the new approach?

Not really. Nine years have passed since they changed the strategy. They still have a hard time winning customers abroad, and in the meantime, they face increased competitive pressure in their domestic market.

My conclusion is that they waited too long to fix the problem. Seven years of pursuing a strategy that doesn't work is a long time in the software industry. If you don't have a clear competitive advantage that can be reflected in the customer's requirement specification, then winning public tenders will remain challenging.

FIRST THE CONTRACT THEN THE LOCALISATION

In 2014 the healthcare authorities at the Capital Region of Copenhagen and the Region of Zealand (RH/RZ) in Denmark decided to buy an EHR solution from American Epic. At one stroke this accelerated Epic from zero to a fifty per cent market share in Denmark. Two Danish software houses that already had solutions running within other regions in Denmark were not selected.

By joining forces, the RH/RZ project became huge. None of the Danish software companies could muster any equivalent references convincing the decision-makers that they were capable of implementing the system and delivering adequate performance. Also, RH/RZ wanted as much out-of-the-box functionality as possible as opposed to entering into a development project with the vendor.

Epic is and was the global market leader in EHR software to large hospitals. They didn't come out of the blue with new technology but offered a tested and proven system installed with a large and comparable customer base. Epic was, despite its lack of representation in the Danish market, nor local language version of the software, and with neither integrations for the local systems or local functionality, still considered the safest choice.

The market for EHR systems to large hospitals is, by nature, global. There are only a handful of vendors available that have a track record of delivering such systems. When there is no established local vendor in a country, then mainstream customers tend to choose among the global market leaders.

In the RH/RZ case Cerner, another US-vendor, came in second, while the Danish vendor, Systematic, for this bid acting as sub-contractor for IBM, came in third. The other Danish healthcare software company, CSC Scandihealth (now DXC Technology), didn't qualify for the final bid.

You can read elsewhere in this book how Epic managed to impact the requirement specifications that made them the safest choice.

FIRST LOCALISATION THEN SALES

When Navision started their internationalisation journey, they understood that localisation was a critical success factor. Being a small software house with just 12 people they knew that the localisation for the individual country had to be undertaken by someone else. Navision would prepare the product platform for internationalisation, and the translation and the country-specific localisation became the job of the distributors.

Deciding upon this approach from the start, the distributors had to undertake local product management and have the technical skills required to develop the local functionality. Without these skills, you couldn't become an NTR, National Territory Responsible, which was the official name of the Navision distributors.

I have written about the success of Navision elsewhere in this book, and it is beyond doubt that the focus on the quality of the localisation played a significant role.

EDLUND AND NORWAY

Edlund, who make software for life insurance companies and pension funds, has been looking at the Norwegian market for some time.

The Norwegian market consists of six potential customers that each have their proprietary system. There is no direct national competitor, but a handful of consulting and software engineering companies serve the industry.

When it comes to life insurance and pension schemes, Norway and Denmark turned out to be the countries in the adjacent markets that have most in common. Edlund's market analysis concluded that the six customers would benefit substantially from moving to their new standard platform. Still, it was hard to assess when they would be ready to start the process.

One of the Norwegian pension companies had already been engaged with a foreign supplier, but three years into the project they pulled out. The incident illustrates how difficult it is for a foreign supplier to comprehend and implement the local market requirements, and it has made the entire industry even more cautious.

Edlund is not the only insurtech (technology for the insurance industry) company that has cast its eyes on Norway. Swedish Itello AB recently acquired Eikos AS, a Norwegian actuarial consulting firm providing systems and services to pension funds and suppliers within the financial industry in Norway and abroad.

There is a very high probability that the first insurtech company to win a project and demonstrate successful implementation will also be the preferred choice for the remaining companies. Only this way can they share the ongoing burden of maintaining legal compliance. Such a "winner takes all" scenario makes Edlund cautious.

"Norway should be an excellent match for us, says Gert Bendsen, "and we are in very close contact with the customers. However, we need to get the timing right. A solution for the Norwegian market must be based on our new platform. Adding specific Norwegian features will require tangible signs of a commitment from at least one of the customers. We do not ask the first customer to take the full investment, but without a live project, the risk for us would be hard to justify."

TAKE-AWAYS FROM THIS CHAPTER

With very few exceptions software companies must provide localised versions of their products to achieve any significant market share. The standards for how to make an international product that is prepared for localisation are well documented, and there are plenty of service providers that can help you with the process. Also, the locale-specific components are well defined through the Unicode initiative and are supported by numerous platform products.

The reference base should always be English, but the questions of for which countries you should localise first, how you obtain sufficient specification of the requirements beyond those covered by the Unicode elements, and to which degree customers are prepared to participate in the development varies from case to case.

In a market where there are no local alternatives available already, it is more likely that the first innovative customers are prepared to work with you in completing the localisation. In hyper-competitive markets, it is less likely.

Chapter Eight - Becoming a Thought Leader - Generating Inbound Leads on a Shoestring Budget

INTRODUCTION

Including a single chapter on how to be found on the Internet is quite ambitious. Thick books have been written on this subject. Nevertheless, I do see untapped potential for most small software companies with limited budgets. In this chapter, I'll give you the quick 10-step shoestring process for becoming a thought leader within your subject matter domain and how to use this position to drive quality traffic from all over the world to your web site.

The thing you have in abundance and which is unrelated to your limited budget is your insight. You know and understand the issues, problems, challenges and opportunities that your customers have within the domain where you operate. You know the difficulties they face with managing the change from their current modus operandi to a situation based on your category of software. You understand the value that your type of solution can release and how to make it happen. That insight is something your potential customers all over the world would like to learn from if they knew you existed and if you shared your wisdom in a non-propaganda and product-agnostic type format.

I admit that the term *thought leadership* is misused. Doing a simple search on LinkedIn returns over 100,000 persons in my immediate network (1st, 2nd and 3rd level) that use the term thought leader to describe themselves. A quick look reveals that most of them don't share any leading thoughts on their LinkedIn profiles or anywhere else for that matter. They claim to be thought leaders, but it doesn't show.

My advice is that you can become a thought leader or a subject matter authority, *and if you follow my advice, you won't have to tell anybody.* Instead, you establish a schedule for thinking, documenting and sharing your thoughts - generously. The key objective is to make others consider you a thought leader or a trustworthy industry authority, and that doesn't require self-inflation. Rather the opposite.

If your global key audience can find and enjoy your documented thoughts, then you are on the right track.

STEP 1: KNOW YOUR TARGET AUDIENCE AND HOW THEY BUY

When you have invested time in understanding and documenting your business model, then you already know your target audience well. If not, then now is the time to become super specific.

First, you define the type of companies or people that get the most value from using your product. Start with the demographic characteristics, and you might as well limit the description to the filter options available in LinkedIn's Sales Navigator, because in step seven, we will use these variables to find them by name.

Now consider if there are any specific challenges that your type of customers face as organisations and individuals. Find industry sources that can help you understand the big picture, but also remember to talk to your customers about generic issues and what they think about them.

When the buying journey for your product is complex, then your target audience consists of several personas within the individual firm. A persona is a generic type of decision-maker, purchaser, end-user or influencer that plays a specific and essential role in acquiring your kind of solution. Decide how many personas you are dealing with and make a generic description of their position, concerns, challenges and success criteria. Again, start the description by using the demographic search options offered by LinkedIn's Sales Navigator.

Now that you know your target audience, then you can define a generic process for how they find, become interested in and end up buying a product like yours. Your revenue generation process then becomes the facilitation of the customers´ buying journey as illustrated in figure 8.

Becoming a thought leader or a trustworthy industry authority requires that you provide content that helps the buying personas in each step of their buying journey. As you are interested in being found, you must have an idea of which keywords or phrases these personas use when they search for information or solution for their problems.

This discipline is called SEO - Search Engine Optimisation. Which words do your key personas use when talking about the problems you solve? Which words will they use when searching for information on the search engines (Google, YouTube, Bing, DuckDuckGo, Baidu and others)?

Before writing this chapter, I was fortunate to get an introduction to SEO by Grit Neumann, a senior online marketing consultant at the German company Ströer. By coincidence, she and her family stayed at the same holiday resort in Croatia as we did, and she was generous and took some hours of her holiday to give me a peek into the mystery of being found on the search engines. After reviewing some of the tools she uses to help her clients get found more often, she made a meaningful conclusion:

No tool in the world will help you unless you produce quality content that your target audience wants to consume.

I will not get into the details of SEO, but before you start writing and producing videos and a podcast, you need to have a good feeling for the vocabulary your customers use. You must use their words to describe their world so that they can relate to it. If you are not familiar with SEO, then you need to become familiar with it. There are plenty of free resources available that will help you understand the concepts and how to use the tools available to explore the key phrases used by your target audience .

STEP 2: CONTENT CREATION

There are two main categories of content produced for revenue generation purposes.

All companies produce *company and product centric content* telling the world who they are and what they do. Some companies also produce *industry-centric content* discussing the problems, challenges and opportunities that their customers are facing now and in the future, and what to do about them at the general solution level.

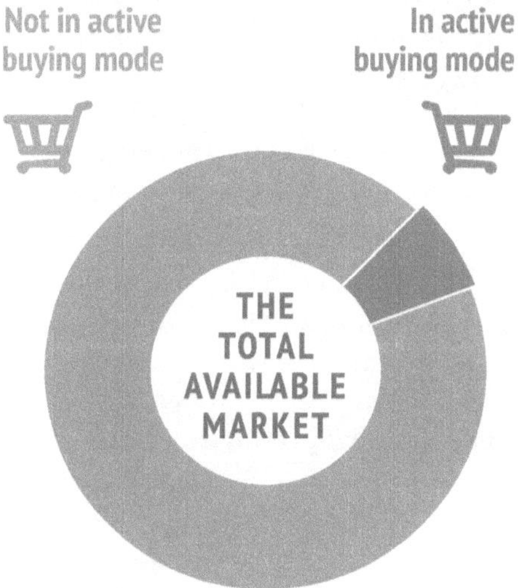

The first category, company and product-centric content, is valuable for people who may consider buying your product. When the customer's buying process is complex, the higher-level decision-makers are not interested in product-centric content. They are more concerned about mitigating risk.

Figure 11: At any point in time, the majority of your potential customers are not in active buying mode.

Industry-centric content is relevant to all customers irrespective of where they are in the buying journey. At any point in time, the bulk of your potential customers are not in active buying mode, which means that your company and your product-centric content doesn't attract their attention. Instead, they may consider it annoying propaganda.

Achieving the status as an internationally recognised thought leader requires that you produce a steady stream of industry-centric content. You can package such content into blog posts or articles, videos, podcasts, white-papers, infographics, ebooks, presentations or some other searchable material that teaches the visitor something valuable in the cross-section of their problems and your area of expertise.

Before you leave step two, I suggest that you produce ten blog posts of at least 1,200 words each, two white-papers or eBooks of at least 4,000 words each and five videos of five minutes each (remember subtitles!). You can start with the white-papers and then break them up into several articles afterwards or the other way around. The videos can be visual presentations of the content from the articles or the white-papers, including your talking head. If some of the material is suited for the podcast format, then do a few of those too.

Reusing the content across formats is perfectly acceptable and advisable. The whole idea of providing text, videos and podcasts is to reach as large a portion of your target audience as possible. Some prefer reading text; some listen to podcasts while commuting or working out, and some prefer watching videos. The same content in different formats extends your reach.

Having created your starter package, you now produce two one-minute videos to introduce the white-papers and some short teaser texts (280 characters including everything) for each piece of content.

When drafting the posts, the white-papers and the scripts for the videos and podcasts, consider which personas you are talking to and where they are in their buying journey. The same content can address more personas and be relevant across several steps of the journey, but looking at the map of people and issues, it seldom covers everything. Over time you should have produced something for all the bases or touch-points in the buying journey.

Try not to mention your product and company in any of this material. You can add a reference at the end of the text, video or podcast, but never at the beginning. Be personable and visible. A thought leader is a human being, not a robot or a company.

Before you move to step three, you must develop a list of subjects for upcoming content and a publication schedule. Publishing once a week is ideal, but once or twice a month will also work if you have limited resources. Less than once a month is too little.

Content production is a problem for most companies, both big and small. Who is going to produce it? How can you take time out of people's busy calendars to write articles, shoot videos and record podcasts? Can you outsource it to external content producers on a freelance basis? What does it cost?

The preferred scenario is to do most of the production in-house. With the tools available today, setting up video and audio studios and post-production facilities are not expensive, and the benefit of having easy access makes it so much faster to get things done. The shoestring approach should focus on content quality over format quality. There is neither room nor need for expensive productions on a shoestring budget. The quality should be acceptable, which isn't difficult with the tools available today. Don't spend your money on being super professional at the format level. You could even argue that a moderate format quality improves the feeling of authenticity. Content is more important than format.

If you don't have the skills in-house, you can outsource the production of illustrations and final formatting. For the proofing of English content, you will, in any case, need a native English-speaking resource.

If you cannot produce the core content in-house, because you don't have the writing skills or are uncomfortable talking to a camera or a microphone, then you have a problem. There are plenty of agencies and freelancers offering to produce content, but only a few are good at communicating complex matters. It also comes down to the quality of the briefings they get, and the budgets allocated. It takes substantial briefing to have a third party write something which the readers consider thought-leading. If you go for the outsourcing option, then invest in a long-term relationship with your freelancers or agency.

There is a considerable upfront investment in briefing your content team to a level where they can produce something genuinely original.

Several of the companies in the case story section of the book are doing excellent jobs creating thought-leading content. The eBook *"10 ways to navigate the implementation maze"* from Tia Technology[53] is an outstanding example of product-agnostic content that addresses the concerns of the customers' top-level decision-makers.

STEP 3: BUILD A BLOG

The purpose of the thought leadership exercise is to drive more traffic to your website. If you want to entertain outbound activities, then you can motivate potential customers to reveal their identity so that you can serve them at their current step in the buying journey. You should first and foremost post your content on your website. Having a blog as a separate subsegment of your website is an established and accepted format, but it also has some real advantages.

Posting on your website gives you full control over the SEO. You can use the same tools with which you're already familiar. If you don't do SEO, then it's time to start now.

While the top priority is to write content that resonates with and brings value to your potential customers and other key stakeholders, there are some communication guidelines to which it is worth paying attention.

A picture paints a thousand language-independent words. Use illustrations to bring variation to the text and use alt text (alternative text) to build SEO authority. Avoid too many stock images. Embed videos and audio and link to internal as well as external content. Maintain your communication style, but respect the rules about reading complexity, passive language and grammar. Writing in English, you can use a tool like Grammarly to improve the quality of your prose. Keep your writing simple. Communicating globally, close to seventy per cent of your target audience will have English as their

---

[53] https://tiatechnology.com/insights/

second language. You gain nothing from using a too sophisticated or academic language style.

The big difference between the blog and the rest of your web site is the type of content posted. The blog should be product and company agnostic. It contains information from which any visitor can benefit without using your product. Of course, you will twist the content to support your position and value propositions. Still, the blog is where you demonstrate your expertise, not where you directly praise and promote your company and products.

Building a reputation as an international thought leader or an industry authority requires that you stop mistaking yelling for selling. Refrain from promoting your company and your products the same way most companies and people do. Stop yelling that you have great products, healthy values, awesome people, lovely customers, brilliant business partners and generous investors. Leave the traditional promotion work to someone else and focus on discussing the problems and opportunities that your customers face.

My recommendation is backed by recent research that indicates a general change in customers' behaviour. Even when customers are in active purchasing mode, they are reluctant to engage with salespeople until very late in the decision-making process, and then only when they can't avoid it. There are two reasons for this change. The first is a general and increasing mistrust in salespeople as a source of valid information, and the second is the easy availability of information through the Internet. Stop acting as a salesperson and become an industry authority instead. Your blog should be the voice of this authority.

It is common wisdom to always include a call-to-action element in your publications. It can be an offer of more information on the same subject in return for a name, company name, email address, telephone number or some other reader-data. I am not a big fan of this wisdom. Asking for personal information is like putting a fence around your content. What will you do with the data? How do I, the visitor, benefit from providing such information? I don't! In contrary I risk being called by a salesperson and being added to mailing list. Offering to be called or to be added to a mailing list is fine, but don't make it a quid pro quo deal. The quality of your content should make people get in touch. If they don't then check the quality of your content first.

STEP 4: PICK YOUR SOCIAL MEDIA PLATFORMS

If you have ambitions of winning supporters for your thought leadership by posting your content on social media, then you will soon be disappointed. The level of noise on social media is enormous, and it's highly unlikely that the platforms' algorithms will help your content to find its niche audience. Working with a global perspective, there are only three potentially relevant platforms: Facebook, Twitter and LinkedIn.

Although probably the vast majority of your customers are on Facebook, how will you make your content appear in their feeds? Facebook's algorithms will not do it for you, no matter how relevant it may be. You can create a business page, but unless you pay Facebook, your posts will be mostly invisible. Facebook is great for paid distribution, and you can probably find your niche audience using their targeting tools. But can you convert them into something valuable? Try it and see if you can make it work. Without an advertising budget to boost your posts, it's most likely that you cannot.

Over time you may get people to follow you on Twitter, but when it comes to searching for and sharing niche content, a 280-character service isn't the best place to go. Unless you have followers that actually do follow you, then Twitter is like shouting into space, hoping to be heard on Mars.

Your best bet is LinkedIn.

Since its incubation in 2002, LinkedIn has grown to become a global database with information about business professionals and companies. As of mid-2020, the platform has almost 700 million members across 150 countries, and the signup rate is about two per minute. Nearly half of the members are active on the platform within a month.

However, be aware that LinkedIn, like Facebook, will not help your content reach the feeds of your target audience. Their algorithms for deciding relevance are lousy, but the real issue is that if they worked well, then they wouldn't make any money from advertising. To reach your target audience, LinkedIn wants you to pay. That's their business model. However, the objective of this book is to help you reach your potential customers without spending too much on it, so let's explore some other options.

The chances are that a significant number of your potential customers have a profile on LinkedIn. If that's the case, then you should be able to find them. Sign up for LinkedIn's Sales Navigator service and use the search function. You can search for companies first and then move on to people next, or vice-versa. Within an hour, you should be able to find the people that would benefit from using your product.

You can study their profiles, see if they are active and follow their activities. You can also reach out to them, but don't do any of this just yet.

STEP 5: REVISE AND ENRICH YOUR LINKEDIN PROFILE

The shoestring approach makes intensive use of LinkedIn, but in a very different way from how most people use the platform. You should invest time and energy in understanding how LinkedIn works and the best resource that I have come across lately is Melonie Dodaro's book *LinkedIn Unlocked.*[54]

Before you start posting anything on LinkedIn and reaching out to potential customers, you should revise and enrich your own personal and then your company's profile first. Melonie Dodaro's book provides a step-by-step process for doing that, so I will not repeat it here.

However, I will say this much. Take a look at your own profile as if you were a potential customer. What do you see? Does your profile leave the impression of someone looking for a new job, or does it leave the

---

[54] Dodaro, M. (2018). LinkedIn unlocked: Unlock the mystery of Linkedin to drive more sales through social selling.

perception of someone capable of solving the challenges experienced by your customers? Because of how LinkedIn started, most people have job-searching profiles. You need to change that if you want to use the platform to position yourself as a subject matter authority and generate business from it.

Where most people fill their LinkedIn profiles with what they do for their employer, you now need to describe what you do for your customers. That's not so easy, and many fall back on generic platitudes such as "helping my customers improve their bottom line" or "driving digital transformation". Everybody can claim that, and many do. Instead, be factual, offer relevant metrics and impact on key performance indicators, and use some of the industry jargon that your customers use.

When you start hacking LinkedIn to build your network, then your job title should not look like a red warning light. Most of your potential customers are not in buying mode, and the last person in the universe that they want to connect or talk to on LinkedIn is a salesperson.

As you change your title to something more meaningful to the customer, you should also change your behaviour and stop pitching to anything with a pulse. Stop yelling and start listening.

STEP 6: POST AND ENGAGE REGULARLY

With your profile revised and enriched, now comes the time to start being active.

Noise and propaganda account for most (over ninety per cent) of the content on social media. LinkedIn is filled with company- and product-centric material that doesn't bring any value to the reader. Companies announce that they have hired a new sales manager, have closed a funding round, are running a partner event, promoting a newsletter, announcing a free webinar, calling applications for a job or some other "look at me, I'm awesome" posts. Check your LinkedIn home feed, and you will find that most of the content is organic or paid noise and propaganda.

Your strategy shouldn't rely on noise and propaganda. You won't stand a chance of attracting your target audience, and if you do get the engagement, you won't gain anything. Unless what you do is relevant for hundreds of millions of people on LinkedIn, then you shouldn't rely on showing up in their home feeds. You are competing with cat videos, celebrities and social media experts. You don't stand a chance of getting the attention of your key audience this way.

Do start posting regularly (once a day), but don't expect to get much attention. There are tools such as Buffer and Hootsuite that can help you schedule your posts, but when it comes to posting on LinkedIn, you will also want to use tagging. Tagging will increase the reach of your post but use it only when relevant.

You don't always have to only post your own content. Posting content of other experts in your industry and tagging them will help build and promote your reputation and will create more invitations to connect.

Remember hashtags! If you don't know what that is or how it works, then search the term and learn about it. Never post anything without a hashtag. A thought leader not using hashtags can hardly be an authority. Don't overdo them. Two to three is ideal.

STEP 7: FOLLOW YOUR CUSTOMERS

When you have your content production and posting schedule up and running, and your profile reflects your industry authority, then it is time to start following some of the people and companies that you have found through your search using Sales Navigator.

Not all of them will be active, but some will be, and you can like, comment and share their posts and articles. From time to time and when relevant, you can include a reference to content on the same subject that you or someone else has produced. Use a mobile device (smartphone or tablet) to insert the reference link in the comment and watch what happens! Instead of just a text link, LinkedIn now generates a nice preview snippet of the post. Delete the text link, and the reference looks more like a signature element. Use this referral activity with care and stay relevant. You should add value to the discussion, not interrupt or derail it or worst of all, come across as spammy.

As you increase your activities following other people, you will see an increase in invitations to connect. Although you are eager to expand your network, you should take a close look at each invitation and decide if it is relevant. There is no point in having a vast network of people outside your target industry. If you choose to accept the invitation, then send them a welcome message. If you decline, then send them a friendly message urging them to follow you instead. Some of them will, and that will increase your number of followers without devaluating the quality of your 1st level network. You can use a tool such as TextExpander to have prepared messages, then it will only take a few seconds to respond.

STEP 8: INCREASING YOUR 1ST LEVEL NETWORK

When you have been active for a few months enriching your profile with quality content and enlarging your network, then comes the time where you can apply a very productive hack.

There are tools available - robots - that can auto visit LinkedIn profiles. When you use such a service, then between ten (USA) and twenty (outside the USA) per cent of those visited will look back at your profile. If you have a professional and compelling profile, then about five per cent will invite you to connect. Again, don't just accept any invitation. Although the Sales Navigator is a powerful tool, the search results are based on profile data that people have filled in themselves. Only you can decide if a person may be a relevant connection or not. Don't rely on LinkedIn's suggestions and recommendations. They are the result of automatic algorithms and are not very reliable. Carefully qualifying each new connection may not seem so important when you only have a few thousand connections. Still, as you approach the 30,000 limit, which is the maximum number of connections LinkedIn allows, then it does become an issue. With the method I am outlining in this chapter, 30,000 connections is not an unrealistic target over time.

You can accelerate building your network by letting such robots submit invitations to connect. However, you will quickly find that crafting a personalised message with the invitation will significantly increase your acceptance rate. Once someone has connected to you, send them a welcome note such as:

> *Hi [First-Name],*
>
> *Thanks for accepting my invitation.*
>
> *I am looking forward to following your posts and hope that you also can benefit from the material I produce.*
>
> *Best regards*
>
> *Your name*

By using a tool such as TextExpander, it will only take a few seconds to do that.

WARNING: Using robots are against LinkedIn's service terms, and you should not use them too aggressively. Follow the guidelines recommended by the robots or LinkedIn will restrict your options or deactivate your account. Also, if you run them while not using your computer for other activities, then you should have an app such as Caffeinated active in the background. Remember to delete open invitations every week or LinkedIn will punish you. I am not recommending you use robots. I am only telling you that they exist ;-)

As you increase the size of your LinkedIn network, you may consider downloading their contact information which also includes their email addresses. You can import the email list into Facebook and target them and a lookalike audience with boosted ads of your blog posts. This will expose them to your blogs inexpensively and increase your reach as they share with others in their network. Advertising on Facebook is much less expensive than on LinkedIn.

STEP 9: INTERACTING

With a growing network and a growing repository of quality content, you should keep the conversations going.

Don't waste your time on your home feed. This is where LinkedIn's algorithms post messages from advertisers and other users. Based on what shows up in my home feed, LinkedIn is not doing a very good job, but you can judge for yourself. Instead, check your Sales Navigator and observe what your connections and leads are doing and interact directly with them.

Keep in mind that although LinkedIn is the home of millions of professionals, not all of them are active. When you post something, only a tiny fraction of your network will see it. There are two reasons why. The first reason is that they are not on LinkedIn around the time when you post. That often happens if you are in different time zones. A scheduling tool as Buffer or Hootsuite can help you overcome this issue. The second reason is that LinkedIn deliberately exposes your post to only a few connections, around 100. If it doesn't get any engagements within the first couple of hours, then they will kill the visibility of your post. If you only have a small target group, say less than ten million individuals and you post about niche issues, then it is unlikely that you'll get enough organic engagement for LinkedIn to boost it.

The smaller your market is, and the bigger the deals you do, the more personal and specific you should be in the content you share. Narrowing your focus on single companies is called account-based marketing and Sales Navigator is an excellent tool to help you do this. You can pay LinkedIn to post your content in the feeds of a certain type of people within named companies. You can also find these individuals yourself and initiate contact and conversations.

You can use robots to send personalised direct messages to your 1st level connections. However, only do so with messages that have genuine value to the recipient and don't do it too often. Never use direct messages for solicitations or when asking people you don't know for favours.

STEP 10: TAKING THE CONVERSATION OFFLINE

If your revenue process requires you to have an individual conversation with your potential customers, then the relationship must go offline at some point.

A first step in bringing a relationship offline is to offer webinars. You can prepare these so that the presentation part is pre-produced (highly recommended) leaving you free to monitor the chat with questions and comments. After the presentation or interview, then you open up for the Q&A.

Again, I strongly recommend that you distinguish clearly between your product promotion and your thought leadership webinars. It is legitimate to offer product presentations and demonstrations, but don't dress them up to be something else. There are times when people look for inspiration, and there are times when they search for products. Serve those two needs separately.

To which extent you want to chase individual one-on-one calls depends on the situation and your value proposition. If you are successful in establishing yourself as an industry authority, then you will find that you begin to receive more prospects, - inbound leads -, which is an excellent place to be in business.

ORGANIC DISTRIBUTION

As I have mentioned several times, getting quality content for a niche audience distributed organically by social media is tricky. Both Facebook and LinkedIn offer the option of creating special interest groups. However, many of these groups get cluttered by people spreading propaganda, making other members with more serious intentions flee.

There is a hack that can help you bootstrap the distribution process, and it's called employee advocacy. It is simple to understand, doesn't cost anything, but it is challenging to execute, which is why it still works.

If all the people in your company like, comment and share your post within the first hour after publication, then the LinkedIn algorithm believes that the post is valuable and will spread it further. The LinkedIn algorithm will notice that the support is internal, which is not as valuable as an external endorsement, but it is still better than nothing. If you can get someone outside your company, such as your business partners, to like, share and comment, then the impact will be substantial, and the content will have a much broader reach.

Although it sounds like a simple method, experience shows that it is not easy to orchestrate. You need as many people as possible interacting with the post within the first hour or so, and making that happen has proven to be difficult. If you can make it happen, then you have an inexpensive, competitive advantage.

As you build your blog and create a name for yourself in your industry, social media will not be as important. If you work seriously with SEO and produce quality content, most of your traffic will be direct and organic. Taking our own blog as an example, we get 94 per cent of our traffic from direct or organic search and referrals. Only six per cent comes from social media. Social media is great for direct messages but not great for organic distribution.

Don't expect short term miracles and don't give up just because you don't see immediate results. Doing content marketing and building thought leadership are marathon type efforts where you benefit from the accumulated volume of the material you produce and take advantage of the long tail of the Internet.

TAKE-AWAYS FROM THIS CHAPTER

If you are capable of producing quality content that is both company- and product-agnostic, that also discusses the issues your customers are facing and explains how they can address them, then you can become a thought leader and an industry authority. Your content will also help customers that are not in buying mode, and by definition, this is by far the largest group. This will drive quality traffic to your website and support your customer's buying journeys. Eventually, it will fill your pipeline and lead to sales.

The key social media platform for engaging with your customers is LinkedIn. However, to make that work, you need to change the way you use the platform. By changing your LinkedIn profile from being job-search oriented to being customer value-oriented, you can engage and connect with your target audience and start communicating with them on an individual basis. To do that most effectively I would recommend subscribing to the Sales Navigator service. With LinkedIn, you can build an audience for the content you produce.

Social media platforms, including LinkedIn, do not distribute the content for you. If you want organic (as opposed to paid-for) distribution, then you will have to hack or cheat the algorithms and work directly with your communities. There are ways to do this, but they are not explained in the textbooks, because hacks that everybody uses will lose their effectiveness.

An excellent place to start learning how to hack LinkedIn is by reading Melonie Dodaro's book *LinkedIn Unlocked*.

Learn the difference between quality content and propaganda. Stop producing and disseminating propaganda. Use all your energy on quality content.

Chapter Nine - Establishing Productive Partnerships

INTRODUCTION

I frequently facilitate workshops on how to break into foreign markets. The number one question and the subject that all the attendees want to discuss is:

How do we find business partners in the new countries that can do the work for us?

When I ask them to elaborate on their thoughts, they give me 25 benefits for themselves and how leaving all the work to the partners will minimise their risk. They don't mention any benefits to the business partners.

In this chapter, I will discuss the general principles for when and how to use independent channel partner to break into new countries and why that may not be your best option.

THE BUSINESS MODEL IN YOUR BUSINESS MODEL

Using business partners, such as distributors, resellers, system integrators and other third parties, when moving into a new country is often a preferred approach.

If your go-to-market strategy already is indirect, and you have the experience and framework for working with third parties, then replicating this strategy abroad makes good sense. However, as mentioned in chapter seven, you may find the competitive situation and the partner infrastructure quite different across countries which may have consequences for the outcome. An indirect go-to-market approach that works well in one country does not automatically work well in another country.

If you have a direct go-to-market approach at home and now want to apply an indirect approach abroad, then you are facing a fundamentally different business model, which I address in more detail in the book *Building Successful Partner Channels*[55].

Using third parties to perform some of the activities in your business model's front office is not a short cut or shoestring approach to the market. An indirect channel is primarily a scaling tool. It takes additional time and effort recruiting the partners, and it takes extra time and effort onboarding them and making and keeping them thriving. First, when they have travelled the learning curve will they start to produce results on their own. And where some of them will become productive, some will not be able to make it work.

Working successfully with independent partners, that you want to promote, sell and implement your product in a new country, requires two value propositions; a customer value proposition and a partner value proposition. Potential partners may be intrigued by your products. Still, they are motivated by the business it creates, and they first become committed when they experience it generating revenue and profit. Getting to that point requires investments in people, knowledge transfer, marketing and sales.

Selling through third parties that operate in their own name, at their own cost and risk and receive a commission on their sales is like having a foreign business model within your business model, as illustrated in figure 7. The adage *If you have enough money then go direct and if you also have enough time then go indirect* still holds. It takes additional effort to build an indirect channel.

STRATEGIC OR TACTICAL PARTNERSHIPS

Using independent third parties to assume responsibility for some or all of the customer-facing activities in a new country or region leaves you with a couple of options that you must clarify upfront.

---

[55] Bech, H. P. (2015). Building Successful Partner Channels: in the software industry. Copenhagen, Denmark: TBK Publishing®.

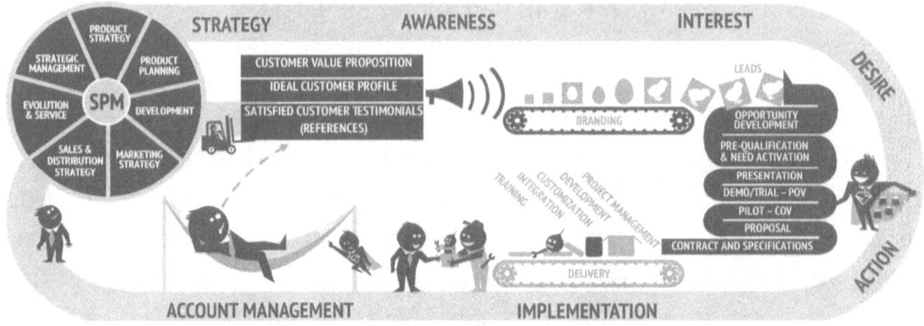

Figure 12: For which activities do you want your business partners to assume responsibility?

Are you looking for one or more business partners?

If you look for more, then how many?

For which activities do you expect the business partners to assume responsibility?

One or more partners

The difference between having one or more partners is fundamental.

If you go for one partner only, then the relationship is de facto exclusive and strategic. The partner should be motivated to invest in market development since all the business generated will come her way. If the partner doesn't perform, you will not make the expected revenue from her territory. Replacing her is not easy and may even require legal action.

If you want many partners, then each of them will be reluctant to invest in market development. Unless you can apply a precise segmentation of the market where they don't overlap, you will immediately receive complaints of over-penetration. Even when they, in reality, don't compete for the same business, they will still complain about the situation and be reluctant to invest. Resellers are very sensitive to competition in a situation where you enjoy no brand awareness, and there is no latent demand from the market.

All software companies that operate an indirect go-to-market approach in their domestic market and want to replicate the model in other countries face this challenge. The lack of a distributor role causes the problem. In the domestic market, you exercise the distributor role, which means that you are responsible for branding and lead generation. The partners operate under your marketing umbrella.

When you move into a new country and want to have more partners, then you also need someone to take the distributor role. Either you do it yourself, or you apply a two-tier model with both a third-party distributor and third-party resellers.

Building a two-tier distribution network is not a shoestring type undertaking. It's something you do because you have ambitions for market leadership. It takes time, skills and money, and it pays off in the long run.

Simple channel principles

If you want someone to do something for you, then you can hire that person or engage that company, pay them for their work and keep the results for yourself. Getting people to do work for you against payment is a well-known and tested concept. Even when you are prepared to pay well, finding people with the relevant skills and an entrepreneurial attitude is still no simple task.

Finding people or companies to do work for you without getting paid along the way is a tad trickier. You need a compelling business proposal to motivate someone to spend their time and money promoting your agenda, only getting paid sometime in the future depending on circumstances that are not entirely within their control. On top, you are asking them to commit at a time where they have no experience with you and your products, and where you enjoy no brand recognition.

This business proposal: *"Sell my unknown product (for which there is currently no demand) from my unknown company to new customers in this new market, and I'll pay you a commission on the results"* is not very attractive. It is essentially asking people to get paid with their own money.

If you are looking for business partners to assume the responsibility for certain portions of your revenue generation process, then you need to develop an investment prospectus. You need to explain why investing time and resources in being part of your ecosystem is a great idea. And you need to translate this idea into hard monetary terms. How much should she be prepared to invest, how soon can she expect to be cash-positive, when does she reach break-even. What is the return on the investment on a three-year timeline, and how will you help make it happen?

Ask someone on your team (or an external party) to play the role of the potential business partner and ask that person to ask all the tough questions. As you develop your business partner value proposition, you should review the details with potential candidates. Ask them what they think about the various elements of the program. Ask additional questions to understand what they mean and why they say it. Collect feedback from 10-15 potential partners before you assess the information. One opinion is not always right.

Even when you follow my advice, finding business partners that are prepared to break a new market for you is hard. You cannot eliminate the risk, and most people are not visionaries and early innovators. You have to keep looking for someone with the right mindset and the resources to make your business proposal work. Be patient and keep looking. Saying yes to the wrong candidate (person or company) can set you back and cost you dearly, as I will explain below.

OEM AND WHITE LABEL

OEM and white label deals may be interesting, and they may also lead to your products being used by companies in foreign countries. However, by the nature of the OEM and white label frameworks, such end-user companies will not know who you are, and therefore you can hardly refer to them as your customers. If you can negotiate the terms giving your brand some transparency, then you can create a Trojan Horse effect. However, this is exactly what most OEM and white label customers want to avoid, and it may also harm your other distribution channels. Be careful with OEM and white label agreements if you also sell through resellers[56].

---

[56] Bech, H. P. (2018). 5,460 Miles from Silicon Valley - The In-depth Case Study of What Became Microsoft's First Billion Dollar Acquisition Outside the USA (S. Quirke Køngerskov, Trans. A. Hagel Ed.). Copenhagen: TBK Publishing®, chapter 7.

STRATEGIC ALLIANCES

A strategic alliance is an arrangement between two or more companies to pursue mutually beneficial objectives while each retains its independence. The alliance can be anything from a non-binding declaration of intentions and the exchange of information to the establishment of an organisation that perform certain activities. In a strategic alliance, the parties do not represent each other, nor do they sell to or buy from one another.

That doesn't mean that such alliances are not necessary.

If you want to sell ERP systems to the SOHO and SMB-market, then an alliance with the chartered accountants is crucial. Most small companies take advice from them and may lean heavily towards their recommendations. It's hard to make chartered accountants recommend something with which they are not familiar, and an arrangement that allows them to use your software is therefore crucial.

When your software is based on platforms from some of the global providers, such as Microsoft, IBM or Oracle, then you may find that cooperating with them can open some doors. Especially if your software is extending their market reach. However, figuring out who can help may be a challenging job, and if you expect them undertake sales and marketing for you, then you will most likely be disappointed.

As I mentioned in chapter three, the market for business software solutions is moving towards a best of breed scenario. Customers combine products from many suppliers to support their business processes. The products exchange data through APIs (application program interfaces), and the ability to connect to peripheral functionality becomes a necessity.

Uniconta, a cloud-based ERP system for the SMB market, offers over a hundred integrations to other products. It allows Uniconta to concentrate on their core functionality and the SDK for their resellers while enabling the customer to get bank integration, creditor invoice workflow, foreign payments, Microsoft 365 integration, warehouse management, salary administration, point of sales functionality, management reporting, e-commerce, EDI and much more. Most of the third-party products are local, which means that Uniconta needs to forge new alliances when they move into a new market.

While strategic alliances don't sell for each other, they do represent important word-of-mouth marketing.

GREAT START, TROUBLESOME ENDING

A software company had over fifteen years established resellers in over fifty countries and distributors in the major markets. Although the company generated a profit of about twenty per cent of revenue, they had experienced flat turnover levels for the last five years, and now new and competitive solutions were beginning to put pressure on the prices. Flat unit sales led to decreasing revenue and profitability.

An analysis of the reseller-base showed that most of them were regular customers and IT-service providers for large enterprises, that had become resellers to get a discount on the products. They were not actively reselling the products.

An analysis of the distributor-base revealed that they were primarily resellers that took advantage of the high distributor discount of seventy per cent. They only entertained a small number of actual resellers and did not actively recruit. The growth-potential of the distributors was limited due to lack of ambitions and management capabilities. They were running a nice business and didn't want to rock the boat.

With the changes in the business model environment and especially with the pressure from declining prices caused by the insurgents, the software company had to rethink their distribution model and find ways to replace their distributors.

Acquiring the distributors turned out not to be an attractive option. They didn't have the management potential that the software company was looking for and probes had revealed that their valuation expectations were unrealistic. Terminating the distributors could generate an unfriendly environment, and it was hard to predict how they would react.

Nevertheless, the software company did decide to terminate the distributors' exclusivity and replace them with subsidiaries. The distributors responded by immediately stopping sales and took on a competitive product instead. That was an emotional reaction and not in their own best business interest; however, that's what they did.

Setting up the new subsidiaries and facing trouble with the revenue stream from the previous distributors proved to be a toxic cocktail that led to further declining revenue and losses. After several years with losses, the board of directors replaced the executive office at the software company and brought in a new management team to restructure the company.

The story shows that using resellers and distributors can sometimes be a quick way to get revenue in foreign countries, especially when your product is hot. However, unless you work very closely with your business partners, they may turn out to become a problem when you want to scale or when the business model environment changes.

TAKE-AWAYS FROM THIS CHAPTER

Using a channel of third-party companies to distribute your product and serve your customers is primarily a scalability tool and seldom a shoestring approach.

If you want to take the indirect route, for instance, when that is your go-to-market approach, then you need to develop attractive partner value propositions and formal terms and conditions for the cooperation. You have a third-party business model within your business model that needs to be managed very carefully.

Unless you can offer exclusivity or apply a two-tier setup with a distributor taking care of brand building and lead generation, then it is implausible that the resellers will invest seriously in market development.

If your challenge is to recruit the first partners, then you may be tempted to provide exclusivity and high margins. However, awarding exclusivity to a business partner you don't know well is risky. When you come to disagree on the market potential or on the level of investment required to grow the market share, then you may have to go separate ways. Changing the agreements with partners that represent a significant revenue stream may stir emotional responses and hurt your business.

Be very careful choosing the partners that share your mindset and that have the same ambitions for growth. A quick fix now may turn out to become a big problem later.

Chapter Ten - Picking the next market

INTRODUCTION

Companies with versions of the simple virtual business model do not pick markets. The markets pick them. As described in chapter six, companies with physical business models may also be selected by the market. Epic is a great example.

For many companies, though, picking the next market or markets is a job on the to-do list. Where should we invest first or next in our global expansion?

Making such decisions require information about the opportunities available. In which market, country or region will our investments provide the fastest and highest payoffs. Quickest and highest seldom coincide, so in a shoestring perspective, we would probably go for the first.

On a shoestring budget, a fast return on the investment is more important than a high return.

In this chapter, I discuss various principles for picking and prioritising markets.

MARKET ANALYSIS

Picking one country over another should be based on some facts that justify the choice. Such facts are usually the result of a market analysis or a market assessment - two expressions for the same thing.

Ideally, you would prefer to have a decision matrix where you can rate the most critical characteristics, called CHA in figure 13, for your type of product across the markets that you consider. Then pick the one with the best match, while you keep exploring new opportunities.

	Value	Market A	Market B	Market C	Market D	Market E
CHA 1	3	5	0	5	3	0
CHA 2	3	3	0	5	5	5
CHA 3	3	5	1	5	0	3
CHA 4	3	0	1	1	3	3
CHA 5	3	0	3	1	3	5
...						
CHA N	1	3	5	0	5	0
Weighted Total:		93	49	51	111	89

Figure 13: Rate the countries you consider according to criteria that you can measure.

The two main questions for designing a market assessment template are:

1. What do we need to know?

2. How do we find the information?

As explained in chapter three, Alexander Osterwalder's business model environment framework can be used as a generic template for market analysis. However, it doesn't answer the two main questions listed above specifically for your product.

A shoestring type of market analysis will focus on answering four questions:

1. How big is the market for your product?

2. Can you use your current position in this market?

3. Can you use your current revenue generation approach in this market?

4. How much localisation is required, and which strategic alliances must you forge to get accepted?

Providing answers to these four questions can be done through a mix of desk research and interviews. Through the desk research, you should be able to identify all the competitors. In some countries, you can get access to their annual reports too, also and check how they are performing.

Getting a take on the size of the market should help you decide if it is worthwhile considering.

From mapping the competitive landscape, you should get a feeling for what your current position will look like in the new market. Will you be sufficiently differentiated, or will you be too much *me too*?

The devil is in the details, and you only get those by talking to potential customers, channel partners and consultants. My experience is that you get much more value out of ten in-depth interviews performed by a seasoned industry professional than you get from 200 interviews done by a telemarketing agency following a script.

Look for local market reports. Each country has its industry consultants that publish market research, which can be relevant for your situation.

As an example, DevoTeam, a Danish consulting company, regularly publishes a report named *ERP System in Denmark*. The most recent version of the report, published in May 2020, reviews the market, 14 vendors and 18 products. Numerous similar reports exist that may help you identify competitors and get a third-party view on market developments.

Doing market analysis requires mastering the local language. Often that entails engaging with a local agency that is familiar with your domain.

GOVERNMENT INCENTIVES

Governments on all levels have programs in place to support exports on the one side and attract foreign investments on the other side.

The purpose of both sets of programs and activities is to help create more jobs and improve national welfare. All governments in the world would like to maintain a surplus on their foreign trade balance and a deficit on their foreign capital balance. Export promotion and investment attraction, therefore, remain political priorities in all countries. The recession caused by Covid-19 have refilled the coffers of the export promotion programs across the world, and it is worthwhile checking out what is available in your country.

Such export promotion is mostly organised around support for individual companies and larger campaigns involving one or more industries. While software companies can benefit from the different programs, I have yet to see a meaningful export promotion of a country's software industry.

Trade missions

When the software industry was born in the 1980s, on the platform of the IBM compatible PC, all countries saw an opportunity for becoming a global leader. Making software was independent of any other natural resource than the human brain. Seeing that the demand for software was exploding, that it travelled easily across borders and that jobs in the industry were paying very well, politicians and business associations saw an opportunity.

Despite all the honourable intentions, none of the industry promotion programs has shown any significant results, and the reason is that the software industry is only an industry on the inside. Promoting a country's agricultural products may make good sense. Pork from Denmark, cheese from the Netherlands, lamb from New Zealand, wine from South Africa and beef from Argentina represent homogenous groups of companies that can meet with distributors and their corresponding trade associations. Companies in the software industry have similarities in the backend of their business models, but not in their frontends. Further, no country can claim a historical, comparative advantage in their software products.

I have seen brochures from national export organisations trying to explain why software developed in their country is of exceptionally high quality. I have been at meetings with trade delegations promoting a dozen national software companies and their products. It doesn't make sense. Who is interested in getting ten minutes presentations of an ERP system, a CRM system, a BI application, a DAM system, a marketing automation platform, an app for managing account payables, an app for managing email signatures and an app for digital signage? It's all software, but it doesn't address a homogenous group of distributors, resellers and customers and no single individual is the relevant contact point for all applications.

While I can understand the promotion of Danish pork in China, I have a hard time seeing the purpose of a campaign for software from Denmark. The Danes write great software, but I have yet to meet a company that has bought a software product because it came from a specific country. Denmark has a very long tradition and very high standards for producing quality pork. The industry is highly regulated, and it is very well organised in trade associations that can represent all suppliers (of which there are very few). The structure of the software industry is entirely different; it consists of thousands of mainly small companies offering very different products for many types of customers.

Due to recent incidents of the African swine fever, there is a shortage of pork in China. The Chinese consume on average 30 kilos of pork meat a year, thus making the country an attractive market for the Danish pork industry. I haven't come across any situations where countries have reported an unmet demand for software.

Although many attempts have been made to justify the opposite, there is nothing special about software because it has been developed in one country rather than in another. Today, most software products are made with components developed in numerous countries.

Individual support programs

The services offered by the export associations and the embassies' trade offices to individual companies make more sense. They typically offer to do market analysis, organise exhibitions and help identify potential business partners or service providers.

Such services were defined before the Internet made the world much more transparent, and before LinkedIn enabled us to find and connect with literally any type of competence anywhere. Most governments will charge for their services, but at the same time offer a grant that reduces the cost, and that is why they're still in demand. If you can get a service at a reduced price, then why not take advantage of it?

Some companies have had very positive experiences with these company-specific services, while others have been disappointed. It comes down to the qualifications and effort rendered by the people involved.

Governments also offer more comprehensive business development programs including training, consulting, market visits and lead generation.

This is a short description of the Danish Vitus-program[57]:

> *Small and medium-sized Danish enterprises often have huge export potential, but they can have difficulty correctly forming a clear market strategy and establishing sales abroad.*
>
> *The Trade Council, therefore, offers export counselling in the form of the VITUS program – a customised year-long process with an export adviser who has detailed knowledge of the particular export market. The aim is to give your company a market strategy and the right tools to secure orders on the chosen market within a year.*
>
> *As part of the export counselling package in the VITUS program, your company also receives a subsidy of 50 per cent of the hourly fee of 265 hours with the export adviser. Workshops and sparring with the external expert panel are also included in the package.*

Other countries have similar programs, and I have been on the consulting and training side of some of them. The immediate advantage

[57] https://thetradecouncil.dk/en/services/export/vitus

is the grant that will reduce the cost of the exercise for the participants. The disadvantage is the disparity and level of commitment among the participating companies. The programs I have been involved in all had a systematic and logical approach, and although the content may not be a perfect match, you always take something away.

Sometimes these programs are directed at export promotion to specific countries, which represents a challenge. Deciding which country to enter before you have done at least a preliminary market analysis seems to be premature. At least you will need to reserve the right to pull out of the program if it turns out that the target market is not a good fit in your current situation.

Investment attraction

As mentioned above, governments on all levels also have programs and teams to help attract foreign investments. With ambitions for entering a new market, you are eligible for their services and support.

However, the prime - and often sole - objective of foreign investment attraction is the creation of jobs. Getting their attention requires that you want to set up a local subsidiary and hire local staff. The more staff and the more investment you will make in buildings and other assets, the more interested they are in your project.

Finding real estate, offices, service providers and recruiting staff is within their charter while helping you find distributors, resellers and customers are not.

Going global on a shoestring means that you are looking for ways to get customers abroad without initially having to build up a base of fixed cost. With such an approach, you will not find much interest from the foreign investment attraction officers.

LANGUAGE

Many companies filter on language first. Where can we go with the language or languages that we already master and support?

That is a legitimate criterion.

It doesn't mean that the countries ending up on your list automatically are more straightforward to penetrate than others. But it does mean that you can test the markets without significant investments in expanding your team, translating your product and extending your marketing platform.

As mentioned above, choosing the language as the guiding principle leads most software companies to focus on the English-speaking markets, making them hyper-competitive.

Nevertheless, I do find it sensible to verify at least if there is a reasonable opportunity in the markets where you already support the languages. For most smaller software companies adding a language is a substantial undertaking.

SOCIAL PHYSICS

Throughout history, countries have always had neighbours as their most important trading partners. With physical products that seems rather obvious, but when the sales and maybe also the implementation and support processes require meeting face-to-face, then proximity does also play an essential role for software companies.

As an example, Southern Sweden, from Göteborg across Jönköping to Västervik, is much closer to Copenhagen than to Stockholm. With the bridge across the sound between Kastrup (DK) and Malmö (SE) and ferries at 15-minute intervals between Helsingør (DK) and Helsingborg (SE) travelling back and forth is no issue. Eastern Poland is closer to Berlin than to Warsaw, and much of Austria is closer to Munich than to Vienna.

Although all Danish software companies master the English language, most are not blind to the opportunities of our big southern neighbour, Germany. The same applies across the world, where countries share borders. USA, Canada and Mexico are also examples of countries that have substantial trade relations.

Social physics is not only a matter of geographical distance. It is also a matter of sharing languages and understanding each other's cultures. However, countries being neighbours doesn't mean that they have identical business model environments. The Nordic countries, for instance, may seem almost identical, but they are not. There are notable differences in the industrial infrastructures, the political landscape and the cultures.

Nevertheless, using social physics as a principle for selecting your first international markets makes a lot of sense. Minimal travel time alone can justify checking out the neighbours first.

MARKET SIZE

Picking a market because of its size is like ordering the most expensive bottle from the wine list. You will know that it cost a lot of money, but you may not get the best value per dollar spent.

Merely picking the largest market is seldom a shoestring approach.

It would also take you to all corners of the world.

2017	2018	2019	2020	2021	Share 2021	Country	Accumulated
2	1	1	1	1	19.22%	China	
1	2	2	2	2	16.36%	USA	
3	3	3	3	3	8.02%	India	50.80%
4	4	4	4	4	4.05%	Japan	
5	5	5	5	5	3.16%	Germany	
6	6	6	6	6	2.96%	Russia	
7	7	7	7	7	2.48%	Brazil	
10	10	10	9	8	2.43%	Indonesia	63.33%
8	8	8	8	9	2.38%	UK	
9	9	9	10	10	2.28%	France	
12	11	11	11	11	1.77%	Mexico	
11	12	12	12	12	1.74%	Italy	
14	14	14	13	13	1.61%	South Korea	71.42%
13	13	13	14	14	1.60%	Turkey	
15	15	15	15	15	1.38%	Spain	
16	16	16	16	16	1.36%	Canada	
17	17	17	17	17	1.25%	Saudi Arabia	
19	19	18	18	18	0.99%	Australia	76.89%
18	18	19	19	19	0.94%	Iran	
23	22	22	20	20	0.93%	Egypt	
20	20	20	21	21	0.93%	Taiwan	
21	21	21	22	22	0.89%	Thailand	
22	23	23	23	23	0.86%	Poland	81.08%
24	24	25	24	24	0.76%	Nigeria	
25	25	N/A	25	25	0.75%	Pakistan	

Figure 14: The 25 largest markets in the world, according to the BECH index.

The global demand for anything[58] is spread across many countries. Twenty-five countries represent more than 80 per cent, but that doesn't mean that those included in the list should be the places you should go first. When it comes to demand for advanced business software, the most potential markets for your product may very well not be all those listed above.

Coming from Denmark, number 53 on the list, Finland (62) or Norway (49), we can enjoy that most countries represent more market potential than we have domestically. However, more than 174[59] countries or territories in the world have a domestic market which is less than one per cent of the total, which means that if you come from a small country, then almost any other country represents an attractive expansion opportunity.

HYPE

Do you recall the abbreviations BRIC, which later became BRICS, and the follower MINT?

BRIC was Brazil, Russia, India and China. Later South Africa was added and the acronym became BRICS. When Goldman Sachs economist Jim O'Neill first coined the term BRIC in a 2001 paper, he projected the group would overtake the collective economic might of the G7 by 2050.

MINT, Mexico, India, Nigeria and Turkey, was initially coined in 2014 by Fidelity Investments, a Boston-based asset management firm and was again made famous by Jim O'Neill.

To understand why Goldman Sachs defines such groups of countries, you have to understand what kind of business they do. Goldman Sachs is an American multinational investment bank and financial

---

[58] Bech, H. P. (2020). *And the Winners Remain China and India* (TBK-WIPA-036). Copenhagen, Denmark. TBK Publishing®
[59] Ibid

services company headquartered in New York City. It offers services in investment management, securities, asset management, prime brokerage, and securities underwriting[60]. When big companies make foreign investments, especially mergers and acquisitions, Goldman Sachs is often a beneficiary.

Goldman Sachs is not playing in the field of helping smaller software companies go global on a shoestring. I don't think Goldman Sachs is particularly happy with shoestring projects.

I have met software companies that subscribed to the assumption that the BRICS and later MINT countries would be perfect opportunities for international expansion. None of them made any significant success in pursuing this strategy. Among the casualties was Daintel, that I have described earlier.

A country's macro-economic growth is of little importance when it comes to deciding market entry on a shoestring budget. You must assess the full business model environment and not just rely on a few arbitrary variables. My advice is to ignore the hype from the big consulting companies and the recommendations from governmental export institutions. Other agendas drive them, and they have never tried going global on a shoestring. Don't go with the flow and consider if you are better off doing exactly the opposite of what the majority does.

THE UNEXPECTED OPPORTUNITY

The unexpected opportunity is an underestimated way to pick the next market. I have already mentioned some of the ways to let a foreign market pick you rather than the other way around. However, many successes (and failures) come from unexpected international opportunities, so let's discuss how you can generate them and how you can decide whether to pursue them or not.

The definition of an *unexpected opportunity* in this context is when an important customer or a potential business partner from a country

---

[60] https://en.wikipedia.org/wiki/Goldman_Sachs

you didn't plan to do anything about suddenly reaches out showing interest in doing business with you.

How do you generate unexpected opportunities?

If you follow my recommendations from chapter eight and become a thought leader and industry authority, then you will create visibility and automatically generate attention. You will regularly receive inquiries in your mailbox.

By making some of your material available in more languages, you can extend your reach and generate even more inquiries. However, it only makes sense broadening your scope if you are prepared to engage in these languages. There are plenty of English-speaking innovators and visionaries around the world that search for new solutions. As long as you are visible with English material, and that what you offer is novel and exceptional, then they will find you and get in touch.

If you don't receive any or only very few inquiries, then you need to find out why your website and the content you produce fail to build SEO authority within your domain. Often it comes down to an unclear value proposition and position statement.

Qualifying the unexpected opportunity

Many of us have experienced the hard work associated with recruiting partners, generating leads and closing sales in new markets. When someone approaches us, then we tend to get flattered and imagine a short sales cycle. Such opportunities often appear more promising than anything we currently have in our pipeline.

Daintel thought they had found an opportunity in Brazil but lost a million Euro on the project.

Euromax got an inquiry from New Zealand, decided to bid and won it.

Navision was approached by three inexperienced entrepreneurs and managed to become market leaders in Germany.

Damgaard Data made a global distribution agreement with IBM and failed.

These examples show that unexpected opportunities can be tough to qualify, but some guidelines may help you.

What is the opportunity cost?

Pursuing an opportunity requires time, effort and money. Something else will suffer while you chase the unexpected opportunity. What is that and what type of risk does it represent? Don't fool yourself by thinking that you can work an unexpected opportunity on top of your already full schedule. Make a sober assessment of the situation before you commit.

Write it down. If I pursue this unexpected opportunity, then I will not accomplish these activities: [Fill in…………..]

If the opportunity cost is high, then you should not pursue it.

Get clear proof of commitment

A genuine opportunity is characterised by the initiator's willingness to commit time and money.

Someone approaches you claiming that they represent a new market (that's not on your priority list) and will develop it for you if you pay them a salary and reimburse their expenses. That's not an opportunity. That's someone looking for a job.

Someone approaches you claiming that they represent a major market and will develop it for you if you give them exclusivity. They will pick up the cost of operations and act as a distributor or reseller. That may be a genuine opportunity, but you should qualify it further before you accept. Even when they pick up the cost of operations, you can stay assured that there will be support requirements along the road. You should do a proper business model and environment analysis and agree on a business plan.

Navision worked a full year on the business plan before entering the German market, and then it took three years to reach break-even. And that was in the days where software licenses were paid for upfront!

When Euromax decided to pursue the opportunity in New Zealand, we suggested the client come to Europe and visit us and some of our current customers. They accepted and paid their own travel and accommodation costs. When we did the first presentation and demonstration in Wellington, the client paid for the conference room and the AV equipment at a hotel.

If the unexpected opportunity is reluctant to make any commitments in the process leading to a potential agreement, then you should back off.

Define a process with milestones

If you find the unexpected opportunity interesting, you should define a schedule for the process leading to a potential agreement and set some milestones at which both parties can back off. When your counterpart misses her milestones, you should be concerned.

People make things happen

It is worthwhile remembering that companies are legal abstractions with no will and no soul. Only people can make things happen, and to do that they must have ambitions and power. They don't have to sit on the very top of the organisation, but they must understand how to navigate to make their company decide in your favour.

For you to assess an unexpected opportunity, you must understand what drives them to pursue this alternative. I recommend using the direct approach and ask them why? Despite all the risk, why do they consider your solution so attractive? It's not difficult to identify all the risk elements that other stakeholders in the organisation will see. You might as well address these risks upfront and assess if you can mitigate them. Does the value you provide compensate for the risk?

Dig below the formal business motives and look for their personal motives. More than often, people do things for other reasons than just financial awards. I have seen people driven by prestige, by the need for the unusual adventure, by the lust for travel and by a craving for revenge. Some of these motivators are fine. Others are not.

TAKE-AWAYS FROM THIS CHAPTER

Picking markets is difficult, but there are approaches that can help do the preliminary market research on shoestring budgets.

It starts with you defining what you want to know - then finding ways to do the desk research. If that requires mastering a new language, then you can engage your government's export promotion program or find a local freelancer through LinkedIn.

There is no better source of market information than potential customers. Performing ten in-depth interviews by a seasoned industry professional should give a good feeling for what the market looks like from the customers' perspective. Which competitors do they mention, which reseller do they use or know of, which consulting companies operate in this domain, is there an industry association? What customers don't mention is probably not so important.

Don't auto-reject the unexpected opportunity. People make a huge difference, and if someone is highly motivated to do business with you, then you should qualify it carefully. Be prepared to invest and engage if you find genuine commitment from the other side.

Chapter Eleven - The human dimension

INTRODUCTION

There is an issue that is rarely included in books on business methodology.

The human dimension.

Individual people make a decisive impact on whether your plan will succeed or not. Especially when you are a small shop. If there is one statement explaining failure in international business that I hear more frequently than any other, then it is *we had the wrong people on the project*. I know that may be a lousy excuse for the lack of leadership or poor judgement, but finding, recruiting and managing the business development team that can execute your international expansion plans is critical.

Provided that you have a competitive offering and that the timing is in your favour, then your success will mostly depend on the quality of the team. The human impact on an early stage international business venture is significant. When you are completely unknown, have few or no references and are not mentioned in the reports from the industry analysts, then it takes a particular breed of people to make customers and partners in other countries listen to you and eventually convince them to use or resell your product. Breaking into new territories requires people with an *entrepreneurial mindset* making the pool from which to recruit quite exclusive.

The pool of available talent that can build an international business from scratch is limited. Not many are prepared to run the risk, and fewer have the broad skill set required. As I mention in several places in this book, even the most carefully crafted plan will not survive the meeting with reality, which means that you depend on the feedback from your business developers to then take corrective actions.

So, in this chapter, I discuss what business developers do, what they look like, how you find them, how you get them on board and how you keep them.

FROM GOOD TO GREAT

Are you familiar with Jim Collins' book *From Good to Great?*[61] It was published in 2001 and studied publicly listed American companies that had been around for many years before they suddenly began performing way better than their peers. Collins and his team searched for companies with at least 15-years returns equal to or below the general market whose performance suddenly changed and then recorded another 15-years returns of at least three times the general market. They found eleven companies that met these criteria and awarded them the title *great*.

As a control group, Collins then identified a "comparison company" for each of the great companies. The criteria for the control group was that they were similarly resourced and positioned as their relative great companies, but their returns remained at or below the general market return after the transition point.

The questions the book attempted to answer were: how did the eleven companies become great, did they do something different than the control group and are those principles repeatable?

Even if you haven't read the book, you will probably not be surprised that he did find distinct commonalities. A business book proving that there is no recipe for success would probably not have found such a broad audience. Still, I do think his findings have some merit.

Collins found six common characteristics:

1. Great performing companies have Level 5 leaders

Level five leaders, first and foremost, think about the success of their organisation. They are never charismatic or prominent personalities

---

[61] Collins, J. (2001). Good to Great : Why Some Companies Make the Leap... and Others Don't: Random House.

but are curious, quiet, shy, deliberate and ambitious. None of the great companies had leaders with big egos.

2. First who, then what

Assemble a team of great people first and then decide on the strategy or vision for the company. Get the wrong people off the bus and the right people on the bus and in their right seats.

3. Confront the brutal facts

Great leaders create a climate where the truth is appreciated. In such companies, bad news travels much faster than good news. Bad news needs swift attention; good news seldom does.

4. Be a hedgehog

The hedgehog is a simple animal, but it has a world-class defence system. Great companies find the thing that they can do better than anyone else and concentrate on that.

5. Nurture a culture of discipline

A culture of discipline requires people to firmly adhere to the strategy, including the policy of saying NO to all the opportunities that do not fit the hedgehog concept.

6. Use technology accelerators

Great companies are not attracted by the buzzwords and blanket promises surrounding new technologies. They give sincere thought to how the application of which technology can improve their performance.

You can find many reasons for discarding Collins' observations. They have been made from a group of large and publicly listed American companies that have been in business for at least thirty years and that have had the resources to make significant changes. As you read the book and its recommendations, you will often think precisely what does that mean? The principles are so general and the terminology so subtle that they offer no clear guidance to what you, in your situation, should do differently. When you use terms such as right and wrong as adjectives, then you help no-one. The example with the bus above sounds grand but it doesn't help you because what precisely distinguishes the wrong people from the right people and what are the characteristics of the right seats?

Finally, the principles in the book only apply when you have Level 5 people on the top. Do you have Level 5 people at the top of your company? If you don't, can you replace them?

I highlight *From Good to Great*, despite its many shortcomings, because I believe that the general conclusion is right: it's all about people.

If Collins found a correlation between the financial results and the characteristics of the management team in big organisations, then I will claim that it is even more prominent in small organisations. Big organisations have momentum. Small companies do not.

There is a tight relationship between what small companies can achieve and the skills, competencies, ambitions, attitudes, curiosity and capacity of their key people. And in small companies most of the staff are vital.

> *People and timing can make a good idea successful,*
> *and a great idea fail.*

Implementing some of the ideas outlined in this book will most likely require skills and competencies that you do not currently have in your organisation. So, you will need to find people that can help you.

THE FOUR INGREDIENTS

As I have indicated before, going global on a shoestring requires four components:

1. A superior value proposition

2. A clear and competitive position

3. Favourable timing

4. A talented business development team

It is the job of the business development team to craft and verify the value proposition and the position statement in a way that takes advantage of or creates the favourable timing.

The value proposition(s)

By the end of the day, companies make all their investments to increase capacity, productivity and profitability. You will, therefore, see many value propositions claiming that they deliver just that.

There are three issues with such statements.

The first issue is that business software cannot deliver on any of these objectives. It's the way people use the software that creates the value, not the software per se. The second issue is that for many stakeholders involved in the buying journey, these objectives are not the most important. And the third issue is that such claims are like setting sail in a bloody red ocean. You compete with all other types of investments that claim to serve the same objectives.

The first job of the business development team is to craft value propositions that resonate with the people that are supposed to use the software. Alexander Osterwalder's value proposition canvas[62] is a great tool to help find the words that relate the features of the product to the jobs the users need to get done. It is unlikely that you will get the wording right first time you try. Test your key words with real users before you commit them to appear in your marketing and sales content.

---

[62] Osterwalder, A., Pigneur, Y., Bernarda, G., & Smith, A. (2014). Value proposition design: How to Create Products and Services Customers Want. Hoboken, New Jersey: John Wiley & Sons Inc.

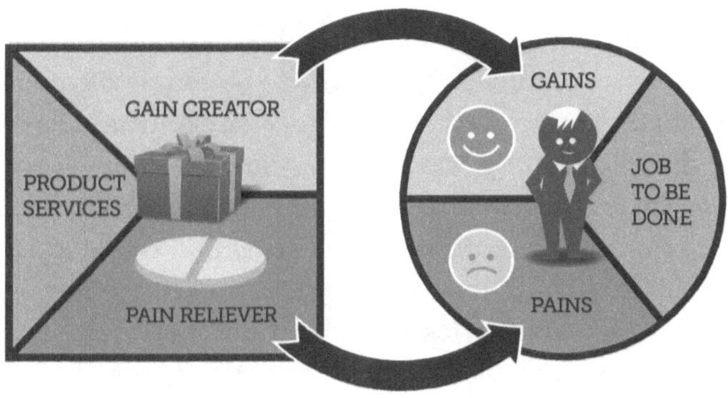

Figure 15: Value propositions should be crafted for the people who are supposed to use the software. As they have different roles and criteria steering their preferences, you need more than one value proposition.

If you use an indirect channel to serve the market, then you need additional value propositions. Your customer value propositions and your partner value propositions are not identical. Your customer value propositions should include the value that the channel adds. Your partner value proposition is mainly focussed on how the resellers can make a profitable business with your products.

Your business development team must understand and be able to explain how your product delivers the value you promise. The fundamental principle is to always tie product-related information to the specific job the user needs to get done and explain how it creates the gains and releases the pains. For marketing purposes, such explanations will be generic, but for sales purposes, where the dialogue is with individual customers, the conversation must follow the SPIN[63] principles.

---

[63] Rackham, N. (1988). SPIN *selling.*

The positioning

Your position statement will explain whom the product is meant for and how it is conceptually different from the competitive alternatives. While changing your product may require substantial time and effort, changing the positioning statements can be done overnight. The objective of the positioning exercise is to place you in a blue ocean. That means finding a position in an existing market or category where potential customers and business partners can immediately recognise what you do, but also quickly understand how you are different. Positioning is done with words and illustrations. You obviously cannot take a position that is not covered by your product, but you can take a position that will be covered by your product in the foreseeable future.

Small companies setting out to win customers in a new market should take clearly defined and narrow positions. It is much better to be the first preference for a small group of customers than just another option for the many.

Favourable timing

Timing is crucial when you are on a shoestring budget. There must be good reasons for why now is the right time for buying your products as opposed to the other alternatives available.

Uniconta, the ERP system in the cloud, was launched in May 2016 just after Microsoft had announced the discontinuation of their Dynamics C5. Behind Uniconta stood the same Erik Damgaard who was the father of the original Concorde C5 that was launched in 1995. Within six months, Uniconta had recruited one hundred resellers, and every second customer came from C5. Uniconta was positioned as a C5 replacement, included comprehensive data migration tools and offered the resellers the same value-add benefits. Within a very short time after the launch, all C5 customers knew of Uniconta, and those who decided to replace their system had it on their shortlist.

Uniconta has started to sell into other markets where partner recruitment and end-user subscriptions cannot benefit from a C5-situation. Therefore, narratives must be developed explaining why market entry now is logical.

Perfect timing is seldom possible to predict. Still, your business development team needs to craft a compelling storyline to make customers, and potential resellers understand why now makes perfect sense and why your product is a logical response to changes in the market and the industry.

FINDING THE MEMBERS FOR THE BUSINESS DEVELOPMENT TEAM

Here are the characteristics of the people you want on your business development team.

The team leader should speak and write English at a B2 or preferably C1 level[64]. That person will be responsible for developing and communicating the positioning statement and the value propositions. The words must be born in her heart, come out of her mouth and flow from her hand.

Look for a person with business acumen who can do many things on her own. Someone that doesn't require a support team to get things done. The person should be self-motivated with no need for specific instructions. Such people, that are self-starters, may do things differently that you would do, so allow them room to manoeuvre.

Team member number two is a technical wizard that also speaks English at a B2 or preferably C1 level. Perfect writing skills are not so critical but take them if you can get them. If you are a start-up, this person may also fill the role as a product manager in the beginning.

These two people should initially be able to cover the entire business development process. Should they lack specific skills, then those can be added using freelancers, until you can afford to extend the team with permanent staff.

---

[64] According to the CEFR classification. https://www.coe.int/en/web/common-european-framework-reference-languages

Should they have tried it before?

What does it mean that they have tried it before? Do we talk about business development in general, in the software industry or into the same markets? If you can find someone who has done the same before, then that would be great, but it will also make the pool of candidates small. There will be few that match the criteria and how many of those will be available now?

No one has a degree in business development, and the technical skills are not particularly difficult to learn. A great business development manager has some personal and interpersonal qualities that in my mind, are much more important than the experience from the exact same type of job. She is curious, empathetic and prefers to listen before she talks. She introduces structure to manage the chaos. She has communication skills that allow her to make the complex appear logical and straightforward.

Should they have industry experience?

Some industries are difficult to understand, and some are not. So, I'll say that it depends on your situation how critical that particular criterion is. The technical whiz-kid should have industry insight and can then help the team leader shorten her learning curve.

Is having worked for a big brand an advantage?

No. Be careful hiring people from big brands. Their experience of working in a large organisation is of little value to you. Being big doesn't mean being professional. That doesn't mean that a candidate couldn't come from one of the big brands, but it is never a justification in itself. If you present someone you have hired to do business development by referring to where she previously worked, then you have made a mistake.

Is age an issue?

Yes. You want someone that has business acumen. Someone that has made enough failures and successes to master the balance of teamwork and getting things done herself. Someone that is not afraid of admitting a mistake, corrects it and carries on. Someone that can make things happen, make people follow her, and doesn't have an inflated ego.

Do academic credentials play a role?

No. There may be rare cases where it helps to be a medical doctor, a lawyer, a nurse or have a certain engineering degree. But in most cases, it doesn't matter.

Are they expensive?

Yes. They are not easy to find; they already have a job, and they can easily find another. They will pick you because they see an opportunity for having fun, learning, growing and becoming successful financially. If you cannot pay them a competitive salary, then you can offer stock options, of which they will understand the potential. Just don't forget that when it comes to hiring the business development team to take your product international, then the difference between getting it right and getting it wrong is humongous. Don't be cheap.

How do you find them?

They seldom apply for open job positions because they are already busy. You have to find them either through your network or by using a head-hunter.

The chances are that you already know whom you want. When there are candidates in your network that have demonstrated the qualities you need, then this is where you should start looking. If no candidates are available in your immediate vicinity, then you should explore your second-level network. Take a one-on-one conversation with people that are in similar positions as you and get names of potential candidates.

Sometimes, they may make unsolicited applications because they have found you. Take an unsolicited application very seriously and understand that these people don't look for a job and a fixed monthly salary. They look for challenges and a personal growth opportunity. You should check their qualifications and motives but understand that they will also qualify you. The risk that they jump ship during the selection process is high if you are sloppy.

I cannot recommend broadcasting a message on LinkedIn that you are looking for a business developer. I have seen many do that, but to me, it comes across as unprofessional, lazy, desperate and cheap. Let the head-hunter use LinkedIn for identifying qualified candidates.

Chemistry is crucial

You are embarking on an expedition into unknown and unmapped territory. There may initially be more surprises and mistakes than successes on the journey. Your attitude and reactions should be based on mutual trust and respect. This book will help you build a common vocabulary and set the expectations, but maintaining a great working relationship and an open and secure atmosphere in the team requires good chemistry among the members. You either trust your people or you will end up parting ways.

MAKE YOURSELF ATTRACTIVE

When I, at the age of 35, landed my first international business development job, as VP marketing and sales for Dataco, I had no experience in doing international business nor did I know anything about building reseller networks. I came from a job as VP of direct sales in the Danish subsidiary of American Control Data Corporation. Maybe my new employer thought that working for a company that operated internationally would make me internationally experienced, but that was not the case. My previous job was selling American made IT in Denmark.

My most recent project with Control Data was building a business unit selling PC-based LAN/WAN systems, which meant that I quickly understood the potential of the product range that Dataco was about to release.

Please note that I didn't apply for the Dataco job. It was advertised, but as I wasn't looking for a job, I didn't see the ad. It wasn't until they approached me that I became interested.

During the first interviews, we spent most of the time talking about Dataco, the vision, the products, the ambition and the very attractive remuneration package. Clearly, they were working on getting me interested, but they also carefully described what the vision was. If we didn't agree on the vision and the ambition, then everything else would be irrelevant.

Dataco was a start-up with no revenue, and there was no job description. I didn't need one. My job was to generate revenue and build an organisation that could make us a global market leader.

Five things caught my attention:

1. The product concept was brilliant. As the products were not released yet, I didn't know if they could deliver, but talking to the CTO and some of the other key members of the staff gave me confidence that they had the right people in the right seats.

2. It was an international job. I was then in a position serving the domestic market, and this job could make me grow. I would do business across the globe.

3. With my experience from Control Data, I found the timing for the Dataco products perfect. The PC was gaining popularity, and there was an enormous base of mainframes and minicomputers that needed to be interconnected.

4. I was to build the organisation from scratch. I hadn't done that before and saw this as a great learning opportunity.

5. The job was well paid with a high base salary and a simple and very attractive bonus scheme that aligned the success of the company with my personal success.

It was only after they got me hooked on the job, that I was asked to explain how I would approach the challenge.

I didn't leave Control Data because I was looking for a new job. I joined Dataco because I understood this unique opportunity and because I could visualise how, in general terms, I would make the company (and thereby myself) an international success. I was not the only candidate for the job, but they picked me because of my credentials and my convincing communications skills.

The Dataco founders had identified some of the potential candidates through their personal network, and this is how they came to know about me. I later learned that none of the candidates that applied for the job based on seeing the advertisement made it to the final round.

There are several lessons to be learnt here:

1. The people you are looking for to spearhead an international business development effort are probably already in a job and not looking at advertisements. You need to find them and make them interested. You can do so through your network or by using a head-hunter.

2. In the first interviews, you have a sales job to do. You need to get the candidates hooked on the vision and the project. At the end of the recruitment process, you want to have at least three highly motivated and qualified candidates from which to choose. Don't let yourself get into a situation where there is only one candidate left that wants the job, and you sign that person up because you need the position filled.

3. Be prepared to pay. You can hardly pay too much for the right candidate. The contribution that person will make to the company's valuation, when successful, can be counted in millions.

GO FOR THE BROAD SKILL SETS

I didn't need a support team to do my job at Dataco. I wrote the first brochures and datasheets in Danish and English. I defined the product names. I put together the first sales presentations. I developed the first reseller program and got a reseller agreement put together. It wasn't all top professional, but it was good enough to get us going, win the first orders and sign up the first resellers. Six months later we could afford to hire more people and gradually they could take over and improve what I had started. I could then devote more time to building and leading my organisation and conducting more international business development.

Our fast, international success was a combination of an excellent range of products, perfect timing and a lucky punch I made in recruiting a brilliant technical person. The combination of him and I could convince any potential resellers or customer that we were the LAN/WAN solution of the future available today. Each of us could do great things, but together we could make miracles. We didn't deliver presentation hell killing people with PowerPoints. Instead, we asked tons of questions enabling us to understand the situation, the concerns and the implications. Then we used the whiteboard to develop the solutions. We applied SPIN®[65] techniques way before those principles became mainstream. My Brother in Arms covered the technical issues, and I covered the commercial side.

Another lucky punch was hiring a young and inexperienced illustrator and giving her the Mac that she asked for. The visuals that she made lifted our presentations and our marketing material to a new level, where we were perceived as a well-established and professional company. Professional we were. Well-established we were not. All this was done on a shoestring budget.

I was given a free hand to hire the people for my team and coach and manage them my way. From my troublesome management job with Control Data[66], where I took over a complete department, I now experienced what it was like building a team of people you have picked yourself. That's two completely different things.

The learnings here are:

> 1. The person you hire to spearhead your internationalisation effort should initially not need a support team to function. If you pick a person from a major company, then make sure that she has

---

[65] Rackham, N. (1988). SPIN *selling*.
[66] https://tbkconsult.com/the-friendly-orange-glow-the-untold-story-of-the-rise-of-cyberculture/

worked with business development before, didn't have a support team and that she can cover many positions.

2. Don't expect anyone to cover both the commercial and the technical aspects of your business equally well. Start with the commercial profile and then let that person choose her technical partner.

AVOID THE NAPOLEONS

After twelve months at Dataco, I recommended that my department was split in two. The technical functions such as product management, documentation, technical training and professional services should report directly to the CEO. I would then concentrate on marketing and sales, which now covered most of Europe and also included plans for overseas activities.

I did so because people management was not my primary interest, and because it would give my technical manager a growth opportunity, a seat on the executive team and a salary increase. Not all my colleagues understood my motives, but when you prefer to be in the field developing the business, you cannot manage many direct reports at the same time.

The reorganisation gave me the room to take on new markets personally and leave them to an area manager once they were bootstrapped.

The people you hire to develop a business may not be the people you need to manage and grow it. Not everyone realises their management shortcomings, and what started out very promising can suddenly become a problem.

When you hire someone to lead a new business venture, such as opening new markets, you need to discuss expectations and aspirations. The first person on the team may not necessarily be the one managing the unit when it has fifty people on the roster. But it could be. You don't want to lose good people because of misaligned expectations, so discuss it openly and help people develop into the positions they aspire to when they have the talent.

Become a great place to work

People working for themselves seem to be more engaged than people working for a salary. Hiring and motivating entrepreneurial talent, which is a prerequisite for going global on a shoestring, requires that you create an environment where they have a decisive say in how things get done and that they can participate in the upside of the venture.

Warrants, stock options or some other equity deal is way better than a bonus or a commission. If you do not expect a liquidity event in the next three to five years, then you need to provide an alternative option for cashing in.

Just as crucial as the equity option is the environment that you provide for your business developers. If they need to be told what to do, then you have the wrong people, or you have the wrong management style. You must give them free rein and agree on which reporting formats make the most sense. Listen to the market feedback they bring home and have a process in place for responding.

Even when you, as a small company, do not enjoy deep pockets and brand recognition, you can still provide a great place to work. I am not talking about the physical office environment and the amenities, but about the way you run the company and how you treat people. I am also not recommending participating in the competitions for titles such as "the greatest place to work." Do that, if you want to, but it will not have any impact on attracting the business development talent you need. A great place to work for a senior business developer is where there is an atmosphere of trust, delegation and an open attitude for changing things.

Great people want to make an impact, and that should also be what you want them to do. Be prepared to listen and change things based on ideas that are not necessarily your own. Remember to recognise others' contributions and celebrate even the smallest successes.

Take-aways from this chapter

Provided that you have a great product, and the timing is right, then failure and success is primarily a matter of the people you assign to develop the new markets.

The people you need will most likely already be working elsewhere. You need to find them through your network or by engaging a head-hunter.

Be careful with hiring people from big companies. People working for great companies are not necessarily great talents in a small company. Don't disqualify candidates from big companies but understand that having worked for a large organisation and recognised brand is not a qualification in itself.

Chose attitude over skills, but don't compromise on business acumen. A business developer must be able to work in a structured and methodical way, have an analytical mind and provide sober feedback from her findings. You want the brutal facts rather a rosy but slightly distorted picture of reality.

Even when you cannot offer a recognised brand and big budgets, you can still be a great place to work. International business development requires people with an entrepreneurial mindset. They want challenges, room to grow and to see their ideas implemented. Providing such an environment doesn't cost anything.

As your international business development team grows, the need for more people management increases as well. The first person hired may not be the best qualified for people management. Adjust expectations, do what's best for the team and the company, but don't lose good people because of misaligned expectations.

CHAPTER TWELVE – CASES

OVERVIEW

THE following case stories are based on interviews conducted over the last couple of years:

Agillic (Omnichannel marketing)

Daintel (Healthcare)

Edlund (Life insurance and pensions)

Epic (Healthcare)

First Agenda (Meeting management)

Forecast (Quote-to-cash)

Fotoware (DAM - Digital Asset Management)

IT Minds (Software engineering)

MapsPeople (Indoor navigation)

Monitor ERP (Cloud ERP)

NetDialog (Data communication optimisation)

NORRIQ (Microsoft Dynamics ERP)

Penneo (Secure document management)

ProManage (Manufacturing Execution and Operations Management)

Pronestor (Meeting management)

RamBase (Cloud ERP)

Sales Force Europe (Business development as-a-service)

Soft4 (Microsoft Dynamics ERP for vertical industries)

SoftScan (Email security and SPAM management)

Solvoyo (Supply chain planning and analytics)

Templafy (Template and document management)

Tia Technology (General insurance)

TimeXtender (Data management)

TrustPilot (Platform for customer reviews)

Uniconta (Cloud ERP)

XINK (email signature management and marketing)

XOLO (ERP and business management for solo-entrepreneurs)

The ones with the most details are those where I have been operationally involved over several years. They are:

Euromax (Newspaper management)

Mercante (Printers)

Damgaard and Navision (ERP)

Scandinavian Dataco (Local and wide area network systems)

AGILLIC – FACILITATING THE BUYER'S JOURNEY

The Customer Problem

When it comes to marketing and revenue generation, all companies face the same challenges. How to communicate effectively through the increasing level of noise and get a response. The remedy is known and requires adapting to the individual customer journey. This may include offering relevant inspiration and making targeted buying suggestions to activate latent needs. The generic name of the solution is omnichannel marketing[67], which allows companies to manage the interaction with their customers across multiple communication channels and adapt it to each customer's individual preferences and mode.

The Agillic Value Proposition

Agillic provides an omnichannel marketing platform that enables their clients to design, manage and maintain high volumes of individualised communication that forms the basis for optimising response and conversion rates. The company can demonstrate how over time their platform improves the clients' revenue generation.

"The software, for which the customer pays a substantial amount of money every year, is, however, not the most significant cost element", explains Rasmus Houlind, CXO[68] at Agillic. "Implementation, integration to internal as well as external data providers and ongoing operational costs are the leading budget items. Executing an omnichannel strategy requires software, such as ours, but it also involves a range of marketing and analytic skills."

Data plays a pivotal role in successful omnichannel marketing. Unique to Agillic is a highly flexible and customer-centric data-structure which can be easily modelled according to the business objectives. The data model is the backbone for the clients' ability to create high levels of personalisation and is directly connected to the execution across channels.

---

[67] Omnichannel marketing is a term covering the ability to communicate in a personalised way across a multitude of marketing channels, digital as well as analogue

[68] CXO – Chief Experience Officer

"Our clients are seldom novices," says Rasmus Houlind. "They are on their first, second or even third system and have generated first-hand experience with omnichannel marketing. With Agillic they get sophisticated software to unleash the potential of personalisation and the full scope of omnichannel marketing. Although there is a new breed of CMOs and CIOs who understand the intersection between business and IT, it may take a series of iterations to get the technical requirements aligned with the marketing goals and the overall business objectives."

The company has earned a solid reputation for enabling a fast time-to-value. Apart from speedy onboarding, this is driven by a user-friendly UX, that empowers the users to perform sophisticated tasks with ease and allowing them to achieve business results fast.

Competition and positioning

The omnichannel systems industry is relatively crowded with an extensive range of software platforms and solution providers, including giants such as Salesforce, Oracle and Adobe. The industry is also the home of several best-of-breed solutions, each with their vertical focus or specialisation on a specific communication channel.

Agillic provides a best-of-breed omnichannel marketing platform. The focus is on enterprise B2C clients within retail, finance, NGOs & Charity, Travel & Leisure and subscription-based businesses across industries, such as fitness centres, media and publishing houses. The ideal client is a mature organisation with a central marketing department that needs a toolbox to implement across all its functional disciplines. The buying centre typically has the CMO (Chief Marketing Officer) as the main driver. The buying process is complex, and the average sales cycle is seven months.

"Our clients are seldom novices," says Rasmus Houlind. "They are on their first, second or even third system and have generated first-hand experience with omnichannel marketing. With Agillic they get sophisticated software to unleash the potential of personalisation and the full scope of omnichannel marketing. Although there is a new breed of CMOs and CIOs who understand the intersection between business and

IT, it may take a series of iterations to get the technical requirements aligned with the marketing goals and the overall business objectives."

Go-to-market approach

Agillic primarily sells directly but have recently started building a channel of implementation and integration partners that can deliver the services required for onboarding and ongoing support of the customers. These services comprise between 50 and 90 per cent of the operations budget. Although this ratio tends to decline as the customers choose to insource the skills required, there is still a substantial need for an assortment of professional services.

"The need for ongoing professional services makes omnichannel software ideal for a partner-based go-to-market approach, says Jesper Valentin Holm. There is an attractive service revenue potential, and the customer relationships are long-lasting. The learning curve for new partners is somewhat steep, but the return on the investment is handsome."

Internationalization

The market for omnichannel marketing software is global, and many of the vendors already have a global presence. Upholding the R&D effort to stay competitive requires an installed base of clients, for which the Danish market is too small. The problems and solutions in the omnichannel domain are identical across countries, and apart from translating the user interface, there are no significant requirements for localisation. Success, however, requires a local presence for delivering the professional services associated with implementation, integration and ongoing support.

Agillic, which has expanded into Norway and Sweden, is currently considering which countries to enter next. The UK, DACH and the Benelux countries are the most prominent candidates.

"We have received some inquiries from potential partners in the US," reveals Rasmus Houlind. "However, our primary focus just now is to consolidate our position in the Nordics and explore further opportunities in the UK, DACH and Benelux."

The international expansion strategy entails building a network of sales, integration and implementation partners.

"On a global level, IT for marketing-driven B2C companies is a fast-growing market," concludes Rasmus Houlind. "However, each country is different in terms of the competitive landscape and service provider infrastructure. We are continually monitoring the market development to identify where and when the timing for market entry is most optimal. Then we will invest in a presence and set up the organisation to support our partners."

DAINTEL – A MATTER OF LIFE OR DEATH

The customer problem

Life intensive care units (ICU) and operating rooms are, by definition, hectic and busy. Like no other places, what happens inside these rooms is a matter of life or death. They are sophisticated operational units that do not know precisely what they must produce today and tomorrow, what skills will be required and what equipment will be needed. The operation plan and procedures change continuously depending on the healing process of their current patients. Both managers and operators can benefit substantially from having access to real-time information on the current status of affairs, which kind of patients they currently have, which facilities and staff are available and when and which type of cases are in the queue. As health care units, they also need to provide detailed documentation for quality control purposes as well as delivering data to national databases for administration, benchmarking and statistical analysis.

The Daintel value proposition

Since 2004 Daintel has, from its base in Copenhagen, Denmark, specialised in developing IT-solutions for emergency and intensive care units solving the problems and challenges described above. They started at a time where the individual healthcare unit in Denmark had the authority to procure their own systems and succeeded in installing their software at over half the intensive care units in Danish hospitals.

The internationalisation challenges

Enjoying a fifty per cent market share by 2010, Daintel decided to expand their activities to international markets and hired a Chief Operational Officer to head up the operations. The endeavour was a complete failure, and four years later, Daintel stopped all international activities, laid-off the staff involved and was left with severe debt. The project almost killed the company.

"In the years 2010-12 we participated in and won several entrepreneurship competitions," explains Patrick Hulsen, CEO and

founder of Daintel. "I was continuously interviewed by the press, invited to deliver keynotes and was even featured in in-flight magazines. The hype around the company was substantial. We mistook this hype for market acceptance. Winning entrepreneurship competitions, delivering keynotes and getting press coverage can lead you to a kind of distorted reality. At least that's what happened to us."

The internationalisation project included penetrating Norway, Sweden, Germany, Switzerland and Brazil all at the same time.

"Brazil came on the plan because we met someone from that country, who convinced us of the opportunities available there," says Patrick Hulsen. "We also managed to get a pilot project running before we fully realised what it would take in time and money to get the official approval for selling to Brazilian health care institutions. There was no way we were capable of supporting and financing such an approval process 10.000 kilometres and four time-zones away. Getting the approval was no guarantee that we could sell anything in the short-term anyway."

Despite dedicated staff, investments and support from the Danish Export Council and the Minister of Industrial Affairs, Daintel were not capable of winning a single international deal. And then the funding dried out.

The main reason for the failure was that Daintel underestimated the time and resources required for being accepted in a business driven by public procurement. In most countries, hospitals make all significant software solutions investments through a traditional procurement process including a requirement specification, a request for proposal (RFP), a pre-qualification stage, a shortlist, a proof-of-concept demonstration and a final contract negotiation. Only if you are known well before the formal RFP is issued do you have a chance of influencing the specifications. Your chances of winning a public tender for a software solution coming out of the blue are very slim.

"The nominal sales process for our type of solution is never less than 24 months," Patrick Hulsen continues, "and we have seen sales processes

that took eight years. That's a genuine challenge for a company coming from a small domestic market like Denmark. We do not have the market potential at home for building the kind of reserves it takes to win foreign markets in head-on competition with the local incumbents. Imagining investing four to five years before you win your first project in an environment where participating in each RFP cost you close to two hundred thousand dollars!"

From 2014 to 2017 Daintel focused on recuperating the losses incurred by the first internationalisation attempt. An administrative reform in 2007 reduced the number of regions in Denmark from 14 to 5. This local reform began to impact how health care information systems were procured, making the domestic market for Daintel more difficult.

In early 2014 the Capital Region of Copenhagen and The Region of Zealand, which represents close to fifty per cent of the Danish population, decided to acquire a new integrated healthcare platform based on the American Epic EHR-system. This solution was to replace 17 Daintel installations in the two regions. Not because the Epic system was better for the IC-units, but because it was an integrated system that should replace all separate systems.

A new global go-to-market approach

In 2017 Daintel won a CIS-project in Iceland and in 2018 they were awarded a data connectivity project in Southern Jutland.

"These two projects are a result of our new go-to-market approach," stresses Patrick Hulsen. "We are no longer the project lead, but the technology sub-contractor to a major player with an established international footprint. We are repeatedly reminded of our technological superiority, but we know that this is not enough. We have learned our lesson and now team up with companies that have the clout, the presence and the relationships required to win the deals."

The market for healthcare information technology solutions are far from saturated, and the need for updating current systems is compelling, but the nature of the market makes customers conservative and cautious. It's a very difficult market for small innovative insurgents.

"This time we start from the top," reveals Patrick Hulsen. "I have identified four senior profiles for a new executive advisory board. Through their network, we will find the partners with whom we can gain entry to foreign markets without the need for massive up-front investments. The projects in Iceland and Southern Denmark have already opened doors to such alliances and we believe this to be a sound approach for a company such as ours."

The project in Southern Denmark was won with Cambio as the lead contractor and Qualcomm as a second subcontractor. It is for a system collecting, filtering, archiving and retrieving patient data from medical devices in Intensive Care Units and Operating Rooms. Daintel will develop and deploy a "Connectivity Platform" collecting patient data from over 9.000 medical devices across all wards in all the region's hospitals.

Daintel was acquired by Cambio in July 2019.

EDLUND A/S - IT-SYSTEMS FOR A VERY EXCLUSIVE MARKET

The customer problem

You do not find life insurance and pension companies (commercial or public) on every street corner. Each country in the world has a limited number of them, they are each quite big and they are heavily regulated. As insurance primarily is information management, the industry was among the first to introduce computer systems and over the years most of them have developed and continue to maintain their own proprietary IT-systems.

Like all other businesses, life insurance and pension companies need to reduce their expenses. If they don't then their customers will suffer in terms of deteriorating insurance coverage and pension payments. Being heavily regulated and overseen by the financial authorities changing the customer pay-outs may not even be an option, which only apply additional pressure on the needs for cutting cost.

The primary source for cost reductions in this industry is the optimisation of business processes including the automation of payments and the introduction of consumer self-service platforms. For any improvements to be made the supporting IT-system must be changed too.

If you conclude that business process optimisation and cost reductions are the top agenda items for the life insurance and pension industry, then you can also conclude that the consequence is a need for replacing the proprietary IT-systems, with preferably standard systems that are easier and less expensive to implement, change and maintain. As the industry doesn't consider their internal IT-system a competitive differentiator, a market for software companies offering standard solutions has slowly evolved.

The liptech industry

Life insurance and pension schemes are the kings of the insurtech industry in terms of complexity and regulation. This is not where you find the agile and fast moving startups. We could assign this section of the industry its own name "liptech" because it is in a league of its own. There are primarily two types of players in liptech:

1. Established software companies that look to expand their footprint beyond the borders of their country of origin.

2. IT-Consulting companies that specialize in bespoke development and in implementing the standard software from the first category.

It seems like each country in the world has its own infrastructure of liptech companies. Smaller countries may have none and bigger countries have more. North America has the most.

With a large base of customers still relying on proprietary systems we may have arrived at pivotal point where demand for more standardised systems provides an opportunity for liptech companies with international appetite and ambitions. However, where the science behind life insurance and pension schemes is universal, the legislative and regulation framework in which it gets implemented in each country differs substantially.

The main reason that the liptech industry is very national is that the market is also very national. There are only few life-insurance and hardly any pension-scheme companies operating across national borders. As is the case in other industries where companies operate internationally there are practically no options available for growing a global business by following the customers.

Liptech companies with international ambitions are therefore facing substantial investments in preparing their platforms for more languages and country specific requirements first and then to decide how much localisation is required for the first customers to come onboard. The price for entering a new country may well run up into USD 20-30 million. Taking liptech companies global requires very deep pockets and visionary customers.

Internationalisation

As mentioned, there is no global market for life insurance and pension products. Each country has their national players and the liptech industry is heavily impacted by national traditions, legislation and regulation. All life insurance and pension companies around the world will at some point replace their current proprietary systems with standard platforms, but how soon it will happen is very hard to predict.

"The core IT-systems are the spine of every life insurance and pension company," says Morten Steiner, CIO with PFA Pension in Denmark. "Leaving a proprietary platform and placing your destiny in the hands of an external software company is no trivial feat. Especially not if you are to be the first customer to do so."

The primary challenge for the software companies considering entering this market is the massive investments that needs to be done up front.

"Hardly any life insurance and pension company are prepared to engage in the development of a core IT-platform from scratch today," explains Morten Steiner. "The risk is too high. We expect our software vendors to show their commitment and present an operational solution that meets at least the most fundamental requirements."

Edlund

The Danish life insurance and pension companies, of which there are 14, started the process of replacing their in-house developed proprietary IT-systems in the 1990s and Edlund was one of the companies that saw the market opportunity. Today, Edlund, a company with a staff of 275 FTEs and annual revenue (2018/19) of almost DKK 300 million (USD 50 million/EUR 40 million), is the undisputed national liptech market leader serving 10 of the 14 operators and providing the IT-solutions for managing over sixty per cent of all pension payments in Denmark.

The company was acquired by KMD (owned by NEC) in august 2016 but continues operating independently under the Edlund brand. KMD, that is one of the largest IT-service providers in Denmark, did the acquisition as a part of its strategy for international growth.

After the acquisition by KMD, Edlund started to analyse the opportunities for international expansion. They engaged one of the big management consulting companies in the spring of 2017 to help with market analysis and recommendations leading to a decision to invest in a redesign of the software and to look at opportunities in the near markets.

Redesigning the software

"In the past we were an IT-consulting company developing software,"
says Gert Bendsen, CEO of Edlund. "This we are changing. In the future
there will be a much larger standard core shared by all customers and
the customisation effort will decline correspondingly. The bottom line is
a much more attractive value proposition for our customers. They will
get more and pay less."

With a more comprehensive standard core Edlund can reduce the
initial implementation price as well as the ongoing maintenance cost
for their customers.

"The life insurance and pension industry is faced with substantial and
steadily changing regulation, "Gert Bendsen stresses. "Sharing the cost
of updating the software correspondingly will mean significant savings
for each customer."

While the changes in regulation are country specific there are other
trends that have impact across national borders. The progress in
operational best practises and the opportunities offered by new
technology are universal. Thus, there is an opportunity for developing
an IT-platform that can serve customers in many countries while still
comply with local legislation.

"The only way life insurance and pension companies can benefit from
the advances in IT-technology without having to face steadily increasing
cost is by using more standard components," Gert Bendsen emphasises.
"Edlund is committed to play the role of the IT-technology partner
providing both the standard software for the core business operation as
well as the IT-consulting required for the individual implementation
and ongoing support."

The transformation from an IT-consulting company to a software company means that the revenue split between licenses and professional
service will change from a 10:90 ratio to about 60:40. Edlund is currently at 50:50 but believe there is room for further standardisation.

"Operational software for life insurance and pension companies will
never be plug and play," says Gert Bendsen, "but getting to a situation

where software accounts for 60 per cent of the solution price and only 40 per cent comes from professional services should be achievable and represents a very attractive value proposition for our customers."

Norway

The Norwegian market consists of six potential customers that each have their own proprietary system. There is no direct national competitor, but a handful of consulting and software engineering companies serve the industry.

When it comes to life insurance and pension schemes Norway and Denmark turned out to be the countries in the near markets that have most in common. Edlund's market analysis concluded that the six customers would benefit substantially from moving to their new standard platform, but it was hard to assess when they would be ready to start the process. One of the Norwegian pension companies had already been engaged with a foreign supplier, but three years into the project they pulled out. The incident illustrates how difficult it is for a foreign supplier to comprehend and implement the local market requirements and it have made the entire industry even more cautious.

Edlund is not the only liptech company that have cast their eyes on Norway. Swedish Itello AB recently acquired Eikos AS, a Norwegian actuarial consultancy firm providing systems and services to pension funds and suppliers within the financial industry in Norway and abroad.

There is a very high probability that the first liptech company to win a project and demonstrate successful implementation will also be the preferred choice for the remaining companies. Only this way can they share the ongoing burden of legal compliance. Such a "winner takes all" scenario makes Edlund cautious.

"Norway should be an excellent match for us, says Gert Bendsen, "and we are in very close contact with market. However, we need to get the timing right. A solution for the Norwegian market must be based on our new platform. Adding specific Norwegian features will require tangible signs of commitment from at least one of the customers. We do not ask the first customer to take the full investment, but without a life project the risk for us would be hard to justify."

EPIC - A GENUINE SHOESTRING APPROACH

Healthcare is primarily IT

Have you ever considered that healthcare is primarily information processing and analytics?

Clinics and hospitals are full of material with buildings, people in uniforms, furniture, machinery, instruments, medicine, syringes, bottles, tubes, blood banks, vehicles and thousands of other physical artefacts. However, all those assets are worth little if you cannot quickly produce the correct diagnosis and allocate the resources and capacity for swift treatment. And doing so re-quires seamless cooperation between the many disciplines involved. Capturing, processing, sharing, storing, finding and analysing information is a core activity of any healthcare system.

Healthcare is expensive. Very expensive. It costs anywhere between ten per cent (Europe) and up to 17 per cent (USA) of GDP. And most of the cost walks on two legs. People. So, although we all admire the developments in medicine, medical equipment and surgery technologies, we often tend to forget that what makes all this effective and affordable is the advances in skills, organisation and information technology.

Any complex organisation – and not much gets more complicated than healthcare – comes with substantial overheads. Wherever many highly specialised people need to cooperate to achieve a single objective, the most significant challenges are always collaboration and information processing. Making correct information flow smoothly and timely is the key to organisational performance and the quality of treatment.

EHR (Electronic Health Record) has become the term for information processing in healthcare, but it is much more than just a record. It's a journey of workflow and data management. The data from the patients, lab tests, x-rays, scanning, prescriptions, from the nurses' and doctors' observations, from the diagnosis and treatments, etc., all come together in the health record. However, to make this possible, every function and discipline in the healthcare organisation must use compatible data formats and have systems in place that can talk to each other and that can best be accommodated by using the same software.

Theoretically, each discipline could use their own system, and integration and compatible data formats ensure that information could flow between them. However, ensuring that so many individual sub-systems and their combinations were always up-to-date, and functioning, would be an astronomical task. Where the cloud-based best-of-breed solutions are gaining ground in other industries, the situation in the healthcare market is different.

The emergence of an international industry

For reasons mentioned above, clinics and hospitals across the globe have preferred to implement integrated EHR systems, where a single vendor is responsible for most of the functionality across many disciplines.

Where the improvement in clinical treatment is the subject of international cooperation among healthcare professionals and, therefore, common standards across the globe, the administrative side (organisation, capacity planning, political prioritisation and who pays for what) differs substantially from country to country. This explains why most countries have their own industry of healthcare informatics providers. Integrated IT in healthcare started with the administrative side (PAS: Patient Administrative Systems) and only later did the systems expand into the clinical workflows.

Developing an integrated EHR system is not unlike putting a man on the moon. Understanding the challenge is simple. Making a working system is anything but simple. It is a gigantic undertaking that can only be done over a long period and in close cooperation with the users. Emerging as the market leaders in EHR systems, we find US-based companies primarily, and in the category serving larger organisations, Epic takes the top position. No other company in the world has more patient information running through their software than Epic.

A shoestring approach

With over 10,000 employees, an annual revenue of over $3B, and over 450 customers in 14 countries (as of March 2020) you would not consider Epic a company using a shoestring approach to internationalisation. However, it always did, and it still does.

"We have never considered the world organised into country-markets that we could proactively decide to approach," says Mercedes McCoy, VP of international business development at Epic. "For us, the market is where customers are active, share our vision for an integrated system, have requirements that match our products and prefer our implementation approach. We are one hundred per cent customer-driven and not market-driven."

Epic, which derives about ten per cent of its total revenue from international activities, was founded in 1979. The company signed its first international customer in Canada in 1994. The next came from The Netherlands in 2007. An organisation in the UAE was added in 2010, Singapore in 2012, the UK and Denmark in 2013, Australia and Saudi Arabia in 2014, Finland and Lebanon in 2016, Belgium and Switzerland in 2017 and Norway in 2018.

"Today, the global market for EHR systems for larger organisations is very transparent," says Mercedes McCoy. "Clinicians and IT-professionals visit each other and attend the same international conventions, conferences, and exhibitions. From industry analysts such as KLAS Research, they have access to vendor-agnostic information and comparisons. For nine years in a row, Epic has earned the top score for Overall Software Suite in the annual Best in KLAS Software & Services report. Most customers in our segment know very well who we are and what we stand for."

At the time of writing Epic does business in 14 countries, and their solution is available in eight languages.

How Epic crossed the chasm

Although Epic started its first international project in Canada in 1994, it wasn't until the beginning of this century that the needle really started moving. And it started moving in the domestic market first.

In 2003, Kaiser Permanente, the largest managed care organisation in the United States, chose Epic as the platform for its new company-wide EHR-system. Over the next seven years, Kaiser Permanente would invest a total of USD $4B in development and implementation, which funded the training of their staff, hardware purchases, the software from Epic, and more. Kaiser Permanente was an innovator and early adopter, and with that project under its belt, Epic crossed the chasm in one single jump. Kaiser Permanente became a global showcase, and healthcare professionals from all over the world made pilgrimages to Kaiser's locations in California and across the United States to see and hear what was going on.

When the Dutch health authorities started looking for EHR-software, Epic was on the list of potential candidates. Epic teamed up with the healthcare division of Philips, and together they won their first major EHR project outside the US, Spaarne Gasthuis, in 2007.

The cooperation with Philips Healthcare didn't continue. Epic realised that it was too complicated to have another company facing the client, and since then, it has been the primary contractor in all new customer projects. The following years it added more customers in the Netherlands and 2010 Cleveland Clinic, Abu Dhabi in the United Arab Emirates, was added to the list. The big breakthrough came in 2013 when significant projects were won in Denmark and the UK, confirming Epic's ability to deliver consistently and successfully outside the USA.

Making sales without marketing

Epic's strategy for international expansion has been and remains reactive. They don't do paid marketing or advertising and don't cold-call prospective clients. They only respond when potential customers invite them to participate in an RFP (request for proposal) and then only when the requirement specifications are close to what they can offer and that they agree on the implementation approach.

In the English-speaking parts of the world, which includes the Nordics, Benelux, and Switzerland, the language used for communicating during the RFP and implementation process is the same. When that is not possible, Epic hires or engages staff that master the local language. Translation of the software user interface first happens when Epic has been awarded the contract.

"With over 450 implementations under our belt, we have refined an implementation approach that we know works," Mercedes McCoy *stresses. "We work closely with our customers to share best practices and lessons learned from these past implementations to help new installs be successful. Implementing a new EHR system is a significant change. By using our project management method, we can bring the system live on-time and on-budget."*

The implementation approach requires that the customer establish a project team, which includes experienced clinicians, that is thoroughly trained and then certified in Epic's software. Initially, the training takes place in Epic's headquarters in Verona, Wisconsin, USA. By attending training at Epic, those working with the system have an opportunity for hands-on learning on a campus designed for creativity and productivity. As expertise is developed locally, the training and certification can also be localised.

Knowing how the software works and the options it offers, the solution architecture, in terms of organisation, workflows and integrations, can be now defined. The customer has to set up her own user support facility, which preferably should be staffed with the people that did the implementation.

"When we take on a project abroad, we also open an office in that country and relocate some of our most experienced people or use an office in a nearby country to support the organisation," Mercedes McCoy explains.

"The average implementation takes around two years – though this can vary depending on the size and scope of the project - and is very much a partnership between the client and us. The client must become intimately familiar with the software as we agree on the configuration and integrations. When have completed the implementation, the customer should be capable of maintaining the system and provide the first line of support."

A matter of life and death

When implementing Epic, organisations seek to improve the quality of patient care and the productivity of health care resources. It typically replaces several disparate systems based on older technology.

Upgrading the core application infrastructure in large organisations is a massive change management undertaking. The recent implementation of Epic in Denmark has 40,000 users, of which 12,000 are expected to be concurrent. New working procedures, new functionality, new user interfaces and new integrations all represent a challenging learning curve for the staff. As the end result affects people's health and recovery, healthcare authorities are known for playing it safe and for preferring solutions that have proven themselves elsewhere.

In the diffusion of innovation perspective, Epic has become the safe choice for healthcare organisations around the world. Customers recognise Epic's track record and experience. Because the non-negotiable priority in changing the workflow and data management backbone in healthcare institutions is based on the first principle of the Hippocratic Oath: Primum non nocere (first do no harm), risk mitigation is a much more serious issue than in other industries.

"We know exactly what is at stake," says Mercedes McCoy, "which is why we consider every invitation to bid very carefully before we say yes or no. It is first and foremost a question about the prospect of a successful implementation. When we are convinced that the projects can be completed successfully, then we commit the resources required to make it happen."

Replacing the workflow and data management platform in a healthcare institution is a significant disruption. It's like renovating an aeroplane while it's airborne. While staff get familiar with the new system, production, quality and safety must not be affected.

Disrupting the industry

The increased global demand for proven EHR solutions is changing the industry. The combination of requirements for tested software functionality and for ensuring that the project can be delivered on time and budget put pressure on the local and smaller vendors that haven't had a project like Kaiser Permanente to bring their products up to date.

As Epic wins more and more international projects, they also become the preferred supplier for new ones. However, according to insiders I have talked to, Epic is not only providing a complete solution, but they also have the most professional organisation to deal with the all the meetings, demos and workshops that take place during the selection and procurement process. Having the best product and the most professional people is an excellent marketing recipe in a highly transparent market.

Epic is a good example of how to go global on a shoestring in a market that was previously dominated by smaller and local vendors. It has happened organically and without the presence of a vast marketing and outbound sales effort.

EUROMAX - A COMPLETE MANAGEMENT SOLUTION FOR NEWSPAPERS

Starting with a lucky punch

VUM (Vlaamse Uitgevers Maatschappij), a Belgian newspaper group, decided in the early 1990s to invest in a new integrated digital prepress system for their newspapers, De Standaard, Het Nieuwsblat, Het Volk and De Gentenaar.

What they wanted wasn't available on the market, and so in 1992, they ended up entering into a development contract with the Danish IT-company DDE (Dansk Data Elektronik). The project agreement was for to develop the solution VUM wanted but also to allow DDE to make the system available as a commercial product. This way VUM would share the ongoing maintenance and development cost with other newspapers.

The main objectives of the project were to optimise the size of the daily newspapers allowing for the best possible mix of advertising and editorial content, to support lean workflows in all corners of the prepress activities and offer superior service to advertising customers. The project was driven by an unusually visionary management team and endorsed by the board of directors. VUM was a company operating at the very forefront of the innovation diffusion curve.

The system architecture was built around a central database (Oracle) holding digital representations of newspapers planned well into the future. Applications were then developed to support the various jobs performed throughout the newspaper organisation. The solution was developed for Unix and used the X-Windows GUI.

From hardware to applications

DDE, founded in 1975, was initially a hardware vendor developing minicomputers. In 1987 the company decided to offer applications. When I joined the company in September 1992, they had shifted their hardware to run on UNIX and provided a broad suite of applications addressing various industries and market segments.

Leading the marketing effort with applications and then delivering the complete infrastructure, including the DDE hardware, worked well in Denmark. However, executing this strategy through wholly-owned subsidiaries failed miserably, and by the time I joined, the company was downsizing its international operations and laying off staff.

Much of DDE's business was with government institutions where the solutions didn't lend themselves well to international markets. However, the failing internationalisation effort was also due to a flawed sales strategy, lack of focus and mismanagement.

With the VUM development contract and the new product, Euromax, DDE had no other choice than to work in the international markets. Denmark was simply too small a market to secure the volume of customers required to keep up development and sustain a competitive position for such a comprehensive product.

Market entry through an acquisition

DDE got into the industry of IT systems for newspaper and magazine publishers through the acquisition of one of their resellers, GMI Data A/S in 1988. GMI had developed a first-generation prepress system and had customers in Denmark, Norway, the UK, Italy and New Zealand. The acquisition proved difficult due to fundamental differences in culture, but also because the companies were located far from each other and DDE didn't have the management skills in place to handle the merger and the remote operations.

The development of GMI's prepress system came to a halt, and the technology soon became obsolete. The contract with VUM represented a significant opportunity for DDE to make a strong comeback, however in a completely different segment of the market from where GMI had their installed base. The usual approach of winning some of your current customers for an upgrade to a new product didn't exist. It was like starting all over again from scratch.

Positioning the solution

Competing for customers in the top end of the newspaper industry required that the Euromax solution was positioned to look very different from the alternatives offered by the leading suppliers, such as ATEX, SII, CCI Europe and a host of other smaller and upcoming software companies.

The early and mid-1990s were marked by a disrupting shift in IT-technology away from mainframes, minicomputers and monolithic systems and towards LAN-based PCs systems with integrated best-of-breed applications. The applications offered for the MAC and the PC were often much more user-friendly and intuitive than their mainframe- and minicomputer-based cousins. Applications such as Microsoft Word and QuarkXPress were already trendy within the publishing community. With the release of the QuarkXPress XTensions API in 1989 and the Microsoft Windows 3.1 version in 1992, the drive for best-of-breed solutions was strong.

The monolithic systems approach, which offered better integration and performance and lower maintenance cost, was still the preferred solution for the major newspapers and the market-leading suppliers remained loyal to this solution architecture, too. The best-of-breed approach was promoted by insurgents and industry analysts that saw an opportunity for consulting assignments, but also recognised the enormous application development effort from which the newspapers could benefit. The ongoing development of a monolithic product depends on a single vendor, while a best-of-breed solution enjoys the outcome of many companies' development efforts.

Euromax was by definition a monolithic system, and its main advantages were its business-focused planning facilities and the support for all the prepress workflows across the editorial and advertising domains. While the objective of competing systems was on how to produce the newspaper satisfying the users' needs for functionality, the Euromax objective was on how to produce the most profitable newspaper. We, therefore, positioned Euromax as a Newspaper Management Solution, which was a new term in the industry. Inventing our own category certainly made us look different, but it also confused the market. No one knew what a Newspaper Management Solution was until we had had an opportunity to explain it.

The international sales strategy

When I was brought in to take care of sales, the company had a subsidiary in the UK, where several customers used the old product, and a subsidiary in Belgium, where the new customer was located. The company had also hired a salesperson in Germany and one in France. The other DDE subsidiaries were not engaged in Euromax activities.

While reviewing the sales strategy for Euromax, we received an inquiry from New Zealand. A previous employee had emigrated there some years before and had implemented the old product at the small newspaper where he now worked.

The owner of the newspaper was INL, a large group with several other publications in New Zealand, Australia and on the US west coast. They were very interested in introducing new technology that could reduce operational cost and provide a better service to their adverting customers. Our ex-employee had told INL management about the project we were doing with the European newspaper group, and they were now interested in talking to us. Were we prepared to come to New Zealand a make a presentation?

After a few additional phone calls, the opportunity was confirmed, and it was also confirmed that our lack of local presence, apparently, wasn't a critical issue that would impact their choice of vendor.

Pursuing this opportunity would require substantial sales, pre-sales and management resources. If we could close the deal, we would have to station some of our most critical support resources in New Zealand for six to nine months. We couldn't fly them back for a day or two to help with pre-sales projects elsewhere. The alternative cost was very high. Looking through the project pipeline, it was clear that we had no other sales opportunities in Europe or elsewhere that was scheduled to close sooner than the one in New Zealand.

I was not in favour of pursuing the opportunity, but my management decided otherwise, and soon I was on a plane to New Zealand.

We did win the business, and after having signed the contract, I finally had time to revisit the general sales strategy. The New Zealand project convinced me that:

- We had a superior value proposition for newspapers with a complex operation (all large newspapers are complex).

- Customers were not very concerned about vendor proximity. Mainly because there were very few vendors in this market and none of them was seldom close by, anyway.

- The market was not particularly national. Even on a global scale, there are not many newspapers with a circulation of over 100.000 daily copies. (The newspaper in New Zealand didn't print 100.000 copies daily, but we accepted to deviate from this threshold as the deal would give us access to the group's other large newspapers. At least that's what we thought).

The opportunity gave us a crucial independent reference and taught me that we were facing what I in this book call a Narrow Gorge scenario.

We would never know where the next project would come from. Euromax was not yet a recognised brand in the newspaper publishing industry, so, we had a brand-building job in front of us. I realised that although we had a different and attractive positioning statement and now two distinguished references to show off, many newspapers would be reluctant to deal with us. Only visionary newspapers with strong management and a risk-willing attitude would be prepared to sign up.

I now recommended that we closed the subsidiaries and terminate our salespeople in Germany and France. Instead, we would drive the business development effort from Copenhagen and fly out to find and develop new project opportunities.

The tactical sales approach

When I was given the responsibility for the Euromax sales effort, I knew nothing about newspapers, apart from reading them. However, I had been in sales long enough to understand there was only one place to go for insight: to the customers. Therefore, I spent half of my time talking to customers and asking them to show me their operation and tell me about their challenges. The other half I spent on developing the sales material conveying our value proposition.

For newspapers to replace their core prepress system is equivalent to spine surgery. You only do it if it is absolutely necessary, and even then it is a delicate affair. Therefore, I had no ambition of convincing potential customers that now was the right time to do so. Our job was to make our brand known and then be available when the customer went into replacement mode.

To support this sales strategy, we used a two-track approach:

- Participate in industry exhibitions

- Make customer visits

Exhibitions

The newspaper industry is mature and therefore very well organised. There were two industry associations that we decided to use: IFRA and FIEJ (now WAN-IFRA). With annual events in Europe, it was possible to meet everyone involved with operational prepress activities as well as many in prepress, editorial and advertising executive positions.

Customer visits

IFRA published a book annually listing all major newspapers in the world describing their key characteristics and the state of their current prepress systems. From this book, we could extract a list of ideal customers and then decide when to get in touch. It quickly turned out that it was challenging to work with newspapers where the key decision-makers didn't speak reasonable English. We, therefore, concentrated our sales activities in New Zealand, Australia, South Africa, the Nordics, the Netherlands, the UK and Ireland.

We invested substantial resources in the development of presentations with visuals and handouts that we used when visiting the potential customers for the first time. It was crucial for us that they understood how we were different from the alternatives. If they liked it, we could continue developing the opportunity. If they did not, then we should move on.

Conveying a message that people remember and pass on requires simple visuals and that's why we spent so much time and effort on getting these right.

Selling Euromax was always a very complex endeavour. Our position statement was directed at the top management of the newspaper. We were primarily a tool to improve the profitability of the business. However, at most newspapers, senior management considered IT a production tool and thus referred any inquiry to their IT or prepress people. It was tough to get the sales process started at the CEO level. By the end of the day, no CEO would sign a contract unless his management team recommended him to do so. We, therefore, decided to make the first contact with the CIO, knowing very well that he or she was not the final decision-maker.

What we were looking for was a systems replacement opportunity. If we found one, we offered to fly in a team of people and run a week of workshops for their staff where they could see and touch the system. This was, obviously, a very expensive approach, but it demystified our offering and allowed us to get acquainted with the decision-makers and hopefully shortcut or at least influence the RFP process.

Jumping the Atlantic

The next opportunity after New Zealand popped up on the US east coast.

During one of the exhibitions in Europe, an early innovator from one of the major North American newspaper groups became interested in our solution. He was so impressed that he recommended a newspaper in Fairfax, Virginia to consider us in an upcoming systems replacement.

We followed our presentation/demo strategy and won the deal. The contract was signed just before Christmas in 1994, at a time where we had our technical implementation resources tied up in Nelson, New Zealand. With these two deals under implementation, we were sold out, but also in need of new projects within the next six to eight-months.

I now devoted most of my time to visiting US newspapers while two colleagues covered New Zealand, Australia, South Africa and the English-speaking parts of Europe.

During the first half of 1995, we managed to line up an impressive pipeline of qualified prospects that were genuinely interested in our solution. Some of them very big names and ready to make a decision.

Sudden death

We were facing three critical issues.

The first one was relatively trivial. When you grow, you need to hire more people, and you face a considerable task with onboarding and skills transfer. The learning curve was pretty steep for a product like Euromax, and new hires would also have to accept being out-stationed for six to eight-months at a time. Such people were not easy to find.

The second issue was the rapid spread of the Internet and the invention of online news. All the newspapers were looking for answers to tons of questions, and we were not prepared to answer any of them.

We would eventually have gotten our act together on those two issues if the third one had not surfaced.

Being a hardware vendor, DDE's application strategy was essentially a cover-up for selling boxes. In the Euromax division, we had downplayed this very tight relationship and even stated in our sales material and our market communication that our software could be delivered on any XPG3 compliant system. That was a lie.

While potential customers were excited about the Euromax software, they were not happy with also being forced to buy the hardware from DDE. VUM, The Nelson Evening Mail and The Journal Newspaper had accepted getting the solution on DDE's Supermax servers, but it seemed as we had reached the end of the line of people with goodwill for this combination.

We, the salespeople, were pushed hard by potential customers to deliver on Sun, IBM, HP and other Unix boxes. Still, when we conveyed this market intelligence back to DDE management, we were critiqued for exercising poor salesmanship.

The downside sticking to the DDE hardware was also that we had no one helping us toot the horn. During a trip visiting several US newspapers, I received a call from a sales executive from HP who had gotten wind of our activities and would like to meet. I was excited about this contact and happily passed it on to my management. Getting in bed with HP would amplify our market communication efforts and help open doors to more customers. The HP opportunity was shot down immediately, and I was ordered to hang up if ever again called by a hardware vendor.

The Euromax solution was based on the Oracle database, so I reached out to Oracle. If we sold a solution in the UK, Australia, South Africa, the USA or somewhere else, it would most likely be a new Oracle customer, too. Sybase was the preferred database system in the publishing industry, so this was an opportunity for Oracle. Why not co-sell? I had a meeting with Oracle at their headquarters in Redwood City just south of San Francisco but was met with little enthusiasm. I later found out that DDE had an OEM agreement with Oracle, where the revenue was recognised in Denmark. There was no incentive for the Oracle salespeople outside Denmark to get involved.

Without the ability to deliver on the customer's preferred hardware platform and with no interest from Oracle, I saw no future for Euromax. It's no fun selling something you don't believe in, so in August 1995 I resigned.

After I left, DDE eventually made a VAR agreement with HP in the US and promised to port Euromax to their servers. But it was too late. The company wasn't able to win any new projects, and they stopped investing in the Euromax activity in 1997, only honouring existing contracts.

The lesson learned

DDE's resistance to make Euromax available on other hardware platforms was not entirely based on poor judgement. DDE's core domestic business was hardware. If customers learned that they could get the applications on hardware from DDE's competitors, many of them would most likely prefer that. There was a very likely risk that such a move would damage DDE's hardware business and internal morale.

The three customers that Euromax was able to win were all early innovators. We were not then familiar with the law of diffusion of innovation nor with Moore's Crossing the Chasm theories, but we knew that without visionary customer management, we could not win new projects. The pipeline, which we developed in the first half of 1995, was all projects with visionary management that subscribed to our value proposition.

It was a genuine dilemma, and management made the wrong decision. Eventually, DDE lost Euromax and then the hardware business as well.

Pursuing a Narrow Gorge market opportunity without any support from a third party is hard.

FIRST AGENDA - SOFTWARE FOR BETTER AND MORE EFFECTIVE MEETINGS

The customer problem

No matter what we do in life, meeting with other people physically or virtually is required from time to time. Many of these meetings are ineffective, and some are even pointless. It always comes down to how well the individual session is prepared, how well it is managed, and what happens afterwards.

Statistics show that the average office worker in the US attends 62 meetings a month of which close to 40 per cent are considered unproductive. She spends 9 hours a week on meetings, her manager in private companies spend 12 hours, and in government, it's 14 hours.

Improving the overall efficiency of meetings is probably the most significant source for productivity improvement across all industries and all types of organisations and at the same time the path to a better and less stressful life for most people. The lack of minutes, a written record of the meeting, is one of the main reasons why so many meetings suck. Without minutes there is a lack of ownership and direction and subsequently confusion on what was agreed. As a consequence, many meetings are held to clarify the outcome of a previous session.

First Agenda's value proposition

First Agenda develops software that can make meetings more productive. The software uses artificial intelligence, neural networks and speech recognition, helping to reduce the number of meetings, facilitating meeting preparation, supporting meeting execution and easing the follow-up considerably. The software is delivered exclusively in a cloud-based SaaS-format.

"Deciding to do something about the meeting culture will have an immediate positive impact in all organisations," says Kasper Lyhr, CEO at First Agenda, "but getting full and lasting value and productivity gains take implementing software like ours."

In addition to providing a structured approach for preparing, running and follow-up on meetings, the First Agenda software also helps automate the tedious job of writing the minutes of the meeting including meeting notes, keywords and a list of action items.

Market segmentation

The more meetings an organisation has, the more value they will get out of First Agenda. Bigger organisations have more meetings, while some organisations have a higher meeting frequency than others. Government organisations tend to have more meetings than private companies and these meetings also have more attendees. Public institutions are, therefore, high on the list of customers.

"We have chosen an inbound approach," says Kasper Lyhr, "and so far, that has generated enough leads to fill out the pipeline. We will continue this approach but may have to add outbound activities to the toolbox, too."

Revenue generation

It can be hard to identify the best contact point and to assess if a company is receptive to the value proposition. Optimising meetings will benefit any organisation, but who should take the initiative, drive the process, pay for the software, and where and how can you measure the outcome?

The go-to-market approach is directly supported by strategic alliances with Microsoft and some of the other technology providers in the industry. The average sales cycle for a team solution is ten days, while a decision to introduce the solution on a corporate level is around six months.

"Corporate purchase initiatives tend to get overly complex," Kasper Lyhr admits. "The more people involved, the longer the process takes, and the more expensive it becomes for the customer and for us. Some potential customers even engage a consulting firm to analyse the situation, design the change process, write the specifications, run the procurement process and assist with the implementation. In my opinion, this is a

waste of time and money. The technology is mature, readily available and can easily be tested in one or two teams, providing data for the PoC (Proof of Concept)."

Internationalisation

"Speech recognition technology is a key part of the solution," explains Kasper Lyhr, "and in this domain, the best-supported language is English. Outside the Nordics, we, therefore, focus all our efforts on the English-speaking markets."

First Agenda is currently operating in Denmark, Germany (R&D) and the USA and 25 per cent of revenue is from abroad. Because English speech-recognition technology is more developed, the company are currently concentrating their efforts on the UK and the USA.

"We are up against the law of diffusion of innovation," Kasper Lyhr stresses. "The technology is mature and the return on the investment attractive and well documented. However, we are an early mover in the industry, and with only a few competitors, we are a small voice in the market. I expect demand to increase substantially over the next couple of years and then we are well-positioned to become the market leader."

The company has established a subsidiary in Boston, MA and relocated their Danish VP of sales to spearhead the build-up in the US.

FORECAST – A SOLUTION FOR PROJECT-DRIVEN COMPANIES.

The problem

Project-driven businesses such as consulting companies, marketing agencies and engineering shops all face a two-sided challenge:

1. Sell enough projects to meet the various budget objectives

2. Have the resources available to deliver the projects sold

If you have been in a project driven business, you will know that getting and keeping this balance right is by no means trivial. Each project requires a certain combination of resources that have to be available at a specific time. However, sales and project managers do not know exactly when projects will be approved, especially if external customers are the prime initiators. Managing a project-based business requires a steadily updated picture of supply and demand for critical resources. You don't want expensive resources sitting idle on the bench and you don't want to overbook, failing to deliver and damaging your customer relationships.

The solution

Forecast is the software that helps companies manage the "quote-to-cash" process. It ties together the sales or project pipeline with the available resources and delivery capacity of the company. It provides a visual perspective of your operations allowing you to manage deliverables from a high-level view on your cross-project timeline.

It helps you achieve a high utilisation rate by scheduling people's available time to unassigned tasks and it helps you foresee when to bring more people onto your team to fully allocate project time. You can track expenses, manage invoices and control the budget from the initial statement of work (SOW) to the final delivery. Team members will know what to work on with their tasks prioritised and project managers have a high-level overview to balance the workload within the constraints of client requests.

Forecast deliver its value by being integrated with the customer's other business management software. Most customers use Forecast to replace proprietary solutions based on Excel.

Revenue Generation

Forecast is the answer to a well-recognized problem in project driven industries and as such they receive a steady stream of inbound inquiries. The prospects are mostly well educated and know what they are looking for.

"We have chosen to focus on the mid-market where companies or departments of larger enterprises have 50-500 FTEs," says Dennis Kayser, CEO and founder of Forecast. *"We deliberately turn down RFPs as we prefer to keep the average sales cycle to no more than a month. From the 500 trials customers run every month approximately 25 decides to go ahead. This results in ACAC (Average Customer Acquisition Cost) in the range of 20% (of revenue) which is acceptable."*

Apart from product training and systems integration there is no further value-add related to the implementation of the product. Despite the short sales cycle the purchasing process is complex.

Scaling the inbound lead generation approach requires optimizing the content marketing activities. There is need for generating both more leads and more leads per invested marketing dollar.

"Effective content marketing requires ongoing optimisation," Dennis Kayser explains. *"Producing quality content, placing it and measuring its' performance require skills that are not abundantly available in the market. Digital marketing and social selling may be hot topics, but there is a lack of talent in the market mastering these new disciplines."*

Most customer contact is performed over the phone and through web-meetings. To increase revenue growth Forecast is in the process of establishing an outbound sales development organisation. The Sales Development team will be an integral part of the revenue generation strategy and will work closely with Account Executives to expand Forecasts customer base by identifying high-potential opportunities.

The role of sales development involves researching companies & contacts to formulate outbound campaigns that create qualified meetings for the account executives. Scaling sales development is a cornerstone in Forecast's growth strategy.

"We believe that a product should sell itself," Dennis Kayser emphasises. "A 30-minute demo should be sufficient allowing the prospect to make an informed decision to test the solution. After a 14-day trial we should be able to convert most prospects to customers. We therefore invest heavily in product development. A beautiful product will make customers come and stay. However, we need to get the message in front of more potential customer."

Getting salespeople capable of helping and guiding prospects to a purchase decision has turned out to be a major challenge for Forecast. So far, the company have had most success with recruiting young people and training them to perform solution selling.

"We are not selling a product, but a solution to a problem that our customers know they need to get a better grip on," Dennis Kayser explains. "The SaaS format and aggressive pricing call for short sales cycles which again calls for salespeople that can quickly identify the potential customer's most urgent needs and guide the demo to address these specific issues. We have experienced that recruiting younger people and training them ourselves is way more productive than using experienced business software salespeople."

Internationalization

The current customer base is spread across more than 40 countries with 70 per cent being located in the USA. European markets are covered by native speaking tele-salespeople out of the Copenhagen office. A deeper penetration of non-English speaking counties will require translation of the UI and documentation, but no further localisation is required.

"We have decided to first take advantage of the US-demand that we are experiencing, Dennis Kayser reveals. "I and five others from the Copenhagen office will move to New York this year and start the operation there. New York is in itself a huge market."

Before establishing the office in the US Dennis needs to get a management structure in place that can handle the global expansion. Managing remote marketing and sales activities and responding to national market requirements will add an additional layer of complexity to the operation.

Forecast has received external funding and the most recent infusion of USD 3M is supposed to support the international growth.

FOTOWARE - DIGITAL ASSET MANAGEMENT (DAM) – MADE IN NORWAY

The birth of a new industry

Pictures and illustrations (images) play an important role in communications. The saying that *a picture is worth a thousand words* was coined more than a hundred years ago and remains an excellent rule of thumb. However, up until the beginning of the 1990s producing and managing images was complicated and expensive. Despite the mass production of cameras and film, making professional pictures and illustrations was costly.

Several unrelated innovations changed the world of images completely: The JPEG format, the Internet, digital photography, graphics software and the price of computer storage. These innovations, that all started in the early 1990s, were commercialised and commoditised in under ten years and resulted in an explosion in the volume of images used in a professional as well as a consumer context. It also changed the image from being an analogue artefact to a digital file. Analogue assets became digital assets.

Whereas the first hundred years of photography was characterised by expensive production, post- and re-production, storage and distribution costs, the most recent thirty years have seen a complete shift in the formula. Making great images is still an art but the unit cost of anything else around the image has been reduced significantly. The outcome has been an eruption in the number of images produced and stored and the emergence of new players in the stock photo industry.

The challenge for organisations is not anymore so much the making of images as it is the management of images, and on the backdrop of this challenge the Digital Asset Management industry was born.

The customer problem

The newspaper and magazine industries (printed media) were among the first to embrace digital photography and graphics software. Producing a consumer-oriented infotainment product benefited substantially from the simplification of the post-production and distribution process that the digital transformation offered.

At the beginning of the 1990s, printed media experienced an eruption in the volume of images produced by their own staff but also in those offered by the news networks and agencies. News is obviously not news for long and working against tough deadlines managing the tsunami of images became a real headache.

Ole Christian Frenning, previously a professional photographer, was, in the late 1980s, the photo editor at the Norwegian newspaper, Aftenposten. With images increasingly born digital, Ole Christian saw the opportunity of using IT to make his job more innovative and productive. To assist with the technical issues, he involved Anders Bergman who was a leader of R&D at Hasselblad Electronic Imaging. This is how FotoWare started as an internal application at Aftenposten. It soon became apparent, however, that other media companies could benefit from the solution.

Ole Christian and Anders left their jobs and joined Interfoto, the agent for Nikon cameras in Norway, to pursue the opportunity, and in 1994 they launched the first version of FotoWare as a commercial product. The term Digital Asset Management (DAM) wasn't even defined then, but FotoWare was among the world's first vendors in this product category.

The media industry is well organised and through Ole Christian's international contacts, newspapers and magazines outside Norway heard about and showed interest in obtaining a FotoWare DAM system. For that purpose, Interfoto was not the right setup and in 1997 FotoWare became an independent company that could concentrate all efforts on developing the product and take advantage of the global market potential.

The requirements for improved management of digital assets turned out to be universal indeed, and the needs were virtually the same across borders. The software travelled very easily, and the global customer base grew accordingly. Today FotoWare has more than 4.000

business customers with over 250.000 users in 34 countries around the world.

Early distribution

Inspired by the distribution approach used by Hasselblad and Nikon, FotoWare initially also chose to work with resellers. The printed media industry was increasingly interested in FotoWare and so resellers were appointed in the Nordics, France, Germany, the UK and in Australia where the company soon enjoyed a very high market share.

There was only one caveat.

The printed media industry was suffering. The rapid proliferation of the Internet was eating big chunks of both the industry's circulation and advertising revenue. Readers were spending more time elsewhere and advertisers always follow the readership. The printed media industry loved FotoWare, but they all had budget challenges.

Ole Christian and Anders saw this coming and understood that there was an untapped market in other industries as well. To dig into this potential, certain product changes were developed, as well as understanding that they would need to do business outside the media industry. What was now needed was to make the resellers start calling on these new types of customers and learn what they wanted and how to sell to them. That wasn't so easy. The resellers were very comfortable dealing with the needs of the printed media industry. Making them call outside their comfort zone turned out to be a genuine challenge.

In 2002, a combination of channel issues and the need for more control made FotoWare decide to set up subsidiaries first in Germany, then in France and later in the UK. The objective of the subsidiaries was to act on behalf of FotoWare AS and expand the reseller networks in their domestic markets, thereby covering more verticals and winning more market share. With this move, FotoWare introduced a two-tier distribution model that would have allowed for managing a much larger reseller network.

However, it didn't happen.

Finding resellers to serve new industries that were not familiar with DAM issues continued to be difficult. Without the critical mass of resellers, the thirty per cent distributor margin was not adequate for making the subsidiaries profitable. The subsidiaries started to serve the clients directly and after some time FotoWare was having the same problems as they set out to avoid, as well as having remote staff on the payroll.

By 2010 the subsidiaries had been closed and the activities passed on to independent resellers. The strategy now called for a one-tier distribution approach with FotoWare AS in Oslo responsible for overall market penetration and non-exclusive resellers responsible for sales, fulfilment, and support.

Software a as service

Around the same time as the distribution strategy was changed, it became apparent that the market and the DAM industry were also changing. A new delivery format, Software-as-a-Service, was introduced and it seemed as though the customers liked it. From 2013 to 2017 FotoWare developed FotoWare SaaS, which is a browser-based application running on the Microsoft Azure cloud platform, and was launched as an alternative to the workstation and server-based products.

With FotoWare SaaS - which requires no installation and implementation and where the pricing is subscription-based - FotoWare could reach many more customers and the company therefore again decided to revise its go-to-market model.

With a much lower initial price tag, instant onboarding and a much larger potential market, FotoWare shifted to an inbound demand generation strategy. More marketing staff were brought on board, a new digital marketing platform (HubSpot) was introduced and the wall between marketing and sales was removed. The objective was revenue generation and that was considered a process where the borders between marketing and sales no longer made any sense.

"Today customers can choose where they want to buy," says Øystein Syversen, business development director at FotoWare. "If they need local support in their own language and time zone, then they are much better served by our partners, but they can buy directly from us if they so choose."

According to Øystein Syversen, it took some time for the resellers to accept the changes in the distribution approach, but as their market is growing rapidly and as the new inbound demand strategy also generates more leads for the resellers, they have come to terms with the changes.

The customer is the king/queen

The DAM category is one of the fastest-growing in the software industry. Virtually all companies irrespective of size need a DAM system and FotoWare is determined to get the lion's share.

"Our inbound demand generation approach is designed to also capture that segment of the market where customers don't want to or don't need to talk to a salesperson," says Anne Gretland, CEO at FotoWare AS. "That's where the SaaS market is rapidly heading, and we are embracing that trend. There will always be customers with more sophisticated needs for systems integration, customisation and ongoing support, and there will always be customers that are more comfortable doing business in their local language and time zone. That's where our resellers have the superior value proposition."

IT MINDS – WHERE YOUNG BRAINS ARE NEEDED

The customer problem

Most organisations need external help with their IT-needs. The bigger the organisation the more help they need. At the same time the IT-technology is developing so fast that all organisations have a steadily increasing backlog of projects that need resources with fresh skills. So while your internal staff is busy maintaining the legacy systems and your pool of external software engineers are tied up in upgrading the operational systems, where do you find the resources required to test and implement artificial intelligence, virtual reality, big data, gamification, responsive webstores, business intelligence, apps and all the other technology initiatives that could improve your productivity, competitiveness and customer and employee satisfaction?

Digital transformation takes place in a space where domain insight and experience are parred with knowledge of the most recent IT-technologies. You obviously cannot harvest the potential of new IT-technology by applying yesterday's frameworks. All organisations are faced with this dilemma. Some of them have resigned and accepted to be followers, while others are actively looking for ways to speed up the experiments and the operational implementation.

IT Minds

IT Minds was started to help fill the need for software engineers with knowledge of the most recent IT-tools and frameworks.

"We employ IT-students and young graduates and expect to have them for five to seven years," says Jonas Vognsen, partner and co-founder of IT-Minds. "Our customer value proposition is the combination of a very fresh skill set in areas where there is very little experience available in the market combined with an attractive price since our consultants are all at the entry point of their careers. We use agile development principles, have a very lean organisation and take advantage of modern technology for internal knowledge sharing and project management."

The company offers young IT-consultants on a T&M basis as resources for projects managed by their clients. They also offer to run the process completely from concept development to handing over the finished solution.

Starting in Denmark in 2010, the company has grown to employ 186 consultants with 286 projects under their belt. The company was acquired by EG A/S in 2014 but continues to operate independently.

Internationalization

The ambition of making IT Minds an international company was always there. In 2013 discussions were initiated on how this could be accomplished. 15 cities in Europe were listed and benchmarked against each other. However, when the company was acquired by EG, that has operations in Norway and Sweden, it was decided to take advantage of this infrastructure and Oslo was chosen as the first international location.

"We are operating in Oslo now, but it took much longer than we had anticipated," explain Jonas Vognsen. "Among the options of relocating a Dane to Oslo or recruit a local country manager we chose the latter. It ended up taking us 18 months to find the right person."

After trying to identify candidates thorough their own personal networks, they engaged a Norwegian head-hunter, but the final candidate did come through the network. The Oslo-operation is now at ten people and going well. Fortunately, they could use the presence of some of their Danish clients in Norway to get the first projects, which helped overcome the scepticism that always faces a new company.

IT Minds have learnt a lot that they will apply when they open the next office.

"We have reviewed our experience with starting up in Oslo," says Jonas Vognsen, "and the result is a process description with 350 action items that we know are required to open our next satellite offices. We are currently considering what the minimum setup looks like and believe

that it takes a team of skills to build a business where it is equally important to get new customers and recruit consultants."

Jonas Vognsen explains that the Oslo-project has consumed considerable management resources. Hiring the country manager and getting the paperwork for opening the subsidiary completed was only top of the iceberg. Getting the new organisation operational required support from all line managers.

"We wanted to replicate the IT Minds' concept in the Oslo-office," concludes Jonas Vognsen. *"That means implementing the same business principles, processes, systems and culture. It's like opening a McDonalds in a new country. There are certain local characteristics you have to respect, but the business model and the modus operandi should be identical everywhere."*

Since starting in Norway, IT Minds has concentrating on consolidating their Danish and Norwegian operations, and the next international office is still in the planning.

MAPSPEOPLE – SHOWING THE WAY TO THE GLOBAL MARKETS

The problem

Finding customer the fastest route from where you are now and being guided to where you want to go next is a problem that we all recognise. Route planning and navigation systems that offer the solution to this problem are technologies that have matured and been commoditised dramatically since the US-government in 2000 released accurate GPS signals for civilian use. Today navigation services are available in the dashboard of our cars and as apps on our smartphones. Most of us use them on a daily basis, but they all stop delivering their magic when we reach the outer perimeter of our destination. And that is a problem.

Finding your way in a building or a set of buildings can be a real challenge. Whether it is locating a specific shop at a factory outlet, finding the place for your MR-scan at 11:30, making sure you're at the podium in the conference room on time to deliver your keynote, finding your way to the gate for your connecting flight and avoiding your name being called on the airport intercom, or locating the desk in the office that is available right now and for the next four hours. Actually, it's not much of a help if your navigation system brings you to your venue in time only to let you down on the final mile of your journey.

The solution

MapsPeople, a Google Maps Partner (reseller) headquartered in Aalborg in the northern part of Denmark, has the solution framework for this challenge. The category is called Indoor Navigation and their platform is named MapsIndoors.

"Finding your way in shopping malls, airports, hospitals, sports venues, corporate headquarters, educational institutions, public buildings, convention centres, campsites and other places outside the reach of GPS signals and Google Maps can be frustrating and time-consuming," says Michael Gram, CEO and founder at MapsPeople. "The information required for a remedy resides with the individual venue owner. Providing indoor navigation is not difficult, but it requires an initiative and a budget for each case."

So far most of the 60 customers with a total of over 250 venues covering more than 18 million square meters located in Azerbaijan, Belgium, Colombia, Denmark, Finland, France, Germany, Hungary, Ireland, Italy, Japan, Netherlands, Norway, Romania, Russia, Switzerland, Spain, Sweden, UK and USA have found MapsPeople. Approximately sixty per cent of revenue is generated outside the domestic market.

"We have invested in inbound marketing activities and receive around 100 leads a month from all over the world," Michael Gram explains. "However, we believe there is a much bigger market out there and have started to build an outbound marketing and sales team."

The AARCV (Average Annual Recurring Contract Value) is USD 30.000 and the expected lifecycle of a site is currently estimated to be five years. The average sales cycle is four months with a spread from one month to a full year. A purchase decision involves several buying centres in the customer's organisation, but it is seldom the IT-department that is the project owner and the key decision maker. A PoC is often the last step of the buying process and MapsPeople have designed a standard PoC for which they charge USD 6.000.

"The drive for an indoor navigation solution primarily came from people caring for the customer experience or for optimising the travel time within the venue," say Michael Gram. "An RoI analysis of indoor navigation always shows very attractive results, but the return is seldom in the form of cash into the same budget that pays for providing the service. For most corporations and government institutions that represents a challenge. The exception being seat and space allocation in corporate headquarters and other large office venues where the utilisation improvement delivered by indoor navigation immediately translates into saved cost."

The software is only one element of the final indoor navigation solution. A map of the venue with a list and specification of destinations must be made. As GPS doesn't work inside buildings, a different positioning technology must be used. There are a range of options available such as beacons, Wi-Fi positioning, positioning via magnetic fields and via lighting. MapsIndoors can be interfaced to any of the above and the most suitable indoor positioning technology depends on the venue type and on the solution requirements. Finally, the solution normally gets integrated with some other key user services which the navigation and routing facilities support.

When you combine your indoor way-finding solution with an indoor positioning technology, you unlock a whole range of added benefits such as "Find nearest". As MapsIndoors is based on Google Maps you get complete and real-time routing to your final destination. You also gain insight into how people move around your venue and can send customers and visitors push notifications based on their current location.

Internationalization

Most of the current customers have been sold to and served virtually and so far, it doesn't seem as though there is a need for meeting physically with the customers. Sales, implementation and project management can be operated remotely using conference calls, web-meeting and other collaboration technologies. However, going forward, Maps-People would prefer to build an ecosystem of SIs, OEM's and VARs.

"We prefer serving the market through SIs, OEMs and VARs, not because we have difficulties finding customers," says Michael Gram. "It's because we need someone to deliver the auxiliary services from a time zone close to the customer and in her local language."

The indirect go-to-market strategy is based on the ambition for achieving global market leadership and is meant to make scaling the global rollout faster. Finding these partners have proven difficult and so far, most of the customers have been handled directly by MapsPeople.

"We have hired pre-sales staff that master the main languages and that have increased the conversion rates considerably," Michael Gram explains. "We will continue to go this route and will cover Europe from our office in Copenhagen and North America from our office in Austin,

Texas. As soon as we see solid demand from Asia, we will establish an office most likely in South Korea, Singapore or Japan."

With the investment in outbound lead generation activities, MapsPeople are convinced they can generate the critical mass of projects required to keep partners busy and justify the employment of dedicated resources for indoor navigation projects.

"The Indoor Navigation market is taking off just now," Michael Gram concludes. "We are investing in the commercial infrastructure to take the major share of this growth and are convinced that the ISs, OEMs and VARs will show increased interest and commitment when the project volume picks up."

MERCANTE

Software as the differentiator

MERCANTE was the second startup where I worked as the VP of marketing and sales. This was in the years 1988 to 1990. The company developed a high-performance printer for the office environment. The founders came from the photocopier business and had recently completed a semi-successful OEM project with Philips. By combining several technologies, Mercante had designed an LED printer that could print 20 pages per minutes (ppm), could hold four times 500 sheets (up to A3), had a 10 or 20 bin sorter and could print three print jobs simultaneously.

The CTO explained that the breakthrough was making a LED printer perform 20 ppm at 300 dpi. Having no intimate experience with printers, I was not impressed by getting toner on to paper at 20 ppm. Any photocopier could do that, and 300 dpi was already the industry standard.

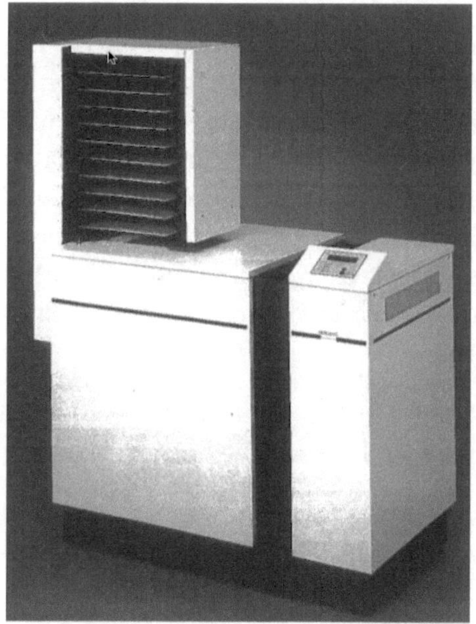

What was new was the four times 500 sheets paper capacity, the 10/20 bin sorter, where each was individually addressable, and the parallel printing capability. No one else could do that, and I saw a real opportunity for value to the customers.

At an executive meeting just after I started, we were reviewing the development plans. The product was still a prototype, and several issues needed fixing before we could release the printer for sale.

Figure 16. The Photon Imager was a high-performance printer with many innovative facilities. Unfortunately, it had serious quality issues.

I wanted the printer made available in three versions; a 15 ppm, a 20 ppm and a 25 ppm model.

HP had a 20 ppm machine with a Canon engine, so I wanted something just below and just above what HP could offer. HP wasn't pushing their product very hard, but if we were successful then I feared that they would flex a muscle or two and make our life miserable. With three basic versions, I could create a portfolio of options coming in low with a 15 ppm/500 sheet version which was less expensive than the HP machine and then upsell to 25 ppm/2000 sheets with 10/20 bin sorters where HP couldn't catch up.

The CTO agreed. This would prove to be a disastrous decision. The CTO should have vetoed my request. Changing a printer from doing 20 ppm to do 25 ppm was not a trivial task. I should have known better, but I didn't.

Fast international roll-out

With several months to commercial release, we started preparing our go-to-market strategy and building the organisation. We decided on an indirect sales strategy. There was an established network of printer distributors and resellers all over Europe. After talking to several of the resellers, it seemed that they all loved the idea of this type of printer. There was very little competition in this segment and the price tag – and thus the margins – were attractive. With this type of printer, the resellers could sell maintenance contracts, and the consumables side of the business was a gold mine.

The printer did things not seen before, so we would have to educate the market to appreciate the features and justify the high price tag.

With my previous success from Dataco[69] under my belt, I saw no reason not to schedule a fast rollout all over Europe. The plan called for a Pan-European rollout within one year after first launch. To support this effort, I started hiring area managers. Before we had shipped the first

---

[69] See the case Scandinavian Dataco

unit, I had built an organisation with three area managers, a marketing team of four people, including a technical writer, plus three secretaries. We divided Europe into four regions, of which I took care of the German-speaking countries and the rest of the world outside Europe.

If you have ever been with a start-up, then you'll know that deciding the commercial launch date (where you take orders and deliver) is no trivial task. I think all of us on the executive team knew that this decision was critical.

Was the product ready? When is a product genuinely ready?

There were issues with the product, but we didn't consider them critical. We could fix these issues within the next 3-6 months. There would be some noise in the beginning, but we would catch up with field engineering changes. The printer was a modular design, and we could replace each module as we improved the reliability.

The pressure was enormous. We had taken outside investment. We had built the organisation. We had lined up resellers and lighthouse customers. Postponing the launch would have been expensive.

Sales material, partner programs, price lists, press releases, posters, and advertising bookings were in place for the commercial launch. We knew how to work the press and got lots of editorial coverage.

We had lighthouse customers in place writing excellent testimonials and the first resellers in Denmark and the Nordics were signed and sealed.

Success

The printer became a huge success.

New partners signed reseller agreements and paid for starter kits, including demo units and training.

We trained the resellers, and they started selling the printers to their customers.

Within the first 12 months, we had signed up resellers all over Europe as planned. Each reseller had invested in a starter kit, including technical training and sales training and was selling to real customers.

We were airborne.

Japan

You cannot be in the printer business without sourcing most of the material from Japan. So did we. Japanese suppliers provided most of the photochemical components. We had excellent relationships in Japan (you usually have excellent relationships with people who sell you things).

Someone suggested that we should use our connections in Japan to make OEM deals there.

I should have vetoed that. I only resisted, then gave in. Big mistake.

We went to Japan, and we wasted lots of money and precious time, but I did learn something.

Unless you are Apple, Armani or Porsche, the Japanese prefer to buy Japanese manufactured products. To penetrate the Japanese printer market, you must do joint ventures. Joint ventures require investment and time. If you want to make it big in Japan, you must have someone on the ground, patience and lots of money. It may pay off handsomely someday, but it is not a quick win for a start-up.

We gave up Japan and returned our focus to Europe.

The Taste of Success

The printers were selling well. Orders came in from several countries.

I remember Alitalia ordering ten units for their maintenance facility in Rome. It was for an application that I had never thought of, but one we could replicate with all other airlines all over the world.

XEROX from El Segundo in California called. They would like to order two units for an OEM test.

XEROX is an excellent company. They have a policy of not squeezing small companies. They were interested in evaluating our printer for an OEM deal and asked us for a quotation including hardware, consumables, training and support. I wrote the proposal and flew off to the US to walk them through the details. The meeting took place over a lovely lunch, and two weeks later I received an order with a PO number. We billed, and they paid. We shipped and trained them, and they started testing.

We participated in the CeBIT circus in Hanover, Germany and came back with bags of business cards from potential customers and resellers. Distributors were knocking on our doors, but we turned them down. We were not ready for a two-tier model just now.

We had regular meetings with our resellers and did sales forecasts, which we passed to the manufacturing department who passed them to our suppliers. I was at the front end of the value chain, and I enjoyed the outlook.

We were successful. Sales were steadily climbing.

Manufacturing was having a hard time keeping up with production when the support hotline started to glow.

The printers were jamming

We knew about the problems. They were there when we released the product for sale. We just hadn't been able to fix them as fast as we thought we could. We shipped more and more printers with built-in problems waiting for it to explode in our faces.

The problem was two-fold. The printer jammed in the fusing unit, and the toner consumption was way over specification.

To help our customers, we shipped spare fuser units that they could have available for replacement on site. We also sent toner free of charge to compensate for the additional consumption. Our pre-sales support people were transferred to post-sales support to help customers fix the problems. Our people were on the road to see customers and help them make - what we had already sold them - work according to our specifications. The support folks returned and filed expense reports that we could not reclaim anywhere. Expenses grew, and sales dropped.

We were treating severe fractures with painkillers.

The real problem with printers that jam is the interruption of production. Not the printer's production, but the customer's production! When Alitalia could not print out work orders to their mechanics, you can probably imagine that the consequences were catastrophic.

Customers became nervous and started rumbling. Resellers became nervous and stopped selling.

My Integrity

All products will malfunction from time to time. The average time between failures never approaches eternity for any product. However, the issues get critical when you cannot fix them. We were a start-up. We were still in high burn-rate mode. Early success had led us to believe we were heading for the tornado. Now we were heading for the abyss.

We were running out of money, goodwill and spirit.

We had been out there with our overhead presentations, posters, press releases and sales material. We had made resellers sign partnership agreements and pay for demo kits and training packages upfront. We had convinced customers that this was a great product. We had accepted an OEM test order from XEROX, who now had the units on stand-by until we could provide a convincing fix for the issues. We had OEM negotiations with other big corporations that we had to stall.

I felt terrible and guilty.

Motivating myself and my team to continue to sell this "great" product was getting increasingly difficult as we proved unable to fix the causes and make our product comply with the specifications.

Decline and Fall

The problems didn't arise from one day to another. We knew about them from the very start. The consequences, however, appeared more slowly. In the beginning, you hope they will go away by themselves. You pray it is a "Monday" machine or something that you can fix quickly. When you are in sales, you must believe in your product. You just don't want to think that this is a design problem.

At a certain point, you realise that this is critical. You realise that it is a design problem. You also realise that R&D cannot deliver on their promises. Your promises to the market are based on the promises R&D made to you. When you cannot trust R&D, you are reluctant to promise the market anything. When you cannot promise the market anything, business comes to a halt.

It may sound as if I am blaming R&D, but that is not the case.

Any start-up must run these risks, but they should mitigate them carefully and not scale too early. We scaled far too soon. We took the risk, and we failed.

I have to take my share of the responsibility. I was on the executive team. I could have quit at any time, but I decided to stay and drive forward. I suggested stopping sales and laying off everyone in sales and marketing until the problems were solved. However, laying off people in Denmark doesn't stop the cash from flowing. There was a three-month notice period. What if we could fix the problems in three months? The discussions went on and on, and we lost time, trust and money.

First, we ran out of trust from the market, then from our investors and then we ran out of cash.

The company filed for bankruptcy.

Printers are high tech devices - we should respect them more!

A printer is a combination of several technology domains.

Mechanics must pick up the paper in the input tray, transport it through the printing process and deliver the sheet in the designated output tray, again, and again, and again without interruption.

Photochemistry must transfer the image to a magnetic drum, which then attracts the toner. As the paper passes through the drum, the toner gets transferred and burnt into the sheet in the fuser.

The software must handle the communication with the print sources (application programs) and control the printing process, including system status monitoring and reporting.

Electronics provide the platform for the software and connect to the sensors controlling the process and monitoring the printer's system status.

All Mercante printers ran at 25 ppm. The 15 and 20 ppm versions had a software delay mechanism that paused the printer momentarily to scale down the speed. A brilliant solution. This way we could upgrade the printers by a simple change in the firmware. The only problem was that the original design was for 20 ppm. Pushing the design to deliver 25 ppm caused all types of technical issues, primarily in the photochemical process.

We should never have embraced all four technologies. That was a big mistake. Photochemistry for printers was already a mature technology. There was no way we could differentiate ourselves by being able to print black toner on paper. Everyone did that day in and day out. We should have sourced the entire printing engine from one of the Japanese suppliers (maybe there was a reason why HP did just that?).

We differentiated ourselves on the three other technologies, and that was more than sufficient.

What did I learn?

When I was with Dataco, I remember that the head of R&D, Peter Videcrantz, always said: "stay clear of mechanics." Peter was obsessed with avoiding field engineering changes. I could now add "stay clear of photochemistry" to my store of knowledge. Never again would I get involved with a start-up relying on mechanics or photochemistry unless they could show off Olympic medals and world records (which a start-up seldom can).

I also learnt that you cannot trust people until you know you can trust them. If you trust people and they fail to deliver, then it is your problem, not theirs. Even though you are "just" the EVP of sales and marketing, you have to dig deep down and form your own opinion. You have to take on those fights, and you must fight hard to make sure that the company is making the right decisions. You represent the entire company and all the stakeholders, not only yourself and your department. Leadership is not a precise science, but I learned that I needed to be a tougher cookie in the executive team in the future.

Never take yes for an answer.

I also learnt that I could not walk on water. I learnt that success is a combination of many things, and you should be careful assigning too much credit to yourself. I was very successful at Dataco, but only because it was a fantastic product, the timing perfect and because the other people on the team were extremely talented.

It was the combination, not me alone.

I learnt that if you want to be an entrepreneur, then you have to come to terms with failure. Take the heat, face the brutal facts and get on with life. As long as people are not losing limbs and lives and you are not behaving unethically, then there is just the business risk left.

I didn't crash in a test flight. I just lost some money and pride. I was alive and had learnt a lot, but I was ashamed of having caused other people to lose money and time believing in me. That was the toughest part. I hope they have forgiven me.

What doesn't kill you only makes you stronger.

And then I went on to do other things.

MONITOR ERP SYSTEM - OPTIMISATION UNDER CONSTRAINTS

The Customer Problem

Manufacturing companies all share the same fundamental challenge: how to manufacture the required quality delivered on time with the lowest possible cost. The mathematical definition of the problem is "optimisation under constraints", and the challenge comes from the complexity of the know variables (your internal resources and processes) and the continually changing constraints. Some customers are more important than others and need priority, some raw materials have varying delivery times and fluctuating prices, and some processes need to be performed by sub-contractors that face the same optimisation challenges.

The support for production simulation, planning, scheduling, costing and reporting was among the first software applications written in the mid-1960s. By the end of the 1980s about one-third of all software sold was for MRP purposes. Then came the PC and the technology became available to SMB companies also.

The Monitor ERP System Value Proposition

Monitor ERP System AB is a company and a solution that exclusively focus on supporting business processes for SMB discrete manufacturing companies. They were among the first to take advantage of the appearance of the microcomputer and have used the popularity of the PC to make advanced MRP functionality available to the SMB market. Over the years Monitor has become a fully-fledged ERP solution, however, maintaining its sharp manufacturing industry focus.

"We speak our customers' language, and we have the functionality that they need," says Johan Holmsten, sales and marketing manager. "We normally don't have to do any customisation at all, which makes implementation times and expenses much lower than our competitors. The combination of a high degree of fit-for-purpose and the attractive cost of ownership makes it easy for our customers to make the vendor selection in our favour."

Johan Holmsten that has been with Monitor for more than twenty years stresses that customers have learned the price of customisation and are increasingly looking for software they can use out of the box. With a 35 per cent market share in Sweden Monitor is always on the short list when manufacturing companies in the SMB segment are on the outlook for a new system to support business processes.

Across their 4.000 customers, the average installation has 15 users, and the initial project price including implementation is EUR 50.000 with a twenty per cent annual charge for support and upgrades.

"We have installations with over 1.000 users and some with just a few users," Johan Holmsten continues, "but we do not inspire to be an alternative to SAP to big enterprises or an alternative to Quickbooks for small businesses. Our strategic focus on the mid-market remains intact."

Currently, the average sales cycle is six months from the time of BANT, but the trend is falling.

"We have recently given our technology a complete overhaul," says Johan Holmsten. "Offering more functionality in a cloud-format will, combined with our leading market position, reduce sales cycles even further. In 2018 we booked 1,5 new customers deals per day and that number will increase to two per day in 2019."

Internationalisation

Monitor has always maintained a direct go-to-market approach and has replicated this model in its international operations.

"Our customers have spearheaded our international activities," explains Johan Holmsten. "Swedish SMB manufacturing companies started setting up operations abroad in the 1980s and asked us to provide Monitor in local languages and with support for the country-specific requirements. The first main hub was Poland, and after building a solid base of customers there, we opened a subsidiary in 1992."

In 2007 the customer base in the Baltics called for local support and Monitor engaged with local companies to represent them in the region. Later came China and Malaysia. When Microsoft announced the discontinuation of Dynamics C5 in Denmark, Danish customers started making inquirers, and in 2016 a strategic alliance was formed with a partner that now operates under the Monitor brand name.

"Apart from Brazil, where we had to pull out, the approach of following our customers has worked wonders for us," Johan Holmsten reveals. "Getting an installed base in a new country without any sales effort makes building the initial bridgehead so much easier."

The challenge for Monitor is finding people with sufficient domain skills and an entrepreneurial mindset.

"That our company is headquartered 300 kilometres north of Stockholm is reflected in our culture," says Johan Holmsten with a smile. "We have been in this business since its very beginning and may not have grown as fast as some of our colleagues, but we are still around, still in control, making good money and believe in the long haul. Finding the right people is the key to the success of our global expansion. It is not a matter of urgency, but rather a matter of taking the right steps one at a time."

Monitor ERP expects high growth in South East Asia where they have subsidiaries in China and Malaysia.

"We have a solid customer base and a great team in place in South East Asia," concludes Johan Holmsten. "This is the fastest growing part of the world, and the competition is primarily Excel. We are well positioned to get our fair share of this market. However, we are also looking at doing more in Europe. Where and how is still under consideration."

NAVISION

A shoestring journey in the ERP industry

IN 2002 Microsoft acquired all the shares in Navision[70] for 1.45 billion dollars. By then, Navision operated an ecosystem of more than 2,000 resellers serving over 100,000 customers though 30 subsidiaries or distributors. When Microsoft took over, the total turnover of and around Navision's products was in the order of 3.4 billion dollars and the entire ecosystem employed over 20,000 people.

Although the Navision story happened in the years 1984 to 2002, there is plenty to take away, even today.

Navision was the name of the company born through the merger of Damgaard and Navision Software in December 2000. Both companies were listed on the Copenhagen Stock Exchange in 1999, both companies were developing an ERP system for the mid-market, and both companies had their headquarters located north of Copenhagen just 13 kilometres apart.

The two companies behind Navision had completely different approaches to internationalisation, although the most successful was off to an early but slow start. Most would have guessed that Damgaard, making a global distribution agreement with IBM in 1994, would be the fastest-growing. However, it turned out that the model used by Navision Software, engaging with small independent entrepreneurs, had significantly more potential.

Navision Software

Navision Software was founded in 1984 by three engineers. In the autumn of 1985, they launched PCPLUS, a single-user bookkeeping system for PC-DOS. The successor, Navigator, a multi-user financial management system, was launched in October 1987 and was to be distributed by IBM Denmark through their Business Centres.

---

[70] Bech, H. P. (2018). 5,460 Miles from Silicon Valley - The In-depth Case Study of What Became Microsoft's First Billion Dollar Acquisition Outside the USA (S. Quirke Køngerskov, Trans. A. Hagel Ed.). Copenhagen: TBK Publishing®.

Although the cooperation with IBM in Denmark was very successful, Navision Software's CEO Jesper Balser soon found out that IBM was not a candidate for the international distribution of their products. IBM made several attempts to acquire Navision Software, but never managed to present a realistic scenario for the global distribution. Nor did the IBM subsidiaries in other European countries show any interest in distributing Navigator.

When Navision Software read the market in the first half of the 1990s, they made their bets on Microsoft Windows rather than on OS/2. They initiated the development of a product for the upcoming operating system, codenamed Chicago.

Disappointed with IBM's commitment to global distribution, Navision Software started looking for other options.

In the late 1980s, Lars Damsgaard Andersen and Jesper Bowman worked as CFO and Controller respectively with a manufacturing company in Jutland, Denmark, where they used an accounting system on an IBM AS/400. In the latter half of the 1980s, they changed to a PC-based platform and chose the DOS-based Navigator, sold by IBM and developed by the small Danish software company Navision Software. Planning to implement a new financial system in their German subsidiary, Lars and Jesper studied various local software solutions but did not find anything to their liking. They, therefore, proposed that the subsidiary should use Navigator. After a demonstration of the Danish software program in an English version, the German staff were very excited; excited enough that Lars, Jesper and Per Grønfeldt, a technical consultant from the IBM reseller of the product, translated the program to German and put it into operation. It worked well, and everyone was happy.

Meanwhile, the company they worked for was acquired by a Swedish group, and Lars and Jesper lost much of the autonomy and influence they had when the company was in Danish hands. They discussed with Per if there was a market for Navigator in Germany, and if they together could develop business there. Per, who already had a good relationship with some of the developers at Navision Software, offered to inquire whether there might be enough interest for the three Jutlanders to start the distribution of Navigator in Germany.

The feedback was positive, and in August 1989 the trio – Lars, Jesper and Per – travelled to Copenhagen to present and discuss the idea with Jesper Balser. Spending a full day getting familiar with each other and talking about the opportunity proved that the chemistry between the four was terrific. The trio returned to Jutland with instructions to prepare a business plan and find the funding needed to get started. They were also told that a new product was in the development pipeline and that a potential launch in Germany must be based on that.

The trio, who all had full-time jobs, now engaged in the research required to write the business plan, as well as finding private investors that would support the funding efforts. After numerous discussions with PC&C in Copenhagen, the business plan for the German distribution activity materialised and the corresponding agreements were signed. The new company, which was to be called Deltacom GmbH, acquired the exclusive Navigator distribution rights, while agreeing that specific sales targets were to be met. Deltacom would be responsible for the translation and localisation of the software to comply with German legislation and market requirements, and the trio had to assume full responsibility for and fund all activities associated with the distribution in Germany. Navision Software, who contributed to the initial funding and made a trade credit available, received a twenty per cent share in Deltacom GmbH, but was otherwise only involved with providing experience and advice, while everything else was in the hands of the trio.

In the spring of 1990, Lars Damsgaard, Jesper Bowman and Per Grønfeldt resigned from their jobs and moved to Germany, and on July 1st, almost a year after the first meeting, they opened the doors of their new office in Hamburg. They started working on making the product ready for the German market, and to avoid wasting precious time the trio used daytime hours driving up and down the German

Autobahns visiting and demonstrating the product for potential resellers and customers all over the Bundesrepublik. The release of the new product Navigator 3.0 was delayed, so even when potential customers and resellers showed interest, they could not deliver. In late spring of 1991, the product was finally ready for the German market, enabling much-needed revenue and cashflow.

The go-to-market model was defined from the very beginning and was based on serving the customers through value-added resellers (VARs). Although the recruitment of VARs and the subsequent sale to their customers was growing very slowly and fell short of any hopes & expectations, the VAR model was maintained, and Navision Software in Copenhagen decided to extend the exclusivity and gave the trio more runway to get the business off the ground.

The sluggish start was very tough on the cash flow, and the trio, working around the clock, had to tighten their belts, while Navision Software in Copenhagen helped by extending their credit. Even Deltacom's German bank had to step in and authorise overdrafts. Still, as they saw that things were going in the right direction - albeit somewhat slower than expected - they exhibited unusual patience.

At that time, Deltacom had recruited around 50 VARs, and some of these were part of nationwide networks with other partners. They also now showed interest. On top of the trio's market-oriented activities, the word-of-mouth machine began to work, and sales took off. When Navision Software launched Navision Financials for Windows in 1995, Jesper Bowman, Lars Damsgaard and Per Grønfeldt had both the organisation and the VAR-base ready. Although the translation and adaptation effort had to be redone for the new product, market acceptance was swift, and the new product became a huge success.

At the end of 1990s, Navision Software prepared for its IPO and decided to acquire all of its distributors. Shares in the German company were swapped for shares in Navision Software A/S at a price negotiated between the parties. After the IPO in the spring of 1999, these shares became liquid. It returned the trio a handsome reward for the initiative they took ten years earlier and for the many hours they had put into the project before being engulfed by the tornado that led to Navision becoming the market leader in the SMB segment in Germany.

What the trio did not know when they made contact with Jesper Balser & Co. back in 1989, was that, based on their successful co-operation with IBM in Denmark, Navision Software had, in 1988, discussed distribution with a wide range of IBM subsidiaries in Europe. Due to their collaboration with other local software vendors, IBM Germany decided to decline the opportunity to use Navigator as an IBM logo-product supporting their PC business. Being under competitive pressure from Damgaard in the small Danish domestic market, Navision Software was extremely keen to grow internationally. With no immediate options for Germany, they were very open to other initiatives. The three hopeful Jutlanders could not match IBM's position in Germany, but history would show that Jesper Balser and company made the right decision when they chose to give the trio a chance. Germany became a massive success for both Navision Software and the trio themselves. It was a unique adventure in the short history of the European software industry and has become a precedent for international expansion under the name of "The Navision Model."

Navision Software entered into similar distribution agreements in 1991 for Spain, Iceland and the USA. Before the launch of Navision Financials for certified for Windows95, they recruited distributors in Belgium, The UK, the Netherlands, Austria, Switzerland, Slovenia, Sweden and the Czech Republic. Most of these were joint ventures with different degrees of ownership, but always with partners demonstrating an entrepreneurial mindset.

From 1984 to 1999, Navision Software grew organically, and all international expansion initiatives were accomplished through shoestring approaches. Before the IPO in May 1999, Navision Software had more than 700 solution centres serving 31,000 customers through 22 subsidiaries or distributors in 75 countries. At this time, their international operations accounted for more than 80 per cent of their revenue.

Damgaard

Damgaard was founded in 1984 by brothers Erik and Preben. Their first single-user bookkeeping app for the CP/M operating system, Danmax, came out in the autumn of 1984 and became an instant success. In 1986, the multi-user system Concorde for PC/MS-DOS followed and in 1991 came Concorde XAL for UNIX and DOS.

By 1994 Damgaard was the undisputed leader in the Danish market for ERP-systems to small and medium-sized companies. They were almost five times bigger than the number two, Navision Software. Their international initiatives, however, hadn't produced any significant results.

The launch of Concorde XAL in 1991 was accompanied by a distribution agreement with Digital Equipment Corporation's Danish subsidiary. The product and the DEC endorsement pushed the product up in the market. Several large international companies, such as Motorola and Continental, made inquiries and ended up implementing the product. However, Damgaard failed in the recruitment of distributors in other countries.

In the autumn of 1993, Erik and Preben were approached by IBM, who wanted to acquire Damgaard and use Concorde XAL to boost their business in the global SMB market. Although that sounded like a good match of ambitions, they couldn't reach an agreement on the purchase price, and the deal fell apart.

In January 1994 IBM returned and offered Damgaard a global distribution agreement in a joint venture setup. In this arrangement, IBM wouldn't interfere with Damgaard's domestic business in Denmark, but would exclusively sell Concorde XAL through their other international subsidiaries. Such a cooperation with IBM, the then undisputed global leader in the IT-industry, seemed to be the perfect answer to Damgaard's distribution challenge.

The letter of intent was signed and publicly announced at the end of January 1994 and was received as an international breakthrough for

Damgaard. With IBM as the global distributor, they had engaged the most significant marketing muscle in the IT-industry. So they thought.

Several events and circumstances rendered the cooperation unsuccessful. Expectations that both parties expressed at the time of signing the agreements were not met.

Windows 3.1, launched in April 1992, quickly became quite popular; the Windows 3.1 version for workgroups, in particular, released at the end of 1993, which enabled the sharing of data, applications and hardware, gained Microsoft serious market share. When the company unveiled its development plans in January 1994, interest and press coverage was substantial. The idea was to release a new 32-bit version of the server product Windows NT (code name Cairo), but of more interest were the plans for the project codenamed Chicago or Windows 4.0, which was the operating system for the individual user's PC. Microsoft expected to release Windows 4.0 at the end of 1994, with the development tools for programming the operating system to be released in the first quarter of 1994.

At the same time as Microsoft gained market share with Windows, Damgaard entered into the partnership with IBM, which pumped billions of dollars into their OS/2 counter-strategy. Concorde Business, which included a number of other DOS-based software packages, was already immensely successful and Concorde XAL was growing at lightning speed. In May 1994, a highly improved XAL Version 2, operating on DOS, OS/2, Ultrix, OSF1 and SCO/UNIX was released, and was available with Damgaard Data's own file system or with the Oracle database. Preparations were also busily underway for the launch of Concorde C5, a downscaled version of XAL, which was initially planned for DOS and OS/2.

Global sales of OS/2 were slow and could in no way keep up with the spread of Microsoft Windows. IBM's Nordic management believed the problem was a lack of applications. If a supply of useful applications could be made available for the OS/2 platform, customers would prefer this platform, as it carried IBM's good name and reputation.

Therefore, the idea of bundling a variety of applications such as word processing, spreadsheets, presentation and database with a financial program in one package was formed. In spring 1995, IBM launched the Azanta product range in Denmark, Norway and Sweden, which was a combination of IBM hardware, Lotus SmartSuite and the new Concorde C5, now translated into Norwegian and Swedish, and adapted to meet national market requirements. The package was based on OS/2 and was meant to be a Microsoft Windows killer.

Azanta was a giant fiasco and demonstrated that small and medium-sized companies simply were not interested in products based on OS/2. After a few months, the product suite was placed on the shelf and received no further attention.

The spread of OS/2 was supposed to have been supported by XAL. However, IBM never succeeded in making any headway in the market that was supposed to use the product. Thus, XAL lost its connection to a strategic IBM product and, therefore, it had difficulty gaining interest internally in IBM. Several attempts were made getting XAL to run on AS/400 and DB/2. Still, both technical challenges and the lack of sufficient demand among small and medium-sized businesses led to the initiatives running into the sand.

Another factor was that the agreement was signed with IBM in Denmark and with people who only had regional management responsibility. Outside of the Nordic region, it was up to the individual IBM subsidiaries if they wanted to join. If they chose to, there were no accompanying resources. Any business areas from which resources were appropriated still had to deliver on their existing budgets. In other words, the activities were to finance themselves within the first year. It takes between three to five years to establish a position on a new market with a product such as XAL, and IBM's subsidiaries were not geared for such long-term projects.

In the 1990s, IBM was primarily a hardware and service company. It had a wide range of software products, but they were all so-called middleware and IT-tools. When it came to application software, such as XAL and later Axapta, IBM worked closely with every supplier to ensure its hardware was included in as many projects as possible.

After the OS/2 project capsized, IBM has no general strategic interest in owning Damgaard. The strategic mismatch became most apparent in the USA, where IBM very cleverly avoided mentioning that it owned half of the company behind Axapta at the product's announcement.

There was also a definite lack of synchronicity on the board of the joint venture. Damgaard's representatives had short chains of command and authority to execute the decisions made, while IBM's representatives had no executive authority at all. For example, they couldn't influence the activities in the individual countries in any way, and despite being in contact with both top area and regional managers within IBM's organisation, it turned out that even their execution authority was limited.

When the partnership began in 1994, Damgaard was in no way ready to deliver national versions of its products to a standard of quality, a schedule and with the level of documentation expected by IBM. It took several years for the processes to be put somewhat into place so that IBM could be told what was coming when. Did that level of immaturity impact on the partnership's lack of results? The situation certainly didn't make it any easier for the few IBM people who were to develop the market in each country. Had IBM won more customers and resellers started sooner, both the pressure and the basis for improving processes and products would probably have secured more resources and greater urgency internally.

Damgaard didn't lack the technical skills to get the job done, but rather the commercial incentive to spend time on those variants for which there was little demand. A combination of a company like Damgaard, which was at the forefront of technology and willing to put it to the test, and a company like IBM, which, wore both belts and braces, created challenges.

Should management have predicted these factors when they entered into negotiations with IBM in 1993? Had Preben Damgaard consulted Jesper Balser from Navision Software, he might have learned something about the inner workings of IBM. Preben couldn't do that for a good reason, and Jesper Balser certainly wasn't thrilled about the situation during the first months after his break with IBM. Keep in mind that Damgaard had been trying – unsuccessfully – for years to find the way onto the international markets and that in 1993-1994, despite enormous deficits in the previous years, IBM continued to enjoy quite special status and respect within the IT industry. That status was substantially eroded during the years of partnership with Damgaard International.

Moreover, IBM in Denmark was significantly different from IBM in the rest of the world. IBM Denmark was the most successful of all IBM's subsidiaries. In the market for PC-based solutions for small and medium-sized businesses alone, IBM in Denmark, through its Business Centres and Navigator from Navision Software, had acquired unusually high market shares. Thus, in 1993-94, management in Damgaard had every reason to see a partnership with IBM as beneficial. Not only as an opportunity to punch competitor Navision Software in the gut, but as simultaneously giving an extra boost to international growth.

Should the management of Damgaard have called off the partnership earlier on? Only six months passed before Preben Damgaard suspected something was wrong. However, the delays were well explained, and IBM's representatives on the board were optimistic, too. There was always the expectation that it would probably get better soon. When an IBM'er came over from the USA and laid big plans and figures on the table, hope and belief that a breakthrough was coming were once again renewed, and when IBM agreed to help get started in the USA, there were more good reasons to wait and see.

In 1998 Damgaard acquired all of IBM's shares in the joint venture and started investing in their own national subsidiaries.

Comparing Navision Software and Damgaard

Navision Software and Damgaard started almost at the same time in the same market with the same type of product, which gives us a unique opportunity for comparing how they developed.

With IBM as the distributor, Navision Software's revenue in Denmark rose from USD 1 million in 1986/87 to over USD 8 million 1994/95. With a gross margin of 30 per cent of the retail price, Navision Software in 1995 sold software for USD 26 million at market prices.

While they were very pleased with the IBM cooperation in Denmark, it did not appear to have any spill-over effect on IBM's other national subsidiaries. Despite several initiatives, it was not possible to convince other IBM subsidiaries to copy the indisputable success that gave IBM Denmark the highest market share among its peers. Therefore, as early as 1990, Navision Software began to find its own way to the international markets and by the end of 1994, when the cooperation with IBM Denmark stopped, more than 50 per cent of Navision Software's turnover came from exports.

Damgaard Data quickly took the position of leader in the Danish market for financial management systems for small and medium-sized enterprises. In 1986/87, they booked almost USD 3 million in revenue and were, therefore, three times larger than Navision Software. The figures may not be completely comparable, as Damgaard Data itself was responsible for the distribution and therefore retained a higher margin. Still, these are the figures reported in the annual accounts.

Damgaard had significant challenges with internationalisation and didn't find the right distributors that could push the train into action. Preben Damgaard consequently gave IBM Denmark a warm welcome when they called him in the second half of 1993 to start a collaboration on internationalisation.

Damgaard's sales rose from USD 30 to USD 93 million in the period 1994 to 1999, while Navision Software's increased from USD 13 to 167 million. During this period, Damgaard Data realised a total net profit of USD 19 million, while Navision Software's corresponding profit totalled 40 million. It is fair to note that Damgaard Data's export performance in the years 1994 to 1997 is not included. These figures were reported separately in the joint venture with IBM, Damgaard Data International A/S, and not consolidated with Damgaard Data A/S. If 50 per cent (not counting the results in Denmark twice) of the Damgaard Data International revenue was added then the Damgaard turnover in 1999 would have been USD 111 million.

All other things being equal (which I know is never the case), Navision Software performed significantly better without IBM than Damgaard Data did with IBM.

When the two companies were listed in 1999, it seemed as though the difference had disappeared. At the time of listing, their market caps were almost identical. However, facing declining demand after the millennium and difficulties associated with the burst of the dot-com-bubble, Navision Software turned out to be far more robust. When the two companies merged, the Damgaard shareholders were left with 28 per cent of shares, while the Navision Software shareholder took 72 per cent.

When working in a small company, one can easily be flattered by an inquiry request from a large and reputable organisation. But you should take it easy and remain calm.

Companies do not cooperate with companies. People work with people, and they do so for concrete reasons. It is worthwhile checking and understanding the motives, positions and responsibilities of the people who make the initial invitation.

Large companies are usually far more bureaucratic than small ones. This means that the small company may risk investing a disproportionate amount of energy in the preliminary clarifications that may (and most likely will) end up in nothing. For the small company, the alternative costs can be significant. For the big company, not so much. Therefore, a small company should insist on a quick decision-making process. A small and paid-for pilot project is far better than big fat birds on the roof. Middle managers in large companies change jobs quite often. With extended negotiations, people may come and go, and new agendas get introduced.

One should limit the number of people involved in the initial clarifications and keep the cards close to the chest until there is something concrete to report. And, finally, you should uncover options for alternatives. Are there any competitors to the big company that might also be interested? What else can you do if an agreement is not reached? An attractive fall-back position makes most people excellent negotiators.

Further, it should be remembered that apart from the top-level senior executives, managers in large companies are white-collar workers with entirely different incentives and far less impact than executives in smaller companies, who are often shareholders, too. When an owner says "yes, we'll do it " then he or she has direct access to pull the levers to make it happen. This is rarely the case in a large company where strategic decisions and operational execution are often distributed across many people in different departments, pursuing various objectives. The small company should, therefore, get firm confirmation that the drive for cooperation is endorsed and sponsored by high-ranking executives in the larger organisation. And that confirmation must be based on an easily understandable, logical, short-term and measurable gain for this person. That person is most likely sitting in the big company's global headquarters and not in a regional or country office.

The Damgaard brothers bought out IBM in the autumn of 1998 for USD 15 million, for what corresponded to 15 per cent of the shares in the holding company. Just 12 months later, when Damgaard was listed at the Copenhagen Stock Exchange, those shares had a value of USD 165 million.

And finally, it should also be emphasised that the Damgaard brothers did say "no thank you" to IBM's two efforts to acquire the entire company. Had IBM succeeded in acquiring Damgaard Data, it would have cost the brothers millions, and it would probably also have killed the company. Not because IBM did not have noble intentions, but because of the rapid development in the industry, forcing IBM to change its strategy in a direction that did not make room for a small Danish software company such as Damgaard Data.

NETDIALOG – WHEN IT-PERFORMANCE MATTERS

The customer problem

Have you ever been on the phone with a customer services representative excusing for the speed of the IT-system? Or have you checked-in at an airport where the IT-system was slow and people in the steadily growing line started to show their impatience?

Today information technology is a critical component in all businesses and a majority of the workforce is actually information workers. Their productivity and quality of life depends heavily on how well their IT-tools perform. In many job-functions it is also the performance of the IT-systems that determine the quality of the service that the organisations' customers experience. Thus, there is a very direct relationship between customer and employee satisfaction and the performance of the IT-systems.

We have come a long way since the first mainframe-based online systems were introduced in the 1970s. And even though the computer power in our smartphones outperforms these mainframes and our Internet subscription way outperforms the 9,600 baud modem we so merrily welcomed in the past; the performance of IT-systems still remains a serious problem for all organisations. Despite the explosion in computer and data communications capacity it seems that the creativity of the software developers and the demand for new applications are always stretching the IT-infrastructure to its' limits. The bigger the organisation is and the more it is spread across separate geographical locations the bigger the problems become.

The NetDialog customer value proposition

Fixing performance problems in IT-systems is no trivial task. The IT-infrastructure is made up of numerous components each with their capacity issues, update cycles and potential bottlenecks. At the same time, the workload at any given time is decided by how the IT-workers are actually using the systems. Troubleshooting requires sophisticated analytical tools that can help the IT-systems support staff understand what is going on and allow them to apply immediate fixes if possible and schedule systemic changes.

NetX from NetDialog is an application suite of monitoring and reporting tools directed at the data communications infrastructure. It provides the IT-systems support staff with the toolbox for monitoring and fixing problems even before the users start to notice the problems. NetX continuously monitors and analyses the performance, user experience and delivery of applications, as well as the general performance of WANs, providing up-to-the-minute, easy-to-understand analytical information.

The pricing of the service is based on the number of information sources, which typically are the physical routers in the customers network. The subscription price for an installation with 100 data sources is in the range of a few thousand Euros per month.

The ideal customer profiles

Although all types of companies are faced with performance issues the consequence of the problems increase with the size of the organisation. The complexity associated with trouble shooting and preventive initiatives grows with the organisation's geographical spread.

NetDialog has defined the ideal customer as any organisation operating on ten or more geographical locations. However, as the value increases with the size of the network, customers with over 100 routers will actively be looking for the type of solution that NetDialog provides. Being present when such needs becomes active is crucial for the company.

Solution components

NetX, that is delivered in a cloud format and on a subscription basis, requires only little implementation effort to become operational. Of the price the customer pays around 90 per cent is for using the software and 10 per cent is for the professional services required for setup and support.

Based on a list of information sources and the naming convention NetDialog prepares their software for receiving the data from the customer. After the customer has configured her network devices to submit the data, NetX starts the analysis and makes the results available as required. Using this approach NetX can provide very detailed insight into the performance of the customers IT resources without installing any software in the clients IT-infrastructure.

Go-to-market approach

NetDialog is a small company serving a market with very large customers. This is normally a toxic cocktail which is why the company has chosen an indirect distribution model.

"We are a small and technology-centred company based in the Netherlands," explains Olaf Hasker, CEO of NetDialog, "and our customers are major corporations and institutions all over the world. We identified a series of companies that already had relationship with our potential customers in the area that NetX addresses and explored how we could improve their customer value proposition."

The business partners are a mix of systems integrators, communication service providers and performance- and security-management providers.

"Most of our partners are very big companies and the revenue they generate with NetX may not seem as much in their books," says Olaf Hasker, "but the revenue it helps generate with other associated products is substantial. NetX is a business enabler that drives many other revenue streams for our partners."

The partners are responding to RFPs from the customer communities. Either these RFPs express a request for network performance monitoring, or the resellers can add this service to differentiate their value proposition. Both ways NetX becomes a central part of the proposed solution.

"NetX may not be a big part of the price of a managed network proposal," says Olaf Hasker, "but it can be a major part of the value delivered. We therefore need to work very closely with our partners' technical staff and with those who manage the ongoing relationship with the customers. It

is important that they are familiar with the service and the value it provides and that they are comfortable proposing it to their customers."

Internationalization

NetX is a technical product that crosses borders very easily. It requires no localisation and as it is used exclusively by IT-specialist in primarily international organisations, there is no need to translate neither the user interface nor the documentation. NetDialog also have had international ambitions from the start and have recruited business partners that could bring the product to potential customers outside The Netherlands. As eighty per cent of the revenue now comes from abroad and while most of the new business comes from international customers the time is ripe for considering what the next steps should be.

"I believe we can continue to manage our business in the near time zones from Amsterdam," Olaf Hasker explains. "Expanding our market share in Asia and the Americas will require that we establish some kind of local representation."

Olaf Hasker is fully aware that setting up satellite offices adds a layer of complexity to the operation and management of his company. He has seen from others how this step can go very wrong, so he is cautious and considers various approaches where he can adjust quickly if required.

"Outsourcing the initial steps may be a way to minimise the risk," Olaf Hasker concludes. "We want to demonstrate our long-term commitment to the international markets, but we don't want to be caught in a trap. Our business is still very project-driven, and we need the ability to adjust according to the actual deal flow."

NORRIQ – AN INTERNATIONAL MICROSOFT DYNAMICS VAR AND ISV

The customer problem

Most international companies prefer to base their IT-infrastructure on technologies that are already available in all the markets where they operate. Microsoft Dynamics represents such a technology platform. The support for the platform, however, is provided by value added resellers of which only very few have an international presence.

NORRIQ is a company created with the sole purpose of providing support for international Microsoft Dynamics customers. It was an idea and an ambition that Bo Martinsen had worked on for some time when he was a channel manager with Microsoft in Denmark. In 2007, he raised $60 million from investors to acquire and merge three Danish Dynamics resellers and acquire a fourth in Belgium and The Netherlands. The outcome was NORRIQ.

The second start

After the merger NORRIQ was ready to deliver on its business plan, when 2008 happened.

"The timing couldn't have been worse," says Bo Martinsen, founder and CEO of NORRIQ. "The financial crisis made it very hard for us to deliver on our business plan. We worked hard and tried everything, but the economy was down, and companies were holding back investments in IT-projects. I had to leave the company by the end of 2011, when the investors put an interim management team in place to dress up NORRIQ for sale."

The business climate in 2012 wasn't much better and although new buyers had shown interest, the decision to sell kept being postponed. When one of the main investors, the Faroese Eik Bank, folded, the remaining NORRIQ owners needed to decide for a buyer. It was Bo Martinsen and a group of investors that acquired the rights to what was left and in October 2012 the company got a second start.

The strategy

Being a Microsoft Dynamics value added reseller and ISV NORRIQ builds its strategy on Microsoft's strategy.

"The alignment with Microsoft is one of our main strategic pillars," Bo Martinsen explains. *"In the IT-industry there is hardly a bigger wave you can surf."*

At home NORRIQ is a broadline implementation partner serving a multitude of verticals covering all horizontal segments in the market. For the lower end of the market a Dynamics Business Central solution has been developed for the thousands of C5 customers that after Microsoft's discontinuation of the product need a migration path. For the higher layers of the market Norriq offers the full portfolio of Dynamics solutions.

"The comprehensive application portfolio offered by Dynamics gives us multiple entry points for new customer projects," Bo Martinsen stresses. *"A new customer engagement can start with HR, CRM, BI or some other area primed for digital transformation. The opening doesn't have to be a full-blown ERP migration project."*

The international strategy

With the acquisition of the Belgian company in 2007 NORRIQ also acquired the intellectual property rights to DrinkIT, a vertical ISV solution for the beverage producing industry.

"DrinkIT is the ticket to the international markets," say Bo Martinsen. *"This is FDA-domain, which means it's complicated and mission critical, and we already have a substantial international customer base that can testify the quality of our offering."*

The challenge facing NORRIQ is how fast they can develop critical mass in a specific country. Customer inquiries are there, but to build national implementation and support organisations requires more than a single customer project. So far NORRIQ has subsidiaries in the UK, Germany and Benelux. A sales office has been opened in China, which may develop into a subsidiary as soon as critical mass has been reached.

"We have a team of highly skilled consultants with domain expertise that we can assign to projects all over the world," Bo Martinsen explains. "However, many customers prefer local support and that we can only deliver when we have the prospect of reaching critical mass in that country."

It's the chicken/egg challenge. The skills required for implementing and supporting a vertical business solution such as DrinkIT are not available on every street corner. It takes years to build. NORRIQ cannot risk making such an investment and then have the resources sitting idle until the next project comes around.

"The solution is to apply the model we have in the Nordics", says Bo Martinsen. "The broadline VAR-business can then bridge the gap until the vertical ISV-business is self-supporting. We are therefore looking for strategic partnerships in all the major markets."

Building a national VAR business from scratch is not easy. The talent required is hard to find and estimating when revenue will start flowing is difficult. The best option therefore seems to be acquiring or forming joint ventures with existing VARs that have an appetite for growth. The carrot for joining forces with NORRIQ should be economy of scale and the capitalisation opportunity. Norriq's ambition with building a global business based on Microsoft Dynamics could have an IPO as the end-spiel, which would pay out handsomely to those who believe in the idea.

"We are working hard on making Norriq a global company," Bo Martinsen says. "That is also the road to success for our strategic partners. Having a share in the success can be exchanged for a financial award if we float the company or engage in some other liquidity model. This will not happen tomorrow, and I am sure the road will be bumpy, long and winding, but seeing the full picture of what we are building will help keeping us all on the same page."

Norriq is not the first company setting out to build a global footprint on top of Microsoft Dynamics and so far, not many have been really successful.

"Cloud and SaaS doesn't make the cash flow side of the project any easier," Bo Martinsen concludes. *"but it does make the market more dynamic and that is what we need. An increasing stream of new customer migration projects is to the benefit of the insurgent. All we need to do is show patience and make sure we team up with partners that share our vision and values."*

PENNEO - CLOUD-BASED DIGITAL SIGNATURES

The customer problem

Getting legal documents signed can be a cumbersome affair. Getting the people, whose signature you need, to show up at the same place within a certain narrow timespan can be outright impossible. Sending the document as a pdf-file asking for the signature to be added, the document printed, scanned and returned isn't very practical either. But even more challenging is handling the process and documents being compliant to GDPR!

The Penneo value proposition

Penneo is a cloud-based digital signature solution to the problems listed. It provides a platform for managing the signature process, applying the signatures and serve as a repository of signed documents. And most importantly being in compliance with GDPR. It's currently available in Scandinavia and is exclusively using the national digital signature standards implemented in Denmark, Norway and Sweden.

The go-to-market approach

The first go-to-market approach was indirect approaching the business software providers serving those types of businesses where getting legal documents signed was expected to be a daily headache. However, the software vendors were not very accommodating or enthusiastic about approaching this particular customer problem. As with most new technology Penneo was considered a solution looking for a problem that customers may have but didn't know for which there was a remedy. The incumbent software vendors were not prepared to put in the missionary effort required for developing the market.

Instead Penneo started to call potential customers directly. The revenue generation approach was based on making outbound cold calls to segments in the market that were known to have a substantial and ongoing need for signing legal documents. The calls were made to line managers and not to the IT department. The pitch was short and simple invoking interest in hearing more about the opportunity for reducing the laborious effort associated with getting legal documents signed.

The approach worked and the team of inside salesreps was scaled to penetrate the market faster. Because of the simple pitch Penneo could recruit inside salesreps without the requirement for technical skills or sales experience. A short training effort was sufficient.

Revenue generation metrics

Today Penneo has more than 1.200 active customers with hardly any churn.

The pricing is based on two variables: users and signatures. The AAS (Average Annual Subscription) amounts to €3.500. ASC (Average Sales Cycle) is eight weeks and CAC (Customer Acquisition Cost) is 20 per cent of AAS.

There is only very little value add required for the implementation of a Penneo solution which may explain why the software providers initially showed little interest. As the market embraced Penneo the software vendors started paying attention also wanting to make sure that integration to their solutions were possible and available. Today Penneo offers such integrations through a REST API.

Internationalisation

Going forward Penneo is investing in inbound marketing activities to capture a larger share of the SMB market too. The company also considers relocating to a place where there is a larger pool of foreign speaking salespeople allowing for penetrating more countries from a single location as long as possible. Driving an outbound inside sales operation requires a very specific culture, critical mass and dedicated management. Transplanting this setup to a new geography has proven difficult and expensive. Building a solid customer base before setting up a local operation can help mitigate the risk and fund the endeavour.

Background

The company was started in 2012 in Aalborg, Denmark, and became operational after receiving seed funding in 2014. In 2016 the founders acquired the shares back from the seed investor. After focusing entirely on the Danish market Penneo started sales into Norway and Sweden in 2017. The activity was managed out of the office in Copenhagen using native Norwegian and Swedish speaking staff to do the calling. Most of the follow up activities could be handled as phone or web meetings with some on-site meetings for larger accounts.

PROMANAGE

The customer problem

Running a company managing physical products is complicated. No matter which aspect of a business that develops, makes, markets and distributes physical products you look at, you will find serious challenges. I am not talking about start-ups that yet need to find out if there is a market for what they plan to do. I am talking about established companies that have been around for a while.

Just consider for a moment the problem of deciding how much to produce. If you make too much, then you'll end up with excessive manufacturing costs and inventories. If you make too little, then you'll disappoint your distributors and customers, who may end up buying from your competitors. And managing the balance between supply and demand is not a one-time optimisation exercise. Market demand fluctuates with the world economy, with your introduction of new products, with new products from your competitors, with changes in consumer preferences, and with new solutions from insurgents. All of these factors may completely change the price/benefit relationship in your industry. Even if you manage to match supply to demand correctly, how do you balance the quality against the manufacturing cost? How do you manage your suppliers, your factories and your workforce when all the variables constantly change?

The complexity of the manufacturing industries has made them prime customers of information technology ever since the computer was invented. Standard software for manufacturing was created initially in 1964 to supply the NASA Polaris program when Joseph Orlicky developed material requirements planning (MRP). The first commercial company to use MRP was Black & Decker, also in 1964. By 1975, MRP was implemented in 700 companies. This number had grown to about 8,000 by 1981. In the 1980s, MRP evolved into Oliver Wight's manufacturing resource planning (MRP II), which includes master scheduling, rough-cut capacity planning, capacity requirements planning and sales & operations planning. By 1989, about one-third of the software industry was MRP II-software, and it was primarily sold to American industrial companies ($1.2 billion worth of software)[71].

As a layman, you would believe that now, 30 years later, and after the invention of the PC, the Internet, barcode readers, sensors, IoT, robots and the development of billions of lines of software code, that most of the problems encountered by manufacturing companies should have been solved. However, that is far from the case. Advancements in technology, the globalisation enabled by the Internet, the rapid shifts in consumer preferences and the increase in regulatory policies have made the issues even more profound.

The challenges motivated the industry and its major customers to work together under the ISA-95 umbrella. ISA-95 aims to define the terminology and models to be used in the integration of business systems at the enterprise level, with control systems at the plant-floor level. ISA-95 was established to deal with three significant issues:

- Integration of business logistics systems to manufacturing systems is difficult and expensive.

- The effective operation of manufacturing is difficult to explain and compare.

- Integration of manufacturing operations systems is difficult and expensive.

The IT-products and -services associated with helping companies control their manufacturing operations have now been assigned as two categories, Manufacturing Execution Systems (MES) and Manufacturing Operations Management (MOM), that are monitored by the industry analysts.

---

[71] Source: https://en.wikipedia.org/wiki/Material_requirements_planning

Today the market is driven under the Industry 4.0 headline, which was coined by the German Government at the beginning of the last decade and presented on 8 April 2013 at the Hannover Fair.

The market for Industry 4.0 solutions is international in so far as the needs and requirements are the same irrespective of the location of a manufacturing facility. Nevertheless, to ease implementation, integration and support, customers prefer to be served by solution providers that have an operation in the local vicinity, can master the native language and are familiar with the local environment. In many aspects, the MES/MOM industry is very much a sister of the ERP industry.

ProManage

ProManage develops IoT-based MES/MOM solutions for Industry 4.0. Through its software, hardware and professional services, ProManage aims to improve the production productivity in the discrete and batch manufacturing industries.

Founded in Istanbul, Turkey, in 1998, by Doruk Automation, ProManage has a staff of more than 100 people. They won their first international contract in 2006 and they now have customers in the USA, Russia, Rumania, Bulgaria, Serbia, Belgium, Algeria and Turkistan. After pursuing a somewhat opportunistic customer acquisition approach, partly based on participating in conferences and exhibitions and partly based on growing with their current customers, ProManage's global expansion has primarily happened in markets with little growth potential. With Turkey being a manufacturing hotspot, most of its revenue still comes from domestic activities.

In 2016, as part of their long-term growth ambitions, Doruk leadership strategised the company to win notable shares in significant foreign markets under their brand "ProManage." Doruk's subsidiary, "ProManage, Smart Manufacturing Solutions Corp.", was founded in 2017 in Chicago, Illinois, USA, to realise this vision. Since then, ProManage has invested in market development in the USA, Japan and Germany.

"Our primary focus is to generate the opportunities in some of the largest manufacturing hubs of which we have chosen to concentrate on the USA, Japan and Germany," says Aylin T. Özden, Managing Director, ProManage. "Sure, addressing the specific needs of our customers in different geographies is another critical area for ProManage".

A key industry segment for ProManage is discrete manufacturing such as automotive, metal processing, plastic injection, textiles, pharmaceuticals and white goods. ProManage's target segments cover customers with more than twenty production units.

The market is changing

Introducing modern technology and especially IT-technology in the manufacturing industries have become national priorities, pushed and supported by governments. In the USA, such activities are organised by the MxD (previously UI Labs) umbrella. In Germany, the events were kicked off by the Industry 4.0 report and are driven on the practical level by the Fraunhofer Society.

"The policymakers interest in keeping their manufacturing industries productive and competitive is a huge opportunity for us," explains Aylin T. Özden. "The political agenda of keeping manufacturing jobs within the countries is important as well as urgent, which open the doors to small tech-companies such as ours. The government initiatives provide communities and demonstration platforms where we can participate on equal terms with the already established and much larger vendors."

According to Aylin T. Ozden, the market for MES/MOM has developed so fast that the established and large players quickly get bogged down by supporting their installed base. It becomes difficult for them to keep up with the advances in technology. It is, therefore, not so difficult to find an interest in ProManage within the communities supported by the government initiatives.

"The innovation is coming from smaller companies such as ours," says Aylin T. Özden. "In the future, we may face the same issues as our larger competitors, but, for now, it gives us a competitive advantage. Additionally, we see partnerships as one of our strongest points to leverage the ProManage platform enhanced with our partners' capabilities. Our biggest challenge is the timing of our investments in the new markets. We know that new customers will require local support, which we are also prepared to provide. But if we ramp up too soon, then we will have high office costs and idle resources on the payroll. We need to establish the right teams for the countries we focus on as well as preparing our corporate headquarters for running an international business with partners and subsidiaries across different time zones and cultures."

PRONESTOR – WHEN PHYSICAL MEETINGS ARE A PART OF YOUR VALUE PROPOSITION

The customer problem

In an age where web meetings and conference calls are replacing the physical face-to-face meetings there are still major areas where the substitution do not and cannot take place. For many organisations, public and private, the physical meeting still plays an important role. For some companies, such as in professional services, the meeting experience is even an important part of the brand and value proposition.

For such organisations there is a need for paying attention to both two sides of the physical meeting: Ensuring the attendees a positive experience and reducing the effort required by the organisers. Where the reduction in secretarial support is a phenomenon happening across all industries the task of organising meetings is left with the operative professionals. These changes in the environment explains why there is increasing demand for meeting management solutions such as Pronestor's.

Pronestor – enhancing the meeting experience

Pronestor offers three modules covering the full spectrum of managing meeting attendance and resources.

The objective of the Planner module, that allows for inviting attendees and book resources such as meeting rooms, equipment, catering etc., is to simplify the administration of meeting.

The objective of the Pronestor Visitor module is to provide the best possible experience for the attendees. It gives the organiser a list of participants, sends automated notifications when they arrive, prints or display visitor badges, gives attendees Wi-Fi access codes (and cancelling the codes when they leave) and other information pertinent to meeting. The module also handles check-out though the reception or self-service scanning.

Pronestor Display is a suite of hardware independent, interactive, and centrally managed display solutions. It dynamically displays the information you wish to convey such as when a room is booked/free, what the meeting is about, who the host is - on a display outside the individual venue, in the meeting area, at the reception, and on your mobile phone.

"Most people are surprised when they learn how much technology can enhance the meeting experience both for the attendee and the organiser," says Karsten Busck, CEO and co-owner of Pronestor. "I think we are all fascinated when visiting or working for organisations that pay attention to the details, such as providing you with a parking permit and a virtual visitors batch for your smart phone all prior to your arrival, displaying your name in the lobby, giving you access to the building, giving directions to the venue and codes for the Wi-Fi etc. Only by using technology can you guarantee the highest level of meeting experience every time."

The revenue generation process

Pronestor was founded in 2002, and systematic market penetration was started in 2015, when the company got new investors. Following primarily an inbound lead generation approach the company today enjoys a forty per cent market share in their domestic market (Denmark). The go-to-market approach at home is direct.

"The forty per cent is measured on those having a meeting management solution," explains Karsten Busck. "Measured against the total market the share is significant smaller. There is still a substantial potential and activating this potential will require an outbound lead generation activity."

The core market segment is defined as all organisations with more than twenty meeting rooms and especially organisations where the physical meeting is an important element of the brand and customer value proposition.

The current average ACV (Average Contract Value) is USD 4,000 but the spread goes from USD 1,500 to USD 150,000. Efforts to increase the ACV to USD 12,000 is underway. The average sales cycle is four months, but again the spread is considerable ranging from a single phone call to several years. The buying process is predominantly complex with several stakeholders of which the IT-department often becomes the final decision maker.

"One of the main challenges with outbound lead generation is identifying the main purchasing centre," says Karsten Busck. *"With the relatively low ACV we need to quickly locate where the need resides and if it can be activated."*

The consulting services required for integrating and implementing the solution ranges from 10 to 30 hours and is billed on a time and material basis.

The international go-to-market approach

Despite operating out of Copenhagen only, Pronestor has customers in Norway, Sweden, Belgium, France, the UK, USA, Canada, Australia, Argentina and Brazil.

"Fifty per cent of our revenue is from international accounts," says Karsten Busck. *"These are either international customers with wold wide representation or national customers that have found us. Our second biggest market is the USA."*

The international go-to-market approach is currently being refined. Pronestor will apply a direct go-to-market approach in some markets while other markets will use an indirect partner model.

"We have learned that getting international customers does not require that we have representations abroad," explains Karsten Busck. *"However, we need that if we want to undertake deeper market penetration and win considerable market shares. And that is our ambition."*

Currently the product is available in the main languages, but the localisation effort is minimal and having a new language in place is a two-week effort only.

"We have partners in place in some countries and we consider expanding this model with more partners and to more markets," says Karsten Busck. "For the larger markets we may need a two-tier approach ensuring that the general market development and management tasks are performed according to our standards. However, we have not decided if we are to take this role ourselves or subcontract to a value-added partner network."

Most of the current partners have found Pronestor and the most successful have the products as their main offering.

RAMBASE - CLOUD-BASED ERP FROM NORWAY

The market challenges

Using standard software to support business process management and control in midsized companies started with the invention of the minicomputer in the late 1970s and got its breakthrough with the IBM-compatible PC-platform in the late 1980s. By the mid 1990s Gartner grouped such software together under the term Enterprise Resource Planning, ERP. In the same period two Danish companies, Damgaard Data and Navision Software, pioneered ERP products with SDKs (Software Development Kit) that allowed individual customisation which again expanded the footprint of PC-based solutions to even more and bigger companies.

With the rapid proliferation of the Internet and the steadily improvement in the price/performance of hardware the idea of offering software and computer capacity as a service entered the hype cycle in 2000 and have gradually matured since then. Cloud computing and SaaS, as it has now been named, are especially attractive to midsized companies as they can convert CAPEX to OPEX, but also because they can enjoy the advantages of not having to have an internal IT-department taking care of systems management and support. However, the adoption rate of cloud-computing and SaaS has been much slower than the IT-industry expected. The Law of Diffusion of Innovation has played its usual role, but other issues have been also holding companies back from this digital transformation.

Migration cost and risk

Moving from an on-premise to a cloud-based ERP platform is a full blow migration project. Only few companies will be motivated to do so unless there is a compelling reason and substantial benefit. Otherwise the business case will not show black numbers over a reasonable period. ERP-systems seem to run until external circumstances bring them to a halt.

The customisation legacy

While the possibility for customisation reduced the cost of developing ERP-systems for many companies it also introduced the legacy liability and debt. Upgrading customised applications with new versions of the underlying software components became expensive without offering any tangible value. Therefore, many companies didn't do it. Cloud-based ERP systems offered on a SaaS basis tend to be much more standardised and mapping a migration path from the past to the future is perceived as a major undertaking.

Implementation partners

On-premise ERP solutions offer an attractive professional services revenue stream for the suppliers. Often the tie to the implementation partner is particularly strong because of the in-depth knowledge of the customisations made. Cloud-based ERP systems are expected to be less expensive to implement and support, which makes the immediate suppliers reluctant to push the customers towards a SaaS migration project.

The market opportunity

Although you would consider the ERP market fairly mature and saturated exactly the shift from on-premise customised solutions to SaaS and cloud-based standard solutions opens the market for insurgents. Vendors with no installed base to protect and a clean technology sheet are currently moving in and take market share from the incumbents. It happens all over the world.

Rambase

Norwegian RamBase is such an insurgent. Starting out as an internal development project for Hatteland in 1992, RamBase was spun-off as an independent ERP-brand in 2016. Since then the company has won 19 domestic and five international customers. Although coming from a small customer base, RamBase outperformed market growth in 2018 (41%) and expect to more than double the growth rate in 2019.

Value Proposition

RamBase is a complete ERP-system offered exclusive in a SaaS format. The primary competitive edges are completeness and fast implementation (less than eight weeks). Country specific localisation is done by RamBase in Norway based on specifications provided by chartered accountants and market analysts in each country.

"You could claim that we are just another ERP-system," says Odd Magne Vea, CSO with RamBase. "However, the change from perpetual on-premise to SaaS in the cloud does open op the market completely. Where the established vendors seem to be adding more and more peripheral applications to their platforms, we have taken the opposite route. We offer core ERP-functionality that can be implemented fast. When the core functions are in place then we can work with the customers to expand the functionality, but we have no ambition of covering all the peripheral application areas for which there are plenty of great products available already".

Simplification seems to be an attractive value proposition for those customers that have experienced the customisation trap and have paid the associated premium.

"Our technology with continuous releases and microservices is still ahead of many competitors", stresses Odd Magne Vea. "Our platform and SDK will be increasingly important to help partners make money on integrations, apps, and modifications. It's not so different from the product direction especially Microsoft is taking. However, many partners and customers prefer a more intimate relationship with their suppliers and that's what we can offer."

The Market segmentation

The main market focus for RamBase is discrete manufacturing and distribution companies in Norway, Sweden, The UK and Poland. The company is open for entering additional countries but have made no priority list yet. Market entrance is highly depending on the quality of people they can find and where their current customers may have a need for local support.

"With RamBase our customers get support for their complex processes and sophisticated functional needs, delivered as a standard cloud-based service" says Odd Magne Vea. "We support really complex manufacturing processes including the needs for detailed traceability, quality control and documentation. Earlier this was only achievable through on-premise installations with lots of customisation. Not anymore. Our customers get an "out of the box" standard SaaS solution. Our competitors may claim that complex needs still require "on-premise" or managed solutions, but that is not the case. They days of customisation hell and vendor lock-in are finally over."

Channel

RamBase has chosen a clean indirect go-to-market approach where implementation partners are responsible for the entire revenue generation process. The first partners in each country receives substantial support from RamBase including co-funding of the entire revenue generation process.

"The competitive situation differs from country to country," explains Odd Magne Vea, "but as far as we can see there are opportunities everywhere. Apart from Sweden, Poland and the UK, where we are currently making heavy investments, the sequence for when to enter which country is very much depending on the people we can find. It takes an entrepreneurial mindset to start up a country operation and there are only so many people for which the task and the timing is right."

When entering a new country RamBase engages a local business development manager to recruit the business and implementation partners and to work closely with them winning the first deals. The cooperation works like a joint venture where the objective is creating a first bridgehead for the product.

"The partners that help us get established in a new country will obviously enjoy co-investments and dedicated support," Odd Magne Vea continues. "We understand that our partners are breaking the ice for us and we will help them protect their investments and commitment. Building an ERP-reseller channel has been done before and we have

learned what it takes to grow the business and keep partners happy at the same time."

Key resources and activities

Maintaining a complete ERP system is not considered the prime challenge at RamBase. They have been working in this domain for 25 years and have more standard functionality than their closest competitors. The challenge is revenue generation and customer success.

"We realize that we from a functionality perspective are operating in a very mature market" admits Odd Magne Vea. "Nevertheless, as soon as potential customers learn about our technology and value proposition the probability for winning a project is high. Our primary challenge is recruiting more partners, that can talk to more customers and building up the support capacity to keep them both happy. We have the technology, now we need to build the marketing and customer success muscle."

SALES FORCE EUROPE - REVENUE GENERATION AS AS SERVICE

THIS is the transcription of my interview with Rick Pizolli, founder and CEO of Sales Force Europe.

Hans Peter: *What is a revenue-generation-as-a-service provider?*

Rick Pizzoli: This is a service that is fully dedicated to delivering revenue for our clients. There's no delays or cost in recruitment, for opening up offices, or for dealing with local taxes. We simply get down to the business of sales. It's a flexible approach where you can drop in well-qualified and trained senior sources in your target countries, focused on your target verticals and quickly develop qualified opportunities. Think of us as the SEAL Team Six of sales.

Hans Peter: *What is the profile of a typical client?*

Rick Pizzoli: If they're coming from the USA, they typically have $2 to $50 million in revenue and maybe the same in funding. If the client is European expanding from one market to the next, probably a bit less. If it's a start up that's founded in Finland, for example, and they want to expand to Sweden or the UK, maybe a million dollars in revenue on their home market is enough. They need to be established in their domestic market, have established processes, happy clients, a differentiated product, and well-organised team and game plan to expand.

They need to be open to new ways of doing business and having the philosophy of "I'm going to do things different to beat my competition to market and not just follow the normal approach." They need to have a product that can be sold or that needs to be sold. So that's typically a product that is more than $10,000 a year if it's a service. Or if its hardware that needs to be sold via channels, so we do a lot of channel work. Assigning a channel is easy but really engaging and enabling the channel is a lot of work. So what probably is less of a fit, are consumer applications or lower cost items that can be sold off the web.

Hans Peter: *How does the business model work?*

Rick Pizzoli: We spend time understanding our clients business. So that can be a couple of calls of really digging deep, understanding their target countries, their target verticals, the positioning of the product, and then we spend time qualifying the right resources on our team to represent the client in the market. Then we present a team to the client. We have another series of calls, and if there's a good fit, we agree on objectives and terms, and the client then onboard that team. They become an extension of the client's team, completely transparent to the outside market.

The fees are based on a monthly fee and a commission. We try to keep that as simple as possible. So there's no recruitment, there's no office costs, there's no incorporating. No additional cost, just a fixed operating costs, and a commission on sales.

Hans Peter: *Do you carry the business cards of your clients?*

Rick Pizzoli: Correct, we were completely transparent. So we use the business cards, emails, the agreements. So for the market, we're an extension of the client's team immediately active in these new markets.

Hans Peter: Let's imagine that we have a technology company. They're out of the startup stage and generating revenue with their current sales and marketing operation in their domestic market. And now it's time to scale the business and grow and they basically have two options:

1. Option one is that they simply hire more people and they open new offices in the new markets.

2. Option two is to engage with an international revenue as a service provider just like you.

What is the difference between those two scenarios?

Rick Pizzoli: With option one, the traditional approach, you first need to get a budget. It's probably $1 million to open up a new region like Europe just to begin with. It can take time to get that budget approved. Then you need to find a recruitment company to start building the team. That could be another two months and distraction from your home business, flights back and forth.

That recruitment company is going to pull typically random CVs off LinkedIn or off the Internet to make a short list of employees. Then there's another couple months of interviewing short list, selecting the person, they need to leave their current job. Then you need to do an office search, office setup, payroll, incorporating, legal, tax. That's six to 12 months of lost time and revenue where you've lost focus on your home market. You've lost focus on the new market, on revenue, because you spent your whole time building this team that you hope is that right team and, you hope, is the right market.

And guess what? Maybe you've landed in London and you're too early or you too late. You've built this establishment that's very difficult and very expensive to move, and if you have to close it because it's wrong, it's also a black eye in the market making it hard to come back later. Whereas if you engage with a revenue-as-a-service company, all you need is couple of calls with the company to share your strategy and business model. They source the team from within their network, and you can interview the team, typically with one or two weeks. If there is a fit, you agree on objectives, agree on the terms, on board the team, bring them to your home market, train them for a few days, you review sales strategies, targets, objectives, etc. And you engage the market. You can be up and running in three to four weeks.

Hans Peter: *How can you make resources available in such a short time frame?*

Rick Pizzoli: We have approximately 70 people engaged with clients today. We have another 70 people that we've interviewed, that we've liked, that we've worked with before, and that are basically in the bullpen. Maybe they're half time working with somebody else, maybe their full time on another assignment that's about to end. So we have a bullpen of very strong people on a per country basis. So in each country, in Spain, for Italy, or UK, or Germany, maybe we have eight, ten people active. And that team has another ten, 20 people that they know that are available or going on jobs, going off jobs.

So these are personal relationships, people that we worked with before, and people that we can bring to the table very quickly.

Hans Peter: *What is required for working successfully with somebody like you?*

Rick Pizzoli: The whole picture needs to be there, right. They need to have a solid product that's differentiated; they need to have a strong sales team, and founders that understand the whole process. They need to have made the evolution from founders doing the sales to being a professional sales team. So that's a big step. The product needs to have the evolution from being a highly customised for each client to a real product, where there's product release plans and documentation around the product. Marketing needs to evolve from just technical marketing to value based marketing and not fluff, but really what's the business justification for these products. Support needs to be there, operations need to be there, and very important is funding.

It takes time and money to open up a new market. If you want to extract revenue of $1 million from a new market, you need to invest a quarter million dollars up front to get there. So we can deliver 300% ROI, but there's an investment up front to get that revenue.

Hans Peter: *Finding competent and skilled marketing and salespeople is extremely difficult for everybody. How do you tackle this challenge better than your clients?*

Rick Pizzoli: It's because we live and breathe this business. We know the hitters in each market. So the verticals we focus on are Telco, Enterprise SaaS, and Channel. So the people that do those sales jobs in London, Paris, or Madrid, we know them all. We know the guys that are very strong. We know the guys that are not so strong. If somebody wants to develop Telefonica in Spain, we know the top two to three salespeople that really know that organisation up and down, and we can bring them to the client sales team immediately when they're ready to go.

Hans Peter: *I assume that you see a growing market for revenue generation as a service?*

Rick Pizzoli: Well, we've seen an explosion of software as a service. Nobody installs enterprise software any more. We've seen an explosion in human resources as a service. We see this as a combination of the two, and it's growing quickly. You wouldn't manufacture your own products today. You leave it to an expert.

Why, if you're an expert in building technology and selling it in San Francisco, why do you believe that you're an expert all of a sudden opening up a new office in London because that's the right spot? Leave it to experts in the market. Find the customers, close the deals, and then build the organisation around the revenue. Don't build an organisation and expect revenue will come.

Hans Peter: *How long should your clients keep on using resources like you? Is there an expiry date for you or is this something that could go on forever?*

Rick Pizzoli: It may continue for the medium to long term, as long as the team is delivering and the business model works for the client, so the ROI is there. You can keep expanding in this scenario. Employment laws in the USA are very flexible, employment laws in Europe are very inflexible. The market was not built for technology, it was built for heavy industry. And so you can work with contractors. Legally, it's exactly the same as a normal employee, full time, fully dedicated, and grow and expand as you need. Focus them on certain verticals and maybe, as a technology company, you get bought by a Cisco or Google, most cases these companies don't want all these employees. They want the customers and the technology.

And so as a younger company, you're actually more valuable to a company who might take you on without the big burden of a European team. So we have clients who we've been with for many years and we just continue to grow with them on the service basis.

Hans Peter: *What are the most common misconceptions that potential clients have when it comes to asking help from somebody like you?*

Rick Pizzoli: First, we can't work in a vacuum. We need active engagements from our clients. You just don't find team like ours and expect them to sell. You need to do road shows; you need to be involved in the sales process. Another misconception is people think that they lose control. They think we as a service company in Europe is like a development team in India. It's outsourced, out there someplace. I believe the clients have more control because it's a service that is integrated into the client's team, and it's very easy for the client to turn this up or down, whereas if you have an employee, you spend a lot of money bringing this person on, and it's very expensive to get rid of them. So it's a big step. Whereas a service that's not a big step, you just turn it up and down.

Another misconception is clients say, "I want our own team. I want my guys." Well, just because she's an employee doesn't mean she's any more of your guy than if she's a full-time service completely dedicated to you. She is still your guy, she's just under a different agreement.

And probably the last thing we see is people will say, "Well, my product is too complex for this type of service." We can source the best people in the business 100 per cent dedicated to our clients. So they are just as capable of selling a complex solution as any other normal full-time employee would be.

Hans Peter: *What I hear you saying is that choosing a revenue generation as a service provider to bring into a new market is not so much a question about saving money, it's about saving time. Maybe in the long run that could be converted into money, but it's not the immediate saving that is the motivator. Is that right?*

Rick Pizzoli: Well, I think there are upfront savings, because if you go to the traditional approach, you have all the recruitment fees, and offices, and flights. So that's a big hit at the very beginning. But yes, it's time, it's beating the competition to market, its flexibility, it's getting the right team, it's a team and the right market, and the right verticals at the right time, and then expanding that. I mean we've had excellent clients that first put a team in London, and guess what? They were selling, in this case, an OTT platform and all the big providers in the UK had already bought one. They got there too late. And so they were making flights around Europe, they could get meetings, but they couldn't penetrate those tier one Telcos. Then they sign with us, and we got them in all those tier one and tier two service providers and broadcasters. Within two years, they were bought by a major manufacturer.

Hans Peter: *Rick, let's just imagine a client has been using you and that they're very happy with that. But they come to a stage where they really want their own team. How do you make that transition?*

Rick Pizzoli: We have two to three clients each year that come to a certain point, maybe it's for political reasons, or maybe their VCs demand it. They want to go through the transition of having this service in these new markets converted to employees. And we're absolutely open to that. They can recruit the people on our team, so they would pay normal recruitment fee, and they bring our people on, and they become employees. And at the same time, we could also help backfill any other positions and do some recruiting as well. We don't position ourselves as a recruiting company, but since we're there, we're engaged in the market, we know their space, we know the people in the market, and we can help facilitate that transition process.

Hans Peter: *If that's what the client wants, and if that's what your people working for the client, if they want that too, then you will facilitate that process?*

Rick Pizzoli: Absolutely, it happened as I said two or three times a year. And those have all been good transitions and the companies have continued to grow from that point.

SCANDINAVIAN DATACO

Jumping the chasm

I won my first genuine experience with international business development in the autumn of 1986. In April the same year I had started in a position as executive vice president, sales and marketing for a startup developing Ethernet-based local and wide area network products (hardware and software). During my onboarding process we had agreed that our go-to-market approach should be indirect through resellers and that, as soon we had consolidated our position in the domestic market, then we should explore international opportunities. We estimated that this could happen in a year or two. Maybe three at the most.

However, immediately upon releasing the first products we were fortunate to win a huge contract with a major local telecom operator, (Jydsk Telefon - JTAS) that decided to use our products to modernise their internal IT-network. This installation, that took place in the autumn of 1986, had several thousand users and made us jump the chasm at the first try. The business division of the telco had decided to become a reseller of our products and undertook the delivery and implementation. The project, therefore, complied fully with our distribution strategy.

I cannot stress enough how important that contract was to us. We were now approached by all the hardware and data communication vendors, including the local subsidiaries of some of the global players, and they all wanted to become resellers. Soon we could add all types of companies to our reference list including some very large organisations. Our market share in Denmark grew fast.

The rapid success at home allowed me to appoint a sales manager for the domestic market and free up my time for getting our international business up and running. I had initially expected that we should start looking at international opportunities at the earliest in 1987, but the success at home made it possible to accelerate those activities and get started right away.

In 1986 there was no Internet and I had no previous experience with international expansion. Where should we start and how could we find and enable resellers?

Based on the experience with our activities at home we made some fundamental strategic decisions:

1. We wanted resellers in other countries and not distributors;

2. We didn't want to grant anyone exclusivity;

3. We only wanted productive resellers

Before approaching potential resellers abroad, we invested a couple of weeks in developing a rather comprehensive business partner program and a business partner agreement that was non-negotiable. The program included a training package for marketing, sales and support people and a starter kit that the reseller had to buy. We also made business planning mandatory and included a number of templates in the package, among those the now famous P&L Model. However, we didn't insist on a fixed format for the business plan and we also gave each reseller a free hand in how to launch the products and how much to invest in sales and marketing. Nevertheless, the up-front investment for the resellers was quite substantial.

Identifying potential resellers

We used three sources for identifying potential resellers:

1. Visiting national IT-exhibitions;

2. Contacting the national industry associations to get a list of their members;

3. Working with IDC in the countries that we choose to look at.

The data communication industry was already very mature, and, in each country, there was a handful of resellers of which there was always a market leader.

We started by approaching potential resellers in Sweden, Norway and Finland. I found the contact information and then my secretary sent them a fax with a short introduction asking for a meeting. The conversion rate was 100 per cent. I don't recall anyone declining a meeting. Upon confirming the meeting, we shipped a short presentation of our partner value proposition.

The meetings had to be scheduled allowing me to visit two or three a day as I travelled to Oslo, Stockholm and Helsinki. The agenda for the meetings were prepared by us and had a fifty-fifty per cent balance of me presenting our company, products, ambitions and partner program and the potential partner presenting their business and ambitions. We always started with the partner presenting first and then us next. Most of the meetings ended with each of us going home to digest the information, but every now and then the potential partner wanted to sign up right away ensuring that we didn't go with her competitor. I remember the meeting with a potential partner in Oslo, Norway. They were so excited that they wanted to sign the reseller agreement immediately. As it didn't become active before the starter kit was paid, they asked their CFO to transfer the money the same day.

Over the following twelve months we used this approach to sign up resellers in all West European countries (the iron curtain didn't fall until 1989).

The non-exclusivity challenge

The reason we were successful with resellers in Denmark was the fact that we did the distributor's work ourselves. We were present at all the relevant conferences and exhibitions; we did intense PR work and we ran advertising in the trade press and in newspapers. It made sense for us since it stimulated demand. We generated leads and passed them on to the resellers. We were involved in sales cases and did special bids, when required. And then we had the best pre- and post-sales support in the industry. Being physically close to the R&D team was a huge advantage that we used extensively, but we also managed to hire what turned out to be one of the best support managers that I have ever met. Having someone on board that combined technical insight with excellent communication skills was a huge advantage.

Moving into a new country, you start without any infrastructure and you cannot expect a reseller to build it unless you protect her investment in such market development. We therefore ended up only appointing one reseller in each of the other Nordics countries and although the agreements were non-exclusive, we made gentlemen's agreements not to appoint a second one if the business developed satisfactorily. We then repeated this approach for Spain, Italy, Austria, Switzerland, The Netherlands and France.

In Germany and the UK, we didn't find any reseller that we believed could cover the entire market, but as none of those we talked to agreed with us, we had endless discussions. After participating in the CeBIT fair in the early spring of 1987, we started getting recognised in the industry across Europe and had to come to a conclusion for these two important markets. To avoid the exclusivity issue, we urged some of the interested parties to do white label deals instead and that turned out to be a good solution. Our white label contacts had a higher upfront commitment compensated by lower ongoing product prices. In a large market, that worked well for the P&L Model. White label customers had to do all the marketing themselves and we had to deliver rebranded products, so the pricing concept could be justified. One of the white label customers in the UK had an international distribution network and grew very fast.

We appointed two resellers in Germany, one in Frankfurt and one in Munich, and both were very unhappy with the situation. After several meetings we decided not to waste any more time on the issue and left them to decide for themselves what to do about it. It never became a happy relationship. We later closed a white label agreement with another German company and that became a huge success also.

Looking back at the outcome we did compromise on two of our three strategic principles. We did appoint de facto distributors and left it to them to recruit resellers if they wanted. We did provide exclusivity although it was on a gentleman's agreement basis. The result was very active business partners (we stopped calling them resellers or distributors and only referred to them as business partners).

Organisation

Eighteen months after releasing our first products, more than fifty per cent of revenue came from international operations and I started looking at overseas markets.

How did we organise the growth?

We managed all activities out of Copenhagen. We didn't hire any staff in the countries where we operated. In the long run that would not have been sustainable, but for getting the business started, it worked well.

For the first six months, I personally took care of marketing and business development. I hired a support manager that also did product marketing and a graphic designer that enabled us to do all the sales and marketing material in-house. I personally wrote the first datasheets and brochures and the designer made them look great. I have never been a big fan of fancy and glossy brochures, anyway, and our focus on quality of content over format was well received by customers and business partners.

I am sure that our investment in business partner training made a significant contribution to our success. I trained the partners' marketing and salespeople and my support manager did all the technical training. It was a one-week program during which we got to know the partner's staff really well. They had no reservations calling us for help when they started talking to potential customers and we were also prepared to jump on a plane to help them out if required.

My part of the training started with discussing where in the market our products were particularly attractive and competitive. As with many products you could theoretically sell them to anyone, but understanding where we had successfully sold them in the past and for which reasons, helped the partner's marketing and salespeople concentrate on those market segments that would offer the best conversion rates. We then went into how to sell the products and how to manage the communication with the various stakeholders in the customer's organisation. Finally, we rehearsed proposal writing, making sure the reseller's people could configure and price the offers correctly.

The sales training took two days and the technical training another two days. The fifth day was for putting together a launch plan that was documented as a who-does-what-when Gantt chart.

I had a status meeting with each reseller every month where we had a set agenda and talked about progress, issues and opportunities. As we added new countries, I hired regional managers to take over the day-to-day account management and moved on to new markets.

Two years into the project we had a marketing department with a manager, three regional sales managers and a support, documentation and product management department. A pool of three secretaries served us all. I had hired most of them and still spent only about a quarter of my time in the office. The rest of the time I was on the road developing new markets and training new resellers. In the long run that was not sustainable, but my main passion is business development and not people management. We solved the issue by taking the support, documentation and product management department out of my organisation and letting it report directly to the CEO. It was my proposal and it worked really well. The support manager and I were good friends and managed working well side-by-side.

The Dataco scenario is typical

To get something started you need an entrepreneurial sales-oriented person such as me. But as the business and organisation grows the need for people management skills increases and it becomes more and more obvious that the guy or gal who did the bootstrapping may not be the person to take it from twenty people to fifty people; especially because managing managers is so much different from just managing people.

Thankfully, I learned about my shortcomings during my tenure with Dataco and was also helped by having people in my organisation that I had hired myself. Splitting the organisation when it grew beyond twenty people was a clever move.

The P&L model

Not long after I started with Dataco we ran out of money. It was the traditional situation where we were later to market than expected and the burn-rate was threatening to finish us off. There was no way we could overcome the cash-flow crisis through organic means (ramping up revenue) and cutting operational expenses would kill the momentum. We had to get outside bridge funding. The owners were already flirting with potential investors, but their valuation expectations were off the charts.

A most unusual thing now happened.

The management team got together and over a two-week period we worked day and night putting together a new investment prospect and pushing the owners to accept a more realistic valuation. Showing that we all believed in the business, we organised to chip in ourselves and created a company that would hold our shares. Dataco Employee Investment Ltd. became an important element in the plan and made several people millionaires when the company was sold four years later. Within thirty days we had the funding in place and could pay all outstanding bills.

It was my job to write the revenue generation portion of the prospect and I decided to develop a business partner model. The model described the process of recruitment, enablement and operation. We then estimated how much the reseller should invest, which type of staff he should assign to the project and what the revenue and cash-flow profile would look like. I then assessed how many partners we could sign up and how fast, given the resources we had available. It was a purely theoretical model, but the level of detail was sufficient to convince the investors.

I now refined what became the Partner P&L Model which turned out to be my most important tool when recruiting new business partners. After getting familiar with our products and the potential they represented, I could ask the potential partner how much money she was interested in making. With the model we could simulate back and forth depending on where the limitations and bottlenecks were. As we got more resellers up and running, the model was modified based on real life experience and became more trustworthy.

The model itself was actually not so important, but the discussions it facilitated were. It moved the perspective of the co-operation away from product nitty-gritty and the short-term investment requirements and added the long-term perspective. It also moved the discussion to the very top of the reseller's organisation. Issues that span more than one budget year typically require top management attention. Our mission changed from just providing great products and became an important part of the partners' overall business plan.

Timing is everything

Dataco was a huge success and grew from nothing to several hundred million DKK in annual revenue within just a few years. Looking back, I believe the success was a combination of five main elements:

1. Products for which there was an active and easily identifiable need in the market;

2. Excellent product marketing concentrating the effort on the segments with the best product/market fit;

3. A business partners program that had a good balance between product and business support;

4. Little requirement for localization;

5. Perfect timing.

1986 was the year when the DOS-based PC finally broke through and Ethernet became the de facto standard for local area networks. There was a substantial installed base of proprietary mainframes and minicomputers for which we provided a data communications infrastructure solution. We connected terminals and PCs across vendor brands and offered terminal protocol conversion. Our solution was application software agnostic and supported Novell Network, which was the most popular PC-network platform in those days. Our technology was essentially proprietary but used the ISO-OSI model.

The ideal customer profile was an organisation with mainframes and minicomputers and the point of contact was the CIO. Not all of these organisations had a need for terminal protocol conversion, but they all had a need for PC-networks. Many of these customers used IBM equipment and although IBM pushed their proprietary Token Ring products hard, the Ethernet had achieved sufficient market coverage and was considered the accepted industry standard. CIOs had no problem buying our products since they adhered to already accepted industry or official standards and were installed in numerous peer-organisations. We had also decided to follow a very aggressive pricing strategy which made us substantially less expensive than alternative solutions based on older technology. And, finally, we had invested in design which made the products pretty to look at, which was very unusual then.

The appearance of the compatible PC had taught all customers an important lesson: The power of standards and a free market. Before the PC, customers were locked into the vendors proprietary platform and had no other choice than to accept their pricing policies. Around 1986, the movement away from proprietary platforms and towards open systems had gained momentum and we surfed that wave. So strong was the wave that most of the mainframe and minicomputer manufacturers, by the beginning of the 1990s, had to close shop and IBM announced all-time record losses. Although our solution was proprietary, we were successful in positioning it as a standard system. Did we deceive our customers? The technical design followed the ISO-OSI specifications and we were carefully referring to this as a public standard. Customers accepted the claim probably because we were significantly less expensive than the alternatives, too.

Dataco products required little localisation to be used in foreign countries. The hardware required certification and the EC mark gave us access to all countries in the European Union. The user manual for the network management program, a fifty-page document, needed translation, but that was a small effort.

The way we designed and implemented the business partners program also contributed to the success. We had a clean go-to-market strategy and used the indirect approach in all our markets, including our domestic market. Being able to focus on and refine a single go-to-market strategy is a huge advantage for a small company.

Most of the partners understood the business potential and followed our product marketing, marketing and sales guidelines, which we taught at the mandatory training. The training took place at the partner's facilities since we wanted them to send as many of their people as possible through the curriculum and eliminating the need for travel and accommodation supported that. Although I believed that we had very professional documentation, the training always revealed that the participants didn't fully understand how the products should be positioned, who the ideal customers were and how to configure and price a solution. After completing the training, most misunderstandings had been eliminated and the marketing and sales strategy aligned. The last day, with an open agenda, was helpful in being specific on what exactly had to happen after we left the room.

Doing a monthly face-to-face status review may sound like overkill, but it worked wonders for Dataco. I always prepared the agenda and took the minutes with an emphasis on the who-what-when part. As we grew, I taught my regional managers to use the same approach and mostly they did.

The first global partner meeting was held in Copenhagen in the fall of 1987 and from then on it became an annual event. At these meetings the partners were treated like VIPs and little was spared to make them feel our appreciation of their effort.

Our commercial approach to market development was very successful, but I have learned from other situations that even the best sales and marketing programs cannot compensate for poor products and timing.

It was the combination of the five elements listed above that made Dataco a fast and solid success.

The timing of Dataco was perfect. Two years before had been too early and two years later would have been too late. 1986 was the right year for launching UniLan, which later was renamed ScaNet. By the beginning of the 1990s the market had changed completely and Dataco had to redesign their entire product range. The company was acquired by a British OEM customer that was acquired by another company that sold off the Dataco activity to Intel.

SOFT4 - FROM LITHUANIA TO THE REST OF THE WORLD

The need for a larger market

Although Lithuania is a small country with just 2.8 million inhabitants, Softera Baltic, a local Microsoft Dynamics NAV value added reseller (VAR) founded in 2008, were capable of building a very successful business in a very short time. Passing employee number fifty in 2012 the founders thought it was time for expanding the market for their NAV-based industry solutions. Realizing that running a service-driven national VAR activity would be very different from running an international ISV activity the subsidiary Soft4 was founded and Ugne Kontare was hired to head the business development activities.

"We had several NAV-based solutions for which we believed there would be a market in other countries," explains Ugne Kontare. "However, we didn't know where to start and on which solutions we should focus."

The go-to-market approach

That the go-to-market approach should be indirect through resellers was decided from the start. The experience working as a NAV-reseller for Microsoft could be used in Soft4, but where, how and for what to recruit resellers was still in the open. Most of the questions answered themselves as the English product websites were released and the solutions were presented at the international Microsoft partner events.

"We teamed up with our first reseller in Canada in 2013," says Ugne Kontare. "There was an opportunity for which Soft4Leasing, our asset finance management and lease accounting module, was a perfect match."

Using local and international Microsoft partner events and joining industry conferences Soft4 tested the market and gradually narrowed down the international product portfolio to four solutions:

- Soft4Lessee
- Soft4Leasing
- Soft4Factoring
- Soft4RealEstate

"It may sound as a big portfolio for a small IT company," admits Ugne Kontare, "but they are all extensions of Microsoft Dynamics 365 Business Central and they address issues related to financial and business management. Some companies need additional functionality – leasing companies also do factoring and some property management companies also make investments, and therefore need leasing functionality"

While Soft4 is chartered with business development, marketing, sales, product management and reseller recruitment and support, the product development is performed by Softera Baltic.

Internationalisation

Soft4 has resellers in Germany, Albania, Estonia, Latvia, France, the UK, Ireland, Benelux, Norway, Romania, Kenya, Canada, USA, Bahrain, UAE, Cambodia, Laos, Myanmar, Philippines, Singapore, Sri Lanka, Maldives, Thailand, Vietnam, Australia, Hong Kong and Indonesia. International revenue is on par with the Lithuanian Softera business.

"All our resellers are recruited based on customer opportunities," stresses Ugne Kontare. "We have learned that it takes three to four projects for a reseller to become familiar with the solution, the industry and the revenue generation process. There is no point in recruiting a reseller and then wait for something to happen. That only leads to disappointment on both sides."

Soft4 invests heavily in global organic and paid inbound lead generation activities and have staff in place to follow up, qualify and develop them into warm prospects. Soft4 does not engage in national marketing and lead generation activities competing with their resellers, but their international activities do generate leads directly. They also close the deals if possible before they hand them over to the resellers for implementation.

"The world has changed," Ugne Kontare explains. "More and more companies are prepared to reach out to and engage with a supplier

abroad. It all depends on the type of solution and the amount of consulting required for implementation and support."

It takes three to four years to build the platform

Ugne Kontare had expected international activities to generate revenue much faster, but she has learned that it takes time to build the marketing frameworks, the partner program, the support organisation and making the resellers comfortable with selling the products with own resources.

"We are capable of winning customers and resellers in most countries," Ugne Kontare says. "Now is the time to decide where and how to scale to market leadership."

So far Soft4 has been able to manage the business out of their office in Kaunas but realise that growing market shares beyond twenty per cent in a country requires a local presence and a wider reseller network. They can easily manage Europe from Kaunas, however Canada, USA and Australia, that are showing the largest potential, will require a different setup. Ugne Kontare knows that remote operations are expensive and difficult to manage. Growing from one or two per cent market share to twenty per cent is not impossible, but it's hard to predict what and how long it takes.

"I think we need deeper pocket before we make that move," Ugne Kontare concludes.

SOFTSCAN

SOFTSCAN was acquired by Symantec in 2009 and merged with Messagelabs.

The customer problem

Virus and other malware were becoming increasingly problematic during the second half of the 1990s, at the same time as email became the primary communication vehicle for businesses and consumers.

At the beginning of this century, most of the malware got distributed through email and the volume of unsolicited spam now accounted for more than ninety per cent of all emails received. Malware had become a severe issue, and the worldwide productivity cost of spam alone was in 2005 estimated to be $50 billion.

SoftScan was started in 2003 as a spin-off from Softcom Solutions (acquired by IT-Relations in 2017), a general IT-service provider, to address the problems with malware and spam. The solution was a managed service, where customers changed their mail exchanger record (MX record) to point at the SoftScan servers that then filtered the incoming email, scanned them for malware and spam and delivered the clean result to the user's mailbox. To address the issue with false positives, users were notified of dubious cases, and by whitelisting sender addresses, the precision would increase over time. Outgoing emails were also scanned and appended a verification stamp.

At the time when SoftScan started their service, most companies had installed virus and malware detectors, but only a few had a solution for managing spam. Where companies usually only used a single detector, SoftScan had implemented several, thereby increasing the probability of catching close to one hundred per cent of malware attacks. Internet service providers had started applying spam filters, but businesses were concerned that filters outside their control would catch too many false positives.

Going for the big deals

Assuming that big organisations (private and public) were hard hit and also very concerned about malware and spam, SoftScan started their revenue generation approach targeting the top enterprise segment of the market. Getting appointments for presenting the solution was not difficult. Still, the sales process always became highly competitive, dragged out, and the proposals often ended up being squeezed by the customer's purchase department. Although SoftScan's solution was conceptually simple to explain and understand, easy to test and was paid for on a monthly per-user subscription basis, large enterprises had complex procurement processes that any new supplier or purchase acquisition had to go through. Such procurement processes demanded to call for competitive bids, and although SoftScan was attractively priced, they always ended up having to do heavy discounting to close the deal.

Being a bootstrapped start-up, the enterprise market took too long to pick up, the sales effort was too high, and the margins too low.

Telesales

It was when the SoftScan founders were reconsidering the revenue generation approach that someone came up with the idea of selling exclusively over the phone. If that could be done, then it would be possible to address the much larger SMB-market where the deal size would be smaller, but the sales cycle shorter. The sales effort would be lower compared to the enterprise deals, and the resulting margins would, potentially, be more attractive.

Two small decisions may be easier to make

Back at the design table, someone came up with the idea of making the test free of charge and waiting to close the deal until there was enough user data, that is malware and spam, to demonstrate the value. Using this approach, the first threshold for customer acceptance would have no financial implications and the second threshold could take advantage of using the customer's data and not some standard demo of which you can always question the relevance. It required closing twice instead of once, but maybe breaking a big decision into two smaller ones could make a difference.

The sales process was defined as follows:

Step 1: Call, confirm and qualify

Step 2: Pitch the solution and convince the customer to accept the free test.

Step 3: Accumulate customer data, demo and close.

Step one involved getting the contact of and verifying that you were talking to the right person. If not, you should ask to be transferred and update the CRM system with the new information.

Step two involved asking SPIN questions to create a receptivity to change and then going through an ultra-short presentation of the solution. Ideally, you should then get the customer to accept the free test. Doing so would require that she would redirect her MX-record.

Step three happened two weeks after having changed the MX-record, where there would be sufficient user data to demonstrate the value of the solution. After the demo, the salesrep should get the customer to keep using the solution. Accepting the deal required no further technical action as the customer already had changed the MX-record. She would only have to take the subscription agreement, which was calculated on a per user per month basis with a discount for paying twelve months in advance.

To verify the assumption, SoftScan engaged a telemarketing company that was asked to run a pilot calling 500 companies. However, by the first day the approach proved to work. It was possible to identify and get through to the decision-maker, which always was the IT-manager or the person responsible for IT and it was possible to make them change their MX-records.

Testing the two-step approach turned out to be promising. The founder responsible for revenue generation now listened into the conversations that the salespeople had with the potential customers and made two fundamental observations:

1. By coaching the salespeople, all steps in the sales process could be further optimised.

2. There were considerable variations in productivity across the sales staff. Some were way more productive than others.

Notably, there were significant variations in the ability to close at step 3, and it was not always easy to pinpoint exactly what made those differences. It seemed as though the high performers managed to create a positive atmosphere and make the customers feel comfortable.

By performing ongoing coaching of the salespeople, the SoftScan founders were convinced they had found the key to a profitable and scalable revenue generation process. Scaling the effort would require many more salesreps, and instead of having this activity outsourced, they decided to build their own call centre.

To run the operation, they now hired a dedicated sales manager.

Crossing the border

Denmark is a small country, and with an internal call centre, SoftScan was capable of calling the entire potential customer base within six months. There was no problem at a later stage re-calling those that didn't respond or sign up the first time, but further growth would require a larger market.

As Copenhagen is located just across the Sound from Malmö in Sweden, SoftScan hired Swedish speaking salesreps, and soon the company was testing if the telesales approach would work in Sweden as well.

It did.

Then followed Norway. It worked there as well.

Then came the UK and later Germany.

Key challenges

By 2006 SoftScan was a company with 150 employees of which one hundred were engaged with telesales. The sales-machine was signing up three new customers every hour of the day. Apart from selling to new customers, a dedicated team now took care of retaining existing customers and upselling subscriptions. It turned out to be quite easy, making customers accept multiyear prepaid contracts, which improved the SoftScan cash position. The company, that was bootstrapped, had sufficient cash to fund further growth.

Running a company heavily dependent on outbound tele-sales was associated with some key challenges.

Employee retainment

Working with outbound telesales is a tough job. Your performance is evident and measurable, and the level of rejection is substantial. Although some of the salesreps were making very good money, many had a hard time.

SoftScan invested money, time and energy in recruitment, onboarding, ongoing training, coaching and knowledge sharing and still the average tenure for salesreps was only 12 months. Understanding the pressure salesreps were experiencing and the discipline it took to be productive, the company created a culture that supported the competitive and performance-oriented environment but also recognised the individual as a human being with needs for acceptance, recognition, security and social belonging. The culture formation was deliberate, formalised and acquired a name, SMILE. The description of the culture can be found at the end of this case story.

The value of increasing employee retainment (or reduce churn) was substantial. If an employee passed the three months anniversary date, it meant that they were productive and made a positive contribution to the company. Otherwise, they would have left or been dismissed. The years when SoftScan entered hyper-growth were characterised by full employment, and it was easy for people to find another job if they weren't satisfied with the one they had.

Recruitment

If you run an outbound call centre with 100 salesreps and the average tenure is 12 months, then you will have to fill 100 open positions each year or a little over eight positions each month. However, the average number is misleading. It covers a large number of people that only stay for a few months and then a smaller number that stay for over two years. In reality, SoftScan had to add ten to twenty new salesreps each month because they were growing and because they knew from experience that even with the best recruitment and onboarding processes one out of four new hires would not be fit for the job.

Adding ten to twenty new sales-reps each month required a massive recruitment effort, and SoftScan, therefore, had an internal team of two full-time staff to take care of the activity. They found that traditional job interviews were utterly useless for predicting sales performance, so instead, they organised two-days assessment centres, where potential candidates were briefed and then put on the phone to call on potential clients. SoftScan staff listened to the conversations and offered advice on what to improve. After the two days, some of the applicants realised that this was not a job for them. Among the remaining candidates, the SoftScan recruitment team choose those with the highest probability of success.

When asking people to spend two full days on a recruitment activity turned out to be an issue, SoftScan offered the attendees a monetary compensation. Paying for disqualifying candidates was less costly than having to let people go after investing in onboarding.

Sales management

Managing an outbound tele-sales activity requires a very high level of supervision and coaching.

Each salesrep had a monthly gross margin budget reflecting her seniority and the sales district to which she was assigned. The reps were free to deviate from the list prices, but they would then have to catch up with more volume to meet their gross margin target. Sales budgets and actual performance were displayed on large monitors on the walls in the salesrooms. Loud music played whenever a new customer signed up. Everyone could see how each salesrep was performing.

The teams met each morning to review the day's budgets and commit to new targets. Sales competitions were announced daily, and sometimes several times a day. The activities were tightly organised. The days started at 08:30 with briefings and target commitments. The hours 9 am to 12 pm were reserved for three times 45 minutes of concentrated calling. Then two times 45 minutes of calling again between 1 and 3 pm. Friday afternoon was reserved for training and knowledge sharing.

Several coaches were available to listen in on the conversations and suggest improvements. Tele-sales is a volume play. The general rule of thumb is that the more people you call the more you will sell. However, success is not a function only of quantity. When you get someone on the line, you must quickly decide if you should invest time in the conversation or say your goodbyes. Spending too much time with someone that just wants to talk but cannot or will not commit for the next step is a waste of your time.

In the SoftScan case, 25 per cent of those reached would listen to the pitch and seven per cent of those would agree to a free test.

The UK was different

All sales activities were run out of the call centre located in central Copenhagen. Each team had their rooms decorated with flags and artefacts identifying the country for which they were responsible.

The team calling into the UK market soon made two observations:

1. If you didn't have the name of the person you wanted to talk to, the operator would not put you through.

2. Many more companies, compared to the Nordics, had outsourced their IT-operations to a third party.

There were tricks to get around the first issue, but it hampered productivity. There was a need for buying lists with the name of the person responsible for IT. That was an additional cost, but not an issue that distorted the margin severely.

The second issue was more critical. Having to deal with a third party that then needed to recommend the solution to the customer was a deal-breaker. That would complicate the sales process unless you could get that third party to also sell the solution to her other clients. Using this approach, you would build a multiplication engine that would offset the more complicated sales process.

Because of these issues, the go-to-market approach in the UK became reseller based. The tele-sales activities out of Copenhagen continued, and whenever a direct sale was possible, it was closed. When an IT-service provider was in-between, she was signed up as a reseller. As the market share in the UK grew, all customers were passed on to the resellers. This turned out to make the recruitment of new resellers much easier.

Germany was very different

Some of the customers in the Nordics had subsidiaries in Germany, and some of those showed an interest in the solution. One of the Swedish speaking salesreps also spoke German and for the fun of it, she took care of those opportunities and closed some deals.

To grow the company even further in Germany with its millions of small companies seemed like an attractive opportunity. There was just one problem. The availability of native German-speaking salesreps was too low to operate the activity out of Copenhagen. If the German market was to be approached, it should be from an office in Germany.

Testing if the German customer behaved differently from the Nordic customer an external call centre in Munich conducted a pilot project. The outcome was not promising. However, SoftScan was convinced that nothing could be seriously verified unless you had a team of at least ten salespeople plus the facilities for coaching. Instead of running expensive tests for which external call centres didn't have the resources, they decided to jump directly into setting up a German activity. With the undisputed success in the Nordics and the UK under their belt, how difficult could it be to crack the German market?

Facilities were rented in Munich; the Danish sales manager was relocated to head the operation, and a recruitment campaign initiated.

After a year the German operation was closed. A few of the employees were given the option of working from home.

Analysing the failure in Germany, the following conclusions were made:

Recruitment

The recruitment strategy used in Denmark was replicated in Germany and gave different results.

Recruiting salespeople in Denmark, SoftScan had noticed that education and experience from previous jobs, including sales jobs, didn't offer any indication of aptitude. Because of the culture, age did seem to play a role. The average age in the sales team was in the early twenties, and the culture, including the social activities, was particularly attractive to a younger audience. The qualification thresholds for making it to a recruitment event were low. Your behaviour and performance during the two-day assessment centre were the critical selection criteria. You didn't need to be a pro from the start, and only a few were, but you needed to demonstrate that you were not afraid of making cold calls and that you were coachable.

Applying this approach in Germany resulted in hiring too many people who had faked the recruitment test. They were not up to making sixty calls a day, and they were difficult to coach and to develop.

Dismissing people in Germany is more complicated and more expensive than in Denmark; thus, the combination of these two factors increased operational expenses and absorbed management attention.

Delegation

It turned out that IT-managers in the SMB-segment in Germany had less delegation rights than in the Nordic countries. They needed to get approval for using a new tool from the owner or managing director. The sales process in Germany thus had more steps, required more calls and had lower conversion rates.

Management support and coaching

Opening a subsidiary in a foreign country requires substantial management support and attention from headquarters. Irrespective of the seniority of the local country manager, there will initially be many surprises and unexpected differences that require analysis and discussions to overcome. It's unrealistic to anticipate that the country manager can fix everything on her own.

The German subsidiary was SoftScan's first, and they underestimated the management support required. Unfortunately, about ten months into the German project, SoftScan was hit by the 2008 recession and experienced a drop in demand from the other markets, which consumed cash and management attention. With the German project being behind schedule, SoftScan management decided to reduce the risk and pull out.

The SMILE philosophy

Running a business model that relies on cold calling potential customers requires a particular culture, where people can thrive and grow despite the substantial amount of rejection that they experience daily.

SoftScan was very conscious of the cultural environment and what it should be. They even gave it a name: SMILE.

Below you'll find a description in their own words of what it was.

Only one critical resource

SoftScan is a company with only one critical resource: People.

To win the market, we need to offer attractive products and services at competitive prices continuously. Our ability to sustain our business ambitions and to continue the growth rates that we have experienced so far depend entirely on the quality of our people, their skills, experience, enthusiasm, commitment and cooperative capacity.

We hire people from the same sources as all other enterprises, but we select our staff using different criteria, and we make them grow using our unique corporate culture: SMILE.

The SMILE concept is not just a company culture - it is the SoftScan philosophy. People working at SoftScan are called Smileys in recognition of the SMILE culture that resides within our people and forms their attitude and behaviour.

SMILE is the core foundation on which SoftScan is built. It is integrated into the way we operate, manage and live every single day. Without SMILE there wouldn't be a SoftScan as it is today. SoftScan is a highly successful, playful, and crazy company turning brain capacity into products and services that customers rush to use. We sign up three new customers up every single hour of the day, and this number is steadily increasing, proving the attractiveness of our services and support and the effectiveness of our sales approach. SMILE makes the difference. It releases ideas and energy at a level yet unseen, which transforms into deliverables that our customers can use to their advantage.

The SMILE culture was defined during the first year of operation. We looked at the way we did business, the way we dealt with our clients, the way we treated each other and the energy and pulse which we knew was critical to sustain long-lasting results and growth in our company.

We realise that SMILE culture is not for everyone. We will do things that some people find awkward, irrelevant or worthless such as morning songs, birthday songs for all team members, Crazy Thursdays where Smileys dress up following a specific theme. We make room for a very high degree of individualism, yet exercise teamwork across the board. The average age at SoftScan is 27, and the culture is reflecting this. But the oldest Smiley is over 60, so the culture is capable of spanning all ages.

The components of the SMILE culture are:

- Social interaction - contribute to a vibrant and diverse community.

- Make a difference - every day. It requires the highest effort to sustain being the best in a fast-changing business and technology environment.

- Integrity - do what you say. We insist on honesty and fairness.

- Listen - consider the needs of customers, team members and other stakeholders alike.

- Exchange knowledge - help each other grow.

Social interaction

A Smiley cares about her colleagues and chooses to spend time with the team or other Smileys both on and off the job.

A Smiley participates in social activities such as the SoftScan's Friday bar or singing a song before the sales activity starts. A Smiley highly appreciates the emphasis that SoftScan places on the social aspects of work.

To illustrate how serious we take the social part of SMILE, we have made it mandatory to be part of at least one social activity per month, even if it means investing two hours of your free time.

In return, SoftScan will encourage and sponsor the organisation of private or semi-private activities such as team dinners, sports activities, charity or a team-building weekend.

Make a difference

At SoftScan, the phrase "making a difference" covers two specific areas:

1. Deliberately do something different instead of what you would typically do in a given situation. See if the new approach serves you and other stakeholders in a better way, thus adding value to the business. We do believe that failure and learning is a critical path to new knowledge and cognition. Therefore, we want people

to combine skills, experience, intuition and courage and suppress the fear of making mistakes when trying something new.

2. Make a difference towards somebody else, such as surprising a client with fantastic service or attention or going out of your way to help co-workers or management breaking the "good enough" pattern positively and constructively.

Making a difference would be picking up that piece of paper lying on the floor, giving a helping hand with cleaning up after a meeting or taking a new Smiley by the hand to give him or her a good start.

Making a difference is doing the unexpected.

- Jogging with your team leader or manager in the morning,

- Singing a song to celebrate a success,

- Showing your parents around the offices,

- Inviting your customer to a business meeting on a crazy Thursday, where you are dressed up like a circus clown,

- Serving refreshments for your fellow Smileys during our SoftScan Academy meetings Friday at 15:00 (a beer, a glass of wine, a soft drink or hot chocolate).

- Invite a reseller for a glass of wine, a cold beer or fresh fruit juice in our SoftScan Bar

- and so, the list goes on

Most important for us is delivering superior service at any point where we interact with our customers, whether its sales, support or finance. Service is a prime competitive parameter for SoftScan.

Integrity

Integrity is the nucleus in all lasting and durable relationships. Integrity never expires.

It is the foundation for being straight and fair with customers, suppliers, management and another Smileys.

We want to exercise high business ethics in all our customer relationships. We do not tolerate overselling, which means creating expectations that we cannot meet.

We are treating our suppliers as if they are Smileys, and expect the same in return.

SMILE requires that all Smileys treat customers, suppliers and each other with respect, and we operate with a zero-gossip tolerance threshold.

Anyone with an issue with a colleague will use the following approach. Go directly to the person with whom you have the problem and try to solve it yourself first. If that doesn't work, go to your team leader or another department's team leader.

We also make sure that employees understand the importance of aligning with our strategies and business objectives.

We operate a flat organisation where Smileys are part of many decisions. However, we are a business and your team, and management may make decisions with which you do not agree. We expect Smileys to apply a holistic view of their job and carry out all decisions with a SMILE.

The formal SoftScan policies & procedures apply to everyone, irrespective of their organisational position. If a junior SMILEY must fly at the lowest possible airfare, the same policy applies to the CEO.

Listen

Listening comes down to 2 major issues:

- Listen to the clients. You are serving them and need to understand their needs and concerns.

- Listen to the voice of your team. Participate actively and play an integrated role in finding solutions that can gain support.

A Smiley must be team fit. We love performers, but we adore Smileys that can empower other Smileys.

The priority of the SoftScan stakeholders is:

1.   Client

2.   SoftScan

3.   Team

4.   Individual

Exchange knowledge

Smileys must continuously learn from customers, suppliers and each other. Smileys must be capable of giving and taking.

Irrespective of whether you are a senior Smiley or a junior Smiley, you must maintain your ability to teach and to learn.

We have created an Exchange Knowledge Friday Academy where we spend time learning from each other while having fun in the process.

Final remarks

SMILE has some fundamental parameters that will never change. However, the implementation of SMILE is constantly evolving and shaped by the Smileys who live and breathe the culture every hour.

Make no mistake of the objectives: We are a business. We have strong ambitions for growth and profitability. SMILE is the framework that can attract, keep and grow the people that we need to make us the better choice for our customers.

SOLVOYO – SUPPLY CHAIN OPTIMISATION

The customer problem

Have you ever wondered how the supermarket can always have all the goods on your shopping list? Well, maybe not always, but then at least almost always. A supermarket has around 50,000 SKUs of which some are bought by many customers every day and others only by some, sometimes. While clothing may carry a ten per cent profit margin, gourmet foodstuffs deliver around five and non-food items much less. Having what you need while keeping costs down is the holy grail of the FMCG industries. So how can the retailers, the wholesalers, the manufacturers and all the other players in the FMCG supply chains keep their costs down and still make sure to stock what you need when you need it? That's the domain of supply chain planning.

The rapid growth of the Internet and consumers' gradual acceptance of e-commerce has increased the complexity of the supply chain issues for all FMCG companies. Not least, Amazon's aggressive global expansion has changed the playing field.

How to produce what when, how much to store where and how to deliver it to the next link in the chain to finally match the demand in the retail end, is what supply chain management is all about.

The Solvoyo value proposition

Matching demand and supply correctly requires a simulation model that incorporates all elements of the supply chain, considers seasonal variations, adjusts for trends and promotional marketing activities as well using situational data from the POS-systems at the end of the line. The outcome should be a plan detailing what to produce when, where to stock it and how to deliver it.

"The primary challenge for most companies is the lack of a single and coherent planning model," explains Nilüfer Durak, COO with Solvoyo. "Having separate planning and optimisation tools for each functional area of the supply chain is still very common across the FMCG industries."

Solvoyo, a supply chain planning and analytics software company headquartered in Boston, MA, USA with R&D facilities in Istanbul, Turkey, has specialised in cross-functional planning solutions delivered in a cloud-based SaaS format.

"Supply chain planning is a computational challenge," says Nilüfer Durak. "The more interdependencies you can include, the more data you can process and the faster it runs, the better results you get."

Solvoyo's supply chain software uses advanced technologies such as big-data analytic tools that employ sophisticated algorithms and machine learning to aggregate and dissect data. The value proposition is making smarter and faster supply chain decisions by using the latest information technology to tightly couple planning and optimisation with execution management systems. Solvoyo claims to offer speedier implementation and a quicker and higher return on investment than any competitive solutions.

"Our software produces insights to empower supply chain managers to make better supply chain decisions," claims Nilüfer Durak. "We typically reduce inventory with up to 25 per cent and transportation cost with up to thirty per cent, increase on-time fulfilment & availability with up to sixty per cent resulting in an overall EBITDA improvement in the range of one to five per cent."

Getting these results requires that the customer is prepared to reorganise the way she performs supply chain planning and that has turned out to be the biggest hurdle. With an average implementation time from initial data collection to go-live of less than 90 days and a payback period average of less than 3 months, with not a single case over 6 months, such a decision should be appealing for C-level executives.

The delivery format is cloud-based software-as-a-service subscriptions with onboarding services (integration and implementation) charged on a time and material basis. Onboarding amounts to approximately sixty per cent of the first-year subscription fee. The AACR is $240,000 and the average sales cycle that used to be 18 months has fallen to nine months.

The early mover dilemma

Solvoyo started in 2005 as a supply chain consulting company and released the first version of its software product, Elevation, in 2011. The approach of optimising across multiple organisational silos was new to the industry, and the large enterprise-type of customers that they pitched to were reluctant to engage. However, after the early innovators at Home Depot and Schneider decided to use the software, venture capitalists approached Solvoyo, and the first round of funding aimed at scaling the company was completed in 2014.

Assuming that the market had now matured, Solvoyo engaged a team of experienced industry software sales executives to build and manage the revenue generation process. This model didn't work. The experience with selling high-priced supply chain software projects with prepaid perpetual licenses and substantial implementation projects was not a good match for a value proposition which has a lean implementation approach and smaller, but recurring monthly subscription fees.

Salespeople with SaaS experience now replaced the industry sales executives, but this approach didn't work either. Customers preferred to have conversations with representatives that mastered the domain jargon, quickly understood their challenges and could engage in solution-oriented dialogue.

It was not easy to pinpoint precisely why the two revenue generation approaches didn't work. Lack of market maturity may have played a role. Nevertheless, the company could not afford to experiment forever, and in 2016 it decided to switch to an inbound approach without a dedicated team for new revenue generation.

In the meantime, the market did mature, and the Solvoyo name became recognised in the market. More and more potential customers identified the need for new ways to optimise their supply chains and realised that the innovative rush might not come from the incumbents. They invited Solvoyo to Shark Tank type beauty contests, which lead to smaller pilot projects followed by large-scale rollouts. Winning a supply chain management project with one of the largest global CPG companies was the result of such a customer initiative.

Internationalisation

The go-to-market approach is now predominantly direct, relying on inbound lead generation and using the customer success team for sales development and sales.

"In an effort to sign up the Microsoft Dynamics AX channel we shifted to Azure", says Nilüfer Durak. "Theoretically Elevation and AX should be the perfect match, but in practice it didn't work. Selling SaaS solutions combined with short and lean implementation projects through the classic ERP channel seems to be a difficult task."

Solvoyo is open to developing partnerships and believe they have an attractive partner value proposition, but they do not plan to invest in outbound recruitment activities for the time being.

Fifty per cent of Solvoyos revenue is generated in North America, while fifty per cent is generated elsewhere, primarily in Turkey, which the company consider as their test market.

"The market for cross-sectional supply chain optimisation using sophisticated information technology is finally taking off," says Nilüfer Durak, "Interest is growing from the upper layers of the SMB market, too. We have an increasing stream of inbound leads that keep us busy. We will continue with this approach."

Solvoyo has made substantial investments in a very informative website and a large portfolio of content marketing assets. Hubspot has been implemented to support lead capture, nurture and qualification.

"Inbound lead generation has several advantages," Nilüfer Durak concludes. "Leads are much better qualified, and they are closer to making a decision. We basically don't need traditional salespeople to close the deals, which makes the model easier to scale."

TEMPLAFY

The customer problem

As organisations grow, they all face the same challenge; document anarchy. Employees use their own templates, illustrations and text snippets when communicating internally or externally, or they spend time looking for the most recent standards from the marketing and legal departments. The result is a confused corporate image, inconsistent communication, infringements and a massive waste of time.

The Templafy value proposition

Templafy offers a cloud-based solution where communications and compliance teams can control, change and update the templates, text snippets and images that should be used in corporate documents and emails. The solution can even make retro-updates to documents that have already been filed. This means that your PowerPoint, Word, email and other templates and documents are automatically updated to comply with corporate ID and legal guidelines.

Market segmentation

"All organisations are exposed to the document anarchy challenge," says Jesper Theill Eriksen, CEO of Templafy. "However, not all organisations consider it a serious issue that needs rectifying now."

Templafy has learned that organisations, where the document is the product and compliance is crucial, are actively looking for solutions to help their employees. So too are the major consumer brands where communication consistency has top priority. Across all industries, it seems that organisations with more than 2,000 employees are most receptive to the need to bring order to their document anarchy.

"After nailing the ideal customer profile, we had to make some changes to our product," explains Jesper Theill Eriksen. "Serving enterprise customers requires an enterprise-grade product, meeting demands for easy roll-out, configuration of user rights, large scale performance, and stability."

Today, Templafy has the certificates and accreditation required by large enterprises, but equally important, they have the lighthouse customers proving that the solution works and they have been accepted by this demanding customer segment.

The revenue generation process

Originally starting with an inbound approach, around 50 per cent of new leads are still the result of on-line marketing efforts.

"Our growth ambitions are better served by adding outbound lead generation activities to the revenue generation toolbox," Jesper Theill Eriksen continues. "Marketing, sales development, sales and customer success now make up more than 50 per cent of our staff and this area will continue to see considerable growth as we expand our footprint in the major markets."

For the outbound lead generation teams, Templafy maintains very restrictive definitions of what an ideal lead looks like and invests in individual research to identify a compelling purchase event and the right contact point. Lead reviews are performed regularly to ensure that sales resources are used effectively, and conversion rates remain healthy along the entire sales pipeline.

"We have proved that our business model works, that we have an attractive value proposition and that we can win key accounts in foreign markets," stresses Jesper Theill Eriksen. "We have crossed the famous chasm. Our current job is scaling the business model in all the major markets and in this respect revenue generation efficiency has the highest priority."

Average sales cycles are six months, the annual contract value starts at $50,000, the average pre-paid period is 18 months, customer churn is close to zero and expected average customer lifetime is six years.

Go-to-market Approach

"Our go-to-market approach is direct," says Jesper Theill Eriksen, "but we work with partners who can provide the services customers need around the product."

Implementing a Templafy solution is often associated with a review of template and content standards, including an optimisation of the document and compliance procedures and integration to other IT-systems. Some professional services, that often have the same contract value as the software, are left to implementation partners. Currently, Templafy has 40 implementation partners and are actively recruiting more to keep pace with sales.

"Implementation partners are like strategic alliances," Jesper Theill Eriksen emphasises. "They play an important role in our customer success strategy, but they also help with lead generation."

Internationalisation

Templafy had international ambitions from the very start. One way to support these aspirations was to recruit staff with very diverse backgrounds.

"We have 21 nationalities represented in our organisation," Jesper Theill Eriksen tells. "We believe that diversity has a value in itself, but mastering the main languages has enabled us to win customers all over the world."

Templafy has proven so attractive that customers in the early innovators' category have been prepared to engage despite the company not having a local office to provide pre- and post-sales support.

"Even enterprise customers have come to appreciate conference calls, webinars and remote help-desks," says Jesper Theill Eriksen with a smile. "Delivering a solution as a cloud-based service reduces the technical complexity considerably, but since the financial crisis, all enterprises have been through a diet where they have come to appreciate their own cost savings offered by virtual engagements. It's not that we refuse to show up in person, but mainly it is neither needed nor required."

Scaling the business in a specific country requires a local presence and that the software U/I is available in the local language. Serving the DACH region, Templafy acquired a company in Germany (Berlin) and is now using this company as the platform for serving the German-speaking markets.

In the USA, that is estimated to represent 66 per cent of Templafy's global market, a subsidiary has been established. Six people from the Danish office have been relocated and a Dane, that used to work for Dropbox in the US, has been put in charge of sales. Jesper Theill Eriksen has relocated to New York for twelve months to help get the business going and learn what changes must be made to win the US market.

To simplify the operation, Templafy has decided to perform all inbound marketing and promotion activities only in English.

"We have a huge market in front of us," says Jesper Theill Eriksen. "For productivity reasons, we have decided to perform all inbound marketing activities in English only. For the type of customers that we target this represents more than 75 per cent of the global potential anyway and should be adequate for the next couple of years."

The decision to only market in English doesn't affect the availability of the software in local languages. Outbound revenue generation activities are also performed in local languages.

Priorities for success

Jesper Theill Eriksen is convinced that Templafy's ability to become and remain the global market leader in their category entirely depends on their ability to keep the focus and hold on to their priorities.

These priorities are:

> 1. Maintain focus on the selected market segments (become the undisputed leader in one segment before spreading out to more segments)

> 2. Stick to their proven lead generation principles and stay clear of all the hyped conferences and exhibitions offered to the enterprise segment

3. Structure and refine the revenue generation process by performing rigorous pre-qualification and follow a common sales process across the company

4. Insist on performing the majority of customers engagements virtually

5. Introduce the systems and processes required to manage the increasing volume of business, the growing number of people and the representation across many time zones, cultures and languages.

TIA TECHNOLOGY – AN INDUSTRY IN DISRUPTION AND GROWTH

The customer problem

I bought a new Volvo a while ago and was surprised when my insurance company, Topdanmark, declined to take it on. "It needs to be retrofitted with a GPS tracker," they said. However, the dealer had confirmed that the car came with such a device factory fitted. We even tested it on delivery. By pressing a button in front of the rear-view mirror, the car called the alarm centre, who immediately knew where I was, how much diesel I had in the tank and some other information about the car's condition. If an airbag got activated, the car would even auto-call the alarm centre and post its position. I could read the same information in the Volvo app on my iPhone, from where I could also start the cabin heater, open and lock the car, blink the lights, honk the horn and get an overview of all my trips.

The Volvo dealer took action, and a few minutes later a representative of the insurance company IF called. Before the end of that day, the car was fully insured, and before the end of the week, all my other insurance policies had got a new home with IF, including my business stuff.

When I sit across from Anders S. Rosenbeck from Tia Technology in his office in Virum north of Copenhagen, I understand that my experience is not representative of the situation in the Danish insurance industry. In spite of the country's tiny, size and its linguistic peculiarity, insurance companies in Denmark and other Nordic countries are fairly advanced, both when it comes to digitising internal processes, offering new products and modernising the relationship with their customers. For Tia, a company that exclusively develops IT solutions for insurance companies, Denmark, despite its modest size, is a technologically advanced domestic market, and an excellent platform for international activities.

An Insurance Company Is an Information Processing Factory

Insurance is at its core about safeguarding assets and lives by sharing risks mutually while processing the information related to it. The insurance industry was among the first to invest in computers and software. By the 1970s and early 1980s, insurance companies had purchased large mainframe computers from IBM, and each of them developed proprietary systems, believing that internal process optimisation would become the prime competitive parameter. These were monster investments tied to IBM's proprietary technologies, leaving insurance companies unable to take advantage of the development and decline in price of the minicomputer and especially the PCs in the 1980s and 1990s. Quite a few insurance companies continue to depend on their home developed and still often mainframe-based core systems, which are both expensive to maintain and hard to adjust when introducing new products. It makes them vulnerable when customers become less loyal, and to insurgents without legacy liabilities when they begin fast-paced innovation.

When Customers Change Behaviour and Technology Makes New Business Models Possible (and vice versa)

The days where customers were loyal, reliable and predictable and could all be treated the same are long gone. The challenge is that no one knows exactly in what direction behavioural changes are going. Simultaneously, how will the industry be affected by the opportunities that technology offers?

Insurance can be sold at multiple consumer touch points – including at sports events. When a sizeable German football club offers its many hundreds of thousands of fan club members an insurance product at a favourable price, it becomes a success because the club already has a positive relationship with its members. The club subcontracts with the insurance companies, who then have to offer wholesale prices and let go of the customer relationship. It is not just sports clubs that have discovered the merchandise potential that members' loyalty allows. Insurance is a service that may be hard to produce; however, it is quite easy to distribute when you already enjoy the customer's loyalty. Today, we can buy insurance from the airline, the bank, the car dealer, the auto club, the Apple Store and our trade organisation. Will we be able to buy from Amazon, Facebook or Google in the future?

The cross-selling opportunities also go the other way, and many insurance companies now offer products and services that prevent or reduce the consequences of an insurance event. That's great for the customer but certainly also for claims ratios making it easier for insurance companies to offer competitive prices. Road assistance, burglar and smoke alarms, moisture meters and child seats for the car are obvious examples, but also newspaper subscriptions have been seen offered.

The American insurance company Lemonade has introduced an entirely new insurance model, where it takes 90 seconds to become a customer, and most of the claims are paid in cash 3 minutes after they are filed. Lemonade is the insurance industry's Apple. Gone are the dark suits, white shirts and silk ties. Lemonade wears jeans and T-shirts – just like their customers.

Will future generations own less and rent more? Will they share more? Now that my car can report my driving behaviour, why can't my insurance company offer me a customised product? Why do I have to tell my insurance company how much I drive when my car automatically reports it? Why doesn't my insurance company ask for access to my home security system? My house can tell if it is locked or not and if I am home or away when flooding can be expected. My smart watch can tell where I am, where I am going and how I am doing. Which insurance products make sense when I travel, buy a new lawnmower, get married, get divorced, have children, have grandchildren, start a company, etc? Through our mobile devices and social media activity, many crucial events can be predicted before they happen, and new relevant insurance products can be offered. It will happen, but who is going to deliver is not yet fully clear.

All Insurance-innovation Requires Information Technology

Many insurance companies have realised that the world is changing and have acknowledged that innovation is an ongoing core activity that has two main outcomes:

A. Improvements to the existing business model that can be incorporated in the current structure with reasonable organisational and IT system adjustments.

B. Innovation that is best handled in a green field set up.

The challenge with A is that it requires a flexible IT platform that can be adapted quickly and cost-effectively to support the changes.

The challenge with B is that you are often mistaken. Rapid testing of the ideas in a small-scale format without massive IT investments is a requirement.

A Change in the Go-to-market Model

In this market in change, we find Danish Tia Technology, which specialises in developing software for the modern insurance company, where the optimisation of internal processes, improved customer relationships and agility weighs equally high. Until a few years ago, Tia was a pure software house that left the implementation of the software to consulting companies, so-called implementation partners. It was the classic go-to-market solution in the software industry and the textbook design for fast global scaling. That model worked well for Tia since 1997 when the company was started and have let to the usage of Tia's software in more than 25 countries around the world.

"The indirect model works fine when there are many small projects in which new partners can practice implementation before they embark on the large projects," says Anders S. Rosenbeck, CEO of Tia Technology. "Today our market is different, as we mainly do large projects. There are not enough such projects in even the big countries to feed a partner channel, and then we become too dependent on the individual partner. Projects in our industry are too few, too big and too critical so we can't leave the responsibility for success to implementation partners only. Our customer projects are typically 25% software, 50% implementation and 25% organisational change. We have to take charge and our customers expect us to have some skin in the game too. Therefore, we decided to take

direct control of implementation projects in our core markets and making sure we are involved in every major Tia projects globally. "

The shift from the indirect to the direct go-to-market approach has paid off and can be read in the company's annual reports. The implementation partners, which have approximately 1,000 Tia consultants, are still important, but their involvement now depends on the market in which the projects are located and the cases where the customer demand having an external system integrator involved.

The Global Strategy

During the Fall of 2019, the Anders S. Rosenbeck led an update of Tia's strategy, defining the guiding north star for the company in the coming years. The leadership also implemented a new organisational structure, which supports the ambitions and goals set out in the strategy.

The strategy is focused on designing and developing best-in-class, standard software for insurers and delivering Tia's professional services to safeguard quality and best practices to the benefit of Tia's customer base. The company will continue to drive digitalisation and work to make Tia Cloud the preferred delivery method for the software solutions. Finally, Tia will continue to focus on developing as a workplace and community where people thrive.

Tia Technology is one of a handful of global players.

"Tia was originally implemented in the UK and then spread into Denmark and Norway in the late 90'ies so we have had an international outlook from the start," emphasises Anders S. Rosenbeck. "Last year, we generated 74% of our turnover outside of Denmark, but we cannot be everywhere and bid on all projects in the world, so we are considering carefully where to focus our resources when prioritising opportunities."

In order to concentrate the effort, Tia Technology has divided the global market into four categories:

Core markets

Category One includes the Nordic countries, the Baltic countries, Poland and South Africa. In these countries, Tia has a solid position with many customers and their own strong representation. They have invested massively in localisation, i.e. integrations to all relevant platforms and systems necessary to run insurance business in these markets, which, in countries with a well-developed administrative infrastructure, can be quite demanding. As such, customer project risk is minimised and therefore the choice of using Tia becomes easy.

Mature markets

Markets where Tia has years of experience and more than one live installation is defined a near-core market. This category includes the UK and Ireland, the Netherlands and Germany. In these markets Tia also own part of the country specific components for localisation facilitating the discussions with potential new customers.

Follow-the-footsteps markets

Opportunities elsewhere in the world are pursued on an opportunistic basis primarily by "following the footsteps" of existing customers. It is well known that selling to people who know you is less expensive than building reputation and trust from scratch. The markets in focus here are in South America, where Tia is already in Brazil, Columbia and Ecuador with a major European based insurer, and in Africa based on expansion out of South Africa. In such markets Tia will always go with an implementation partner, never alone.

No-Go markets

The USA and Asia, which are the world's largest insurance markets, have been designated as no-go territories.

"We might come to them at some point through established relationships, but it's not right now," explains Anders S. Rosenbeck. "We are running at our full capacity in the markets where we are active, and the complexity of those two markets would be a major distraction. We do receive inquiries regularly but politely decline them."

Besides the market dimension Tia uses profiling when prioritizing opportunities to go for or decline. Together with an international management consultancy, Tia has carefully analysed and profiled the "sweet-spot" insurers that are most likely to choose Tia compared to competition. Elements used in the profiling include size of company, lines of business, technology preferences among other things.

TIMEXTENDER

Customer Problem

Business reporting, analytics and intelligence require data that are often not readily available. Data are stored in disparate systems and in incompatible formats. There is a demand for a data extraction, reformatting and consolidation tool that can feed the business reporting, analytics and intelligence applications, providing executives with the insight they need to lead and grow their companies.

The Value Proposition

TimeXtender develops the Discovery Hub® metadata engine platform that can extract, hold and feed data for analytics and presentations tools such as Tableau, Qlik and Microsoft Excel or Power BI. Discovery Hub® is an integrated data management platform, simplifying and automating the implementation and operation of the corporate data infrastructure. It replaces the need for bespoke development, stitching numerous tools together, reducing the time and effort required for mining, holding and managing data for business analytics in complex IT-environments.

The bottom line of the value proposition is reduced consumption of IT-manpower, fewer IT-tools and associated licenses fees and easier and faster access to information.

Market Segments

The need for timely business reporting, analytics and intelligence is universal and compelling in all types of organisations irrespective of industry, location, size and purpose. A data extraction and management platform like Discovery Hub® is mainly relevant for larger organisations and TimeXtender has defined their market as organisations with more than 250 employees that already use reporting, analytics and intelligence tools such as Tableau, Qlik and Microsoft Excel or Power BI.

Channels

From its incubation in 2006 and until 2015, TimeXtender was primarily a data mining consulting company. With the decision to embed their know-how in a software product they also decided to change from a direct to an indirect go-to-market approach. Instead of entertaining a hybrid approach, which most companies do during such a change, they went straight for a business model exclusively based on Value Added Resellers. The decision was supported by the global presence of an almost captive channel of Tableau, Qlik and Microsoft Power BI resellers.

Working with the indirect channel approach for some years now, TimeXtender has concluded that their key resellers are those who consider Discovery Hub® their core product. The value-add opportunity on top of and around the platform is considerable and enables the partners to build and grow a profitable consulting business. As with many modern IT-platforms, the professional services components around Discovery Hub® are shifting from high-coding to low-coding effort and business consulting. Resellers that understand and embrace this change can enjoy better margins and improved customer loyalty. There is hardly any churn among Discovery Hub® customers.

Key Partnerships

Discovery Hub® is based exclusively on Microsoft technology and the cloud-based SaaS version is using the Azure platform. The close alignment with the world's biggest software company is a key element in TimeXtender's global growth strategy and they enjoy dedicated support from Microsoft in all major markets.

Internationalization

Discovery Hub® is a global product with hardly any need for localisation. The Founder and CEO, Heine Krog Iversen, therefore, has an ambition of making TimeXtender the global market leader in his segment. A key milestone on this journey is reaching the $1 billion revenue mark before 2030. The billion-dollar objective has been broken down into annual milestones defining how many new resellers and customers are required. The plans for meeting these milestones are made and adjusted on a regular basis.

The ambition of global leadership is executed by building a presence in the major markets. TimeXtender employs their own business development resources when opening a new market and adds additional business functions as the business grows. Building and growing the channel in any country is undertaken by local staff who also take care of localising the global marketing programs. The local business development managers have been intimately involved in defining the elements of the global partner program and have been instrumental in monitoring and adjusting the strategy when results deviate from expectations.

Values and culture

TimeXtender is a value-based and purpose-driven company. Heine Krog Iversen's wife, Anne Krog Iversen, is the Chief DNA & Culture Officer responsible for building and maintaining the company's culture and for ensuring that people hired understand, match and support it.

The culture and DNA are based on 5 corner-stones; A Core Purpose, a set of Core Beliefs and 3 additional corner-stones that are a means to fulfil a shared and individual purpose; Mindfulness at work, Moments of silence and 7 Habits of Highly Effective People. This acts as a shared language for the way the X-People, as they call themselves, work together as "one global team". All meetings and speaking slots internally and externally start with a moment of silence to ground, focus and connect among the attendees and concentrate on the task at hand. Mindfulness training is a voluntary tool offered to all employees. The mindfulness training comprises knowledge and techniques to balance the individual in a busy work environment and enhance trust, innovation and creativity.

TRUSTPILOT – THE OPEN PLATFORM FOR MANAGING CUSTOMER REVIEWS

The market opportunity

E-commerce is driven by customer reviews. The average consumer and business customer will prefer a product that has many reviews over a product that has a few or none at all. She will also prefer to do business with companies that show and are transparent with customer reviews, both positive and negative. And while we all appreciate other's reviews, we are reluctant to submit any ourselves. It is only a tiny fraction of customers that submit reviews and left to its' own destiny, unsolicited reviews could paint a biased and mainly negative picture of any business.

E-commerce businesses need a platform for handling customer reviews. Motivating customers to submit a review, follow up, interact and manage genuine problems are crucial, but by no means trivial tasks. In addition, there is the work associated with angry, fake and unreasonable reviews.

Having a generic 3rd party platform that consumers and business customers trust seems to be a much better option than each company making a proprietary solution, with different user interfaces, different policies and no external validation and compliance oversight.

This need for an independent platform used by both buyers and sellers is filled by Trustpilot.

The consumer (or business customer) side of Trustpilot is free and can be used by anyone to review anything, though all reviews must comply with Trustpilot's guidelines. The business side has a free version that covers up to 100 invitations per month along with other features like responding to reviews, reporting reviews and access to basic review statistics. When you need more invitations or can benefit from integrating customer reviews into your revenue generation flow and want to customise the user experience, then you can upgrade to Lite, Pro and Enterprise which are paid plans.

The revenue generation process

From the early days, Trustpilot followed an outbound lead generation approach which has remained the main source for acquiring new customers. About two-thirds of all new customers are generated by the now 270 people employed in Sales across Trustpilot's global offices. One third is generated through inbound marketing activities managed by a staff of about 50 people. Another 100 people are taking care of customer success.

Communication with potential and current customers is predominantly carried out on the phone and through electronic communication means such as webinars and web meetings. Sales cycles are 90 days on average, with substantial deviations ranging from one day to several years.

"For smaller companies deciding on Trustpilot is a simple and fast process that may just require a short conversation on the phone," says Peter Mühlmann, founder and CEO of Trustpilot. *"For larger companies, the process involves more people and takes more time, often involving a pilot project."*

To speed up market penetration early on, Trustpilot engaged external call centres, only to learn that this approach didn't work. Making an outbound call centre approach work requires attention to even the most subtle minutiae of how the individual call is made, which questions are used to understand the potential customer's issues and objectives and of what is said how and when. Leaving that to a third party proved unproductive.

"Customer acquisition and retention are the most crucial elements of scaling your business to global market leadership," Peter Mühlmann stresses. *"Building a productive sales and marketing muscle that scales fast is a key competence for a company like Trustpilot. Leaving that in the hands of others is giving away the control of our most critical business process."*

The international approach

Peter Mühlmann started Trustpilot in 2007 to give consumers shopping online more of a voice and help companies engage with their customers to learn and improve – turning customer feedback into business results. He knew that the business problem he addressed was generic and his ambition for the company was global from the very start.

For the first two years, Trustpilot focused on building a solid position in their domestic market (Denmark) and in 2009 Peter Mühlmann started calling potential customers in the UK. That was difficult, so he hired a native English speaking salesperson and continued the outbound activities from the office in Aarhus. A similar concept was introduced for The Netherlands, Germany and France. With a growing need for foreign-speaking sales staff, the company relocated to Copenhagen.

In the period 2009 to 2013, Trustpilot ran all sales and marketing activities for their European markets out of the Copenhagen office. It was the decision to enter the US market that led to the opening of the first office abroad, in New York, USA.

"I expected that operating offices abroad would add a substantial layer of complexity to our business," says Peter Mühlmann. "However, penetrating a market six to nine time zones away could not be seriously executed and managed out of Copenhagen. We hired an American sales manager and relocated some of our best people to help build the US-operation. With a bit of luck and a lot of hard work, we succeeded."

Since the start in New York in 2013, Trustpilot has opened offices in London (U.K.), Denver (Colorado, USA), Berlin (Germany), Melbourne (Australia) and Vilnius (Lithuania).

"We have the footprint required for consolidating our position as the undisputed market leader in Europe, North America and Australia," says Peter Mühlmann. "We have learned that it is much better to have a leading position in a few markets than just being present in many. While it is possible to bootstrap a market from the outside it is not possible to build a leading position unless you have a serious local operation."

Trustpilot may decide to open offices in more countries, but before making such a decision a thorough market analysis is performed. The need for the company's services is present in all markets and the local competition identified so far is not the main obstacle. The new market must provide the growth potential for rapidly building a business of a certain size.

"A new office must gain critical mass fast," explains Peter Mühlmann. "The initial crew of five must grow to ten within six months and at least twenty within the first year; then we are on the right trajectory. If we fail to achieve this momentum, then we need to invest significant resources in fixing the problems and that will also hurt the attention we have available for other markets."

Finding the right people

Getting market entry right the first time depends entirely on finding the right people to spearhead the endeavour. Trustpilot's policy is to hire a local sales-oriented country manager and relocate two or three experienced salespeople to help build the initial marketing and sales effort. The Trustpilot services require little localisation to match the legal requirements of a new country. These changes can be in place prior to starting outbound activities, but then the company must respond fast to feedback from the market ensuring that sales are not halted by product-related issues.

"Making a hiring mistake on the country manager level is an expensive and time-consuming affair, Peter Mühlmann admits, "It will cause us at least a 12-month setback. There is no silver bullet solution for finding the right country manager other than spending a lot of time with the top candidates before you make the final choice, and then provide them with all the support you can muster."

Another crucial resource in Trustpilot's business model is outbound salespeople, that are also difficult to find. The company, therefore, has a major recruitment and training function that continuously brings in new recruits and trains them for the jobs.

"Predicting if someone can thrive and be productive in an outbound sales job is very difficult," says Peter Mühlmann. "We have found that hiring

junior people and training them ourselves is the fastest way to build the teams we need. Apart from being a software company and a sales machine we also have a sophisticated recruitment and training engine."

A metric-driven revenue generation approach

Using primarily online marketing channels and outbound selling on the phone gives Trustpilot a unique opportunity to monitor and measure performance and their approach to customer acquisition is highly metric-driven.

"Our path to global market leadership is all about fine-tuning our go-to-market approach and the numbers don't lie," says Peter Mühlmann. "If one marketing channel converts better than another, then we need to understand why, fix it or shift our spending. The same goes for sales and customer success."

Optimising the customer acquisition and retention processes are based on learning what produces the best results and then testing and implementing best practises across the board. In addition to measuring the number of calls and milestones achieved, Trustpilot sales-coaches also listen in and help the individual salesperson improve his or her sales performance. Developing successful salespeople is a win-win for both parties. They are more content, make more money and stay longer. Outbound telesales is a tough profession; however, those who master it can stay in the job for many years.

The strategy for global market leadership

Trustpilot's strive for global market leadership is supported by the vision of providing a transparent and managed platform for both sides of the market. Anyone can review any website, and the reviews are visible to the end of time. Reviews can be disputed and Trustpilot's compliance team will look into the matter. Removing reviews can only be done by Trustpilot and not by the party reviewed.

"Trust and transparency are key philosophies of ours," says Peter Mühlmann, "We have customised software that scans the platform around the clock to identify and remove fake reviews and we invest

heavily in making sure you can trust what you read on Trustpilot. To support the software, we have a Compliance Team of around 50 people that investigate all reports of misuse. Allowing our paying customers to filter and suppress reviews would be the end of our commitment to transparency and we would lose the market's trust. That is a road we will never take. What happens on Trustpilot stays on Trustpilot and reviews are published instantly. You cannot pay us to remove a review."

Trustpilot knows better than most that reviews can be faked and that some may be unreasonable and unfair. To manage this side of the business they have established a Compliance Team which is part of a larger unit called Trust & Transparency. The team operates out of Copenhagen, London, New York, Vilnius and Denver. Any company on Trustpilot, whether they are using the Free service or subscribing to one of the paid plans, can report a review if it violates Trustpilot's guidelines. The review is then temporarily hidden while the Compliance Team investigates. If the review can be updated so it complies with Trustpilot's guidelines, the reviewer will be contacted and asked to make the necessary changes. If the review is or can be brought within the guidelines, it will go back online and if it's not, it will stay offline.

Based on the number of reviews and companies reviewed, Trustpilot is the global market leader for non-travel related activities (where TripAdvisor is the market leader). Roughly 1.5 million new reviews are posted each month. This position has been achieved following a very aggressive market expansion strategy supported by venture capital. So far, the company has raised USD 173 million in venture funding.

"Raising USD 173 million can hardly be called a shoestring," Peter Mühlmann concludes. "However, you cannot win this market by bootstrapping growth. It's a race for the pole position and she who comes first will clear the table."

UNICONTA – ERP FOR THE SMB IN THE CLOUD

The customer challenges

Millions of SMB companies and smaller public institutions have a customised ERP system running on in-house servers. Many of them have not upgraded the software to new releases, which has also restricted them from updating the underlying software components. Although the systems run and do the job, they become more and more fragile as the people supporting them move along and the software vendors discontinue updates and bug-fixes. At some point in time, these companies must decide to replace their ERP system and the vast majority of them will move to the cloud-based SaaS format.

Uniconta

However, while many customers do not want to repeat the lock-in situation associated with individual customisations, they still need some special features that the standard systems do not offer. Seeing the move to the cloud-based SaaS format as an opportunity to reduce IT-spending, many of them also don't want in-house IT-staff on the payroll anymore.

"No matter how you spin the marketing lingo, moving from an on-premise solution to the cloud is a fully-fledged migration project," says Erik Damgaard founder and CEO of Uniconta. "Standard out-of-the-box systems are ideal for small companies with just one or very few users, but there are millions of SMB businesses that need customisations and extensions. I have designed Uniconta to satisfy such needs, delivered from the cloud and in a SaaS format."

When Microsoft announced the discontinuation of Dynamics C5 in Denmark and Norway, Erik Damgaard (the architect behind C5) saw an opportunity. He developed Uniconta and included dedicated migration tools for Dynamics C5, e-conomic and Dynamics NAV, the leading ERP-systems for small business in Denmark.

"Data migration has always been a challenge," Erik Damgaard explains. *"It is our strategy to make migration tools available helping customers move to Uniconta with as little effort as possible."*

Customer Value Proposition

The Uniconta customer value proposition has two main elements:

- A comprehensive yet affordable cloud-based standard ERP-system designed for customers in the SMB-market that have individual requirements.

- A channel of Value-Added Resellers that can help customers with extensions, implementation and support.

"SMB customers are not fascinated by IT-technology," Erik Damgaard says. *"But I am, and this passion drives me to make comprehensive and user-friendly software that provides high value for little money. The cloud is a godsend for the SMB-market while it simplifies their use of software and lowers their cost."*

The technical architecture facilitates two types of "customisations":

- Configuration of the standard software package

- Extensions communicating with the core ERP package through an Application Program Interface

"The days of customisations of the core are over," Erik Damgaard stresses. *"It was the solution path we took in the previous century, but not anymore. Instead, we keep adding more configuration options in the standard core and offer an open API for extensions."*

Go-to-market approach

Uniconta has chosen an indirect go-to-market approach through value-added resellers, also called partners. They are primarily responsible for pre-sales, implementation, extensions and post-sales support.

"We take care of building brand awareness and the vast majority of new customers start by downloading a trial version from our web site," says Per Pedersen, EVP sales & marketing. *"Our partners are*

a vital resource for our customers as they provide the extension and implementation support. I prefer calling them ecosystem partners."

Starting out in Denmark, Uniconta has invested heavily in marketing and enjoys very high brand awareness. The one hundred plus partners that signed up just after the launch in 2016 are now productive and have started generating their own customers. Chartered accountants, auditors, documentation authors, free-lance consultants and other service providers are extending the ecosystem.

The Market segmentation

The key market segment for Uniconta is the lower end of the SMB market with 5-20 users across most verticals.

"The market segmentation is primarily decided by the ecosystem," explains Per Pedersen, *"Our partners extend the Uniconta functionality, which brings the software into all corners of the market. This way the partners can differentiate and enjoy high market shares in a specific vertical with little competition from other partners."*

Internationalization

Uniconta was designed as a global product and is distributed in Denmark, Norway, Estonia, Iceland, The Netherlands, Germany, Austria, The UK, South Africa and Egypt.

"We have chosen an international go-to-market approach through distributors," says Per Pedersen. *"Each distributor has exclusive rights and are committed to build brand awareness and recruit partners in her territory."*

The global rollout has primarily been decided by where there were committed people available.

"Building a market for a SaaS product is an entrepreneurial long-term effort," says Per Pedersen. *"It requires experience, stamina, patience, hard work and deep pockets. Such people are hard to find and most of the time they find us."*

The customer acquisition approach is inbound. While all SMB companies are potential customers it is difficult to apply a segmentation that will narrow down on those prepared to migrate within the next 12 months.

"Outbound lead generation is ineffective in this market," Per Pedersen says. "We charge €17 per user per month which makes $2,000 per year for a 10-user subscription. An outbound salesperson should on average be able to close one deal a day if that model should work. We can produce a new customer for less using the outbound approach and improve brand awareness at the same time."

XINK – AN INBOUND SUCCESS STORY

The customer problem

The managing director of a major British company noticed that her staff all had a variety of signature styles in their emails. No two styles were the same. On internal emails that was not a big deal, but on external emails, she found it left an impression of unprofessionalism. She talked to the marketing director about the issue and was told that standards had been designed and distributed for all employees to implement. That was a couple of years ago. Not knowing how to apply an email signature herself, the CEO asked the marketing director to come up with a solution that didn't require intervention by every employee.

The marketing director took the issue to the company's CIO who was responsible for the IT-systems, including the Microsoft Office platform from where all emails were written and submitted. The CIO chartered one of his staff members to search the web for possible solutions.

Among the options was XINK.

The XINK value proposition

Today XINK is a cloud-based email signature solution for companies using Microsoft Office 365 and the G Suite. It moves the task of setting up email signatures away from the individual user and places it at a central point. This is usually in the marketing department. While many companies and government institutions saw the need for maintaining certain corporate identity standards in their emails, using corporate emails for marketing purposes took longer to spread.

"When we started in the autumn of 2003, we already had the idea that corporate email is a marketing channel," says Jesper Frier, COO and co-founder of XINK. "We added campaign management as one of the first features to the platform. However, we were way ahead of the market, and it took some years before marketing managers began to understand the advantage and include it in the requirement specification for an email signature solution."

XINK, that was initially launched under the name eMailSignature, was an on-premise prepaid application and today is exclusively delivered as a cloud-based service. The on-premise version was discontinued in 2018, and support ended as of December 31st, 2018. The price now starts at $1 per user per month and gets discounted with increasing volume. The average sales cycle is one month but varies primarily with the size of the customer. Most deals are closed within the 14-day trial period. The customer base includes all types of companies ranging from 50 and up to 80.000 users. Four thousand customers with a total of two million users are using XINK.

"The acceptance of services like XINK originally had two drivers," Jesper Frier explains. "The need for a consistent corporate identity and the productivity gained from not having thousands of staff members trying to figure out how to implement and maintain manual signature templates. The third driver, the benefits of using emails for marketing purposes, took much longer to mature."

Revenue generation – a complex purchase process

Although the style of corporate emails is a marketing issue, the process for finding a tool for central template management has mostly been left to the IT-department.

"Most purchase processes involve two or three buying centres," Jesper Frier stresses. "Marketing and IT are always involved. Sometimes the CFO also has a say if not only to decide from which budget to pay."

Even though the first contact is from a marketing person, XINK always recommends that the IT-department get involved right from the start. Involving them at the end of the selection process often makes the process come to a halt and delays the decision.

The revenue generation approach was initially outbound and directed at potential customers that the founders already knew or knew of. Later, a call centre was engaged to book meetings with potential customers. The initial sales meeting, which was always face-to-face, was also a learning session as only a few potential customers were aware of the issues and potential around corporate email signatures.

"Our initial approach was expensive and difficult to scale," explains Jesper Frier. "We needed salespeople that could cover the marketing side of the solution and also answer the questions associated with the technical implementation. The price of the solution didn't justify having two people involved. Finding salespeople that could bridge the two domains was difficult, if not impossible, to find."

It was a pilot project selling into the German market in 2007 that demonstrated the potential of outbound telesales. Following an EU directive requiring that all business emails must include an authorised EU email disclaimer with the company's registration number, the place of registration and the registered office address, XINK engaged a telesales centre in Wilhelmshaven to call potential customers. Interested prospects were directed to a German version of the website from where they could download a trial. Face-to-face meetings were not offered, but a German-speaking person would answer questions. The pilot project paid for itself but was not scaled (see below). After stopping the outbound call activity in Germany, leads continued to appear. The EU directive stimulated the search for email signature solutions, and XINK's German website attracted the traffic.

"It was around 2005, and especially following the activity in Germany, that we started investing in online marketing activities," remembers Jesper Frier. "The market had matured, and through organic and paid search we could generate a substantial flow of visits and trial-downloads. Now we just needed to find ways to improve the conversion rates."

From 2005 to 2014, XINK refined their online marketing activities and primarily followed an inbound revenue generation process. The primary challenge remained the need for dealing with the two purchase centres, marketing and IT, of which IT was the most difficult to handle. IT-departments are typically overloaded with work and can be very restrictive when introducing new software applications.

To reduce the IT-component of the solution, XINK launched a cloud-based version at the end of 2013. The IT effort was now reduced to a 45-minute activity.

"With the cloud version we were convinced that we could sell to the marketing team without the need to involve the IT-department," says Jesper Frier. *"We, therefore, invested heavily in outbound lead generation activities, only to find out that we were wrong."*

Running outbound lead generation and sales activities in 2014 and 2015, XINK learned that too many cases were lost because the IT-department didn't get involved upfront. Although the market had matured considerably since the start in 2003, it was also still difficult to predict which types of customers would be most receptive to introducing central email signature template management and which kind of customers would consider corporate emails a marketing channel. Summing up, the conversion rates were too low for the outbound approach to yield a positive ROI.

"We were not able to make the outbound revenue generation approach profitable," admits Jesper Frier. *"We tried all types of variations but couldn't find the right mix of market segmentation and sales approach. One reason may also be that none of us enjoyed performing the tight sales management that an outbound approach requires."*

In 2016, XINK returned to the inbound approach and have since managed to maintain a thirty per cent annual growth rate. Significant investments were made in the web site, and live chat is now available 24/7 in all time zones where XINK can respond instantly to questions from potential customers worldwide.

"The inbound revenue generation approach, with virtual meetings only, works very well for us," Jesper Frier says. *"It is much easier to manage and doesn't require that our people gather at the same locations."*

To complete the picture, XINK also tried to build an indirect channel of resellers, which wasn't successful either.

"Today we have 50 resellers, and the secret behind their success is that they approached us," says Jesper Frier. "Outbound reseller recruitment never worked for us. Finding the level of engagement required was like finding the famous needle in a haystack. Potential resellers continually approach us, and we can now pick those with whom we have a shared mindset."

Internationalisation

XINK has customers in more than 100 countries, and the internationalisation started when XINK launched its first English website in 2005. Over the years XINK has had operations in Denmark, Germany, Australia, the UK and the USA with various types of setups and engagement formats.

"Neither Bjarne Mess (founder and CTO) nor I have an appetite or a talent for people management," Jesper Frier emphases. "In our current setup, all our people invoice us. We pay a fair fixed monthly fee and then a result-based commission or bonus on top."

All XINK people work out of their home and enjoy this type of arrangement. Meetings are virtual, and most of the "staff" have never met each other in person.

"There are plenty of highly qualified people looking for a flexible workspace," says Jesper Frier. "We have never believed in the value of the traditional office, spending time on commuting and conducting annual performance reviews. We deal with issues here and now and leave it to the individual how to perform his or her tasks. We start with a high level of trust and then see where that takes us."

Today XINK is operating from multiple locations covering all time zones (sales/support).

"With our current approach we don't care where people are located," says Jesper Frier. "We also don't need to meet in person before we hire someone. It is done online. We offer competitive remuneration packages

and freedom that you don't find in most other jobs. That freedom is something people all over the world enjoy and appreciate."

Going forward, Jesper and Bjarne realise that penetrating the non-English speaking markets (such as Germany, France, Italy, China etc.) require localisation and different operational setups. However, as long as the demand from the English-speaking markets supports an annual growth of 30-50 per cent, they see little reason for diverting from their current business model.

"We are becoming masters of inbound revenue generation and the virtual global operational setup," Jesper Frier concludes. "Global demand is picking up, and we have a profitable model for getting our fair share. Compared to our competitors, our setup is by far the most profitable. For the foreseeable future, we will continue down that path."

XOLO - SUPPORTING THE GIG-ECONOMY

The customer problem

The term gig-economy covers the phenomenon where more and more people choose to work as freelancers. They are paid by the hour, for a project or a delivery and do not have an exclusive arrangement with any employer. The term is borrowed from the entertainment industry where musicians are paid per performance – the gig.

Just as in the entertainment industry, the variations in pay and engagement conditions in the gig-economy are enormous. Some join it because they cannot find permanent employment, and some choose it because it pays better and offers more attractive working conditions than permanent employment. Driving for Uber in New Delhi is a gig. Playing for an audience of 100,000 people at Wembley is a gig.

A substantial chunk of the gig-economy is organised around digital marketplaces where supply can meet demand. Uber is such a marketplace for transportation services, Meploy for manual labour, Toptal for software engineering, Upwork for all sorts of professional services, while Codeable is a marketplace for vetted WordPress experts.

At the very top of the gig-economy, we find the Rolling Stones, Barack Obama, Oprah Winfrey and other celebrities who basically decide what they will charge. Behind them are a team of people taking care of business.

In the next layer, you have the thousands of specialised solo professionals that can also charge attractive fees for their work. Still, they don't want to spend on the administrative overheads that running a business requires. They typically organise as a limited company from which they invoice their clients and from where they pay expenses, a salary to themselves and take out a profit.

The advantages for the specialised solo professional are apparent. You can work where and when you prefer. Provided you understand how to promote and sell your services, you can live a comfortable life without needing to go to the same office every day, without a boss that you don't like or respect and without getting embroiled in corporate politics. If your services are in high demand, you can decide to work on the projects of your choice and only the hours you prefer.

On the demand side of the market, companies increasingly use specialised solo professionals for projects where they don't have the expertise inhouse, where the type and duration of the activity doesn't justify a permanent headcount or where there is an outspoken shortage of talent. If there was a fire on the oil rig, you called Red Adair (1915-2004), and you didn't negotiate the price. He is the originator of the famous quote:

"If you think it's expensive to hire a professional to do the job, wait until you hire an amateur."

The gig-economy for specialised professionals grows because both sides of the market like the idea and can benefit from a project-driven relationship.

The dark side of gig-economy where you as an individual become a company is the administrative overheads that follows. As a solo freelancer, you are responsible for all activities including business development, marketing, sales, invoicing, accounting, tax and VAT-reporting, salary payments (to yourself) and the closing and filing of the annual report and tax forms. Performing all the back-office administration and ensuring that you comply with the legislation can be both tedious, time-consuming and costly. And more often than not, this is not what the specialised professional is best at.

The Estonian e-citizenship

In December 2014 the Estonian government launched a program that allows non-Estonians access to services such as company formation, banking, payment processing, and taxation. Anyone can apply and, provided you are qualified, receive the e-citizen package, including the smart card that allows you to interact with government services and sign official documents such as registering a company.

This allows anyone to start and run a company out of Estonia without ever having to set foot on Estonian soil. Everything can be done electronically using the digital infrastructure and signature that has been implemented throughout the country.

While the e-citizen program is available to anyone, it is particularly attractive to residents of other EU countries. Because of the Single Market and SEPA legislation within the EU, it is easy and inexpensive to do business across borders, including issuing invoices and moving funds. You can invoice a business client in another EU country without the need for paying withholding tax or adding VAT. You can pay out a salary to yourself and have it taxed in your country of residence and Estonia doesn't tax profits that stay within the company. Only when you pay out dividends do you have to pay the twenty per cent corporation tax and whatever rate for which your country of residence asks. Most, and all EU, countries have tax agreements with Estonia so that double taxation can be avoided.

XOLO - taking care of business

With this backdrop, XOLO, in the fall of 2015 (then named LeapIN), launched a software platform for people who would like to take advantage of the Estonian e-citizen opportunity. XOLO includes company registration, a bank account, a credit card, a bookkeeping system and all the services required to comply with Estonian legislation such as tax and VAT reporting and the filing of the annual report. All for a fixed monthly fee of €79. All you have to do is issue your invoices and upload your expenses. XOLO takes care of the rest. It's a managed service, and all interactions are performed electronically.

Although there are no restrictions on what type of business you can run out of your Estonian company (provided it's legal!), XOLO has decided to focus entirely on the solo-entrepreneur, boutique-consultant and the freelancer.

"It is a strategic marketing decision," says Allan Martinson, CEO at XOLO. "We specialise in making the life of the individual business operator as easy and inexpensive as possible. They all want to spend

their time on client projects. We offer to take care of the back-office and do the housekeeping for them."

The narrow focus seems to have paid off. With a website in English only, XOLO has managed to attract several thousand customers from over a hundred different countries.

XOLO GO

In 2019 XOLO launched the new product GO offering the full package of services without the need for the e-citizenship. The GO service is designed for residents of EU countries provided they do business with customers that have a valid VAT number (B2B transactions). Freelancers now run their businesses in a partnership from a dedicated XOLO registered company. Invoices are issued from the XOLO legal entity, and expenses are also paid by the same. The individual GO account has a dedicated bank account to where revenue flows and from where expenses are paid. The freelancer can withdraw any available amount from his or her GO account at any time. The charge is five per cent of outgoing payments, and there is no initial setup fee.

"With XOLO GO we have lowered the threshold for freelancers substantially," says Allan Martinson. "Our clients are up and running in less than half an hour, and there is no fixed monthly fee to worry about. When the business picks up, GO customers can switch to LEAP and enjoy the same service at a fixed monthly flat rate."

Shoptech.media

Benny Holgaard, a Danish national, became a XOLO user in 2019. Since 2012 he has been running Shoptech.media, a company specialising in building and managing web-shops. In 2014 he decided to leave Denmark and travel the world. Since his work didn't require him to be at any specific place at any particular time, he was looking for an administrative platform from where he could run his business.

"Taking care of my clients while on the road is not a problem at all," explains Benny Holgaard, currently locked down due to the Coronavirus in Cordova in the Philippines. "However, maintaining the

administrative back-office cores with payments, bank transfers and taxation turned out to be a nightmare."

Leaving Denmark, Benny Holgaard incorporated in Seychelles while still having his bank account in Denmark. That combination turned out to be toxic, and the overheads associated with continually having to prove that his business activities were legitimate kept growing.

"The Estonian E-citizenship was exactly what I needed," says Benny Holgaard," and the combination of XOLO and Transferwise has taken all my back-office troubles away."

The clients are invoiced from the Estonian company, and payments are made via Transferwise to an account by a German bank. Serving his clients' different web-shops, Benny uses a pool of freelancers with whom he has long-lasting relationships. They need to be paid on time, and with Transferwise he can ensure both swift turnaround and low transaction fees.

"I picked up my E-citizen package last year at the Estonian Embassy in Tokyo where I was passing through at the time," says Benny Holgaard. "Getting incorporated and setting up the XOLO back-office was easy. They have also helped me streamline my contractual relationships with the freelancers, which was previously based on oral or email agreements. XOLO takes care of the administration, leaving me free to travel and take care of my clients."

Shoptech.media is a simple virtual business, and all the clients have found Benny Holgaard either through word of mouth or through the online groups in which he is very active. At the beginning his clients were Danish, but this year the mix will be fifty-fifty.

"We have built a reputation of being technically competent, business savvy and highly responsive," explains Benny Holgaard. "People that are serious about e-commerce find us and become our clients."

Building and maintaining web-shops is a global industry, and the needs of the clients are identical across national borders and cultures.

It's about attracting traffic, improving conversion rates and increasing basket size. Benny Holgaard's approach to helping his clients make more money seems to work.

Windjammer IT Services OÜ

Christoffer Bjørg Pedersen is an IT freelancer currently based in Brazil. He runs his business under the name Windjammer IT Services OÜ.

"I was actually based in Portugal," says Christoffer. "We were just visiting Brazil for a few months, but due to the Corona-crisis I don't know when we can leave again."

Christoffer does freelance gigs as an IT-consultant and is currently in a long-term engagement with a client incorporated in the UK.

"My client is fully virtual," Christoffer explains. "The people are scattered all over the globe, and I am not even sure anyone is working out of the UK."

Leaving Denmark in 2011, Christoffer first settled in Sweden and then in Latvia. When he relocated to Montenegro, he also registered a legal entity there. The bureaucracy was significant and expensive, and as he decided to travel on, the Estonian e-citizenship seemed the right solution.

"For a digital nomad such as me, XOLO and the Estonian e-citizenship is perfect," says Christoffer. "XOLO takes care of all the back-office duties and they are also accommodating with questions related to payments and taxation."

For the time being, Christoffer has a Transferwise account and credit card for his business activities. Customers pay invoices to this account, and from there he can pay his business expenses and transfer funds to his private accounts in Sweden and Portugal.

"The bigger issues associated with being a digital nomad are banking and personal taxation," Christoffer explains. "There are two options for taking out funds from the Estonian company. As a salary or as a profit.

Either way, you will have to decide where you declare the personal income for taxation, and that is not easy if you are not a permanent resident anywhere."

So far Christoffer has, with help from friends familiar with the paperwork, filed tax reports in Montenegro, Sweden, and Brazil.

"The number of digital nomads such as me is growing very fast, and we need more flexible frameworks for the money side of our activities," Christoffer concludes. *"Being a digital nomad is a lifestyle and not a tax avoidance scheme."*

APPENDIX 1

THE list of software below is by no means meant as an endorsement. I am sure there are alternatives with which I am not familiar and that may be just as good or even better. I have found or been recommended all the software products or services listed and for most of them I have never been in touch with the vendor.

Mindmanager from Mindjet (Corel)

I use Mindmanager for brainstorming and organising ideas. It's one of the most expensive apps that I use, but when it comes to developing ideas and organising my thoughts, it does the job.

https://www.mindjet.com

FreeConferenceCall

Most of the interviews have been made with FreeConferenceCall. It's the only web meeting app that I know of that offers free dial-in with local numbers from most countries. For a few interviews I used Skype.

https://www.freeconferencecall.com

Scrivener from Latte & Literature

This and my other books are primarily written using the app Scrivener, which is developed specifically for authors.

I have Scrivener on both of my Macs and my iPad and can write from wherever I happen to be.

https://www.literatureandlatte.com/scrivener/overview

Microsoft 365

Being an Apple Mac user I don't often use Microsoft Office. However, as the Microsoft file formats are widely used it makes sense to have the apps. I would like to use Microsoft teams but haven't figured out how to upgrade from my current package.

https://www.office.com

Apple Apps

With an Apple Mac comes a series of free apps such as Mail, Calendar, Reminders, Notes, Contacts, Pages, Numbers, Keynote, iMovie, Photos, Dictionary, Maps, Music, Podcasts, TV, Preview, Voice Memos, Books, Time Machine and many, many more. I use most of these on a daily basis.

I prefer to use Apple Pages as the common file format for editors and proofreaders. The track changes facility in Pages is much better than in Word.

https://www.apple.com

EndNote X9

EndNote X9 is a citation management app. Although my writing is not academic and scientific, I do like to give credit to the authors that I read and use for inspiration. EndNote helps me do that.

https://endnote.com

Trello

My support team of freelancers is spread across the globe and Trello is the tool we use for assigning and managing tasks.

https://trello.com

Snagit

Although not used in this book, Snagit is my favourite tool for capturing images from websites.

https://www.techsmith.com/screen-capture.html

TextExpander

This simple tool allows me to assign text strings to a few keystrokes. For example when I type the letters bd TextExpander replaces the two letters with business development and bme is replaced with business model environment. When using the same phrases repeatedly TextExpander is a genuine timesaver.

https://textexpander.com

CopyPaste Pro

CopyPaste Pro gives you a library of the most recent text strings that you have copied. Again, a lovely timesaver.

https://plumamazing.com/product/copypaste-pro-for-mac/

Adobe Acrobat Pro

When I have completed the manuscript for the book I export the text and illustrations to a Word document that I submit to my graphic designer, Jelena Galkina in Tallinn. She does the pagination and returns a PDF-file. From this point forward PDF become the working format and I have found that Adobe Acrobat is the best tool for collaboration in this format.

https://acrobat.adobe.com/us/en/acrobat/acrobat-pro.html

Kindle Previewer

From Scrivener I can export directly to the mobi format. I use the Kindle Preview App to verify the quality and spot any corrections that are required.

ACKNOWLEDGEMENTS

THANK you to Nabil Freij and Sérgio Baptista for reviewing the manuscript and offering great suggestions for editorial precisions and improvements.

My colleague at TBK Consult, Steen Helmer, has helped find the cases for the book. I also want to thank those that volunteered to tell their stories. They are Mercedes McCoy (Epic), Ashley Gibson (Epic), Jesper Valentin Holm and Rasmus Houlind (Agillic), Patrick Hulsen (Cambio, previously Daintel), Morten Steiner (CIO at PFA Pension in Denmark), Gert Bendsen (Edlund), Kasper Lyhr (First Agenda), Dennis Kayser (Forecast), Jonas Vognsen (IT-Minds), Michael Gram (MapsPeople), Johan Holmsten (Monitor ERP), Olaf Hasker (NetDialog), Bo Martinsen (Norriq), Aylin T. Özden (ProManage), Karsten Busck (Pronestor), Odd Magne Vea (RamBase), Rick Pizzoli (Sales Force Europe), Ugne Kontare (Soft4), Allan Thorvaldsen (SoftScan), Nilüfer Durak (Solvoyo), Jesper Theill Eriksen (Templafy), Anders S. Rosenbeck (Tia Technology), Heine Krog Iversen (TimeXtender), Peter Mühlmann (Trustpilot), Per Steen Pedersen (Uniconta), Jesper Frier (XINK), Allan Martinson (XOLO), Niels Henrik Rasmussen (Penneo), Gönül Kamali (YASAD), Øystein Syversen (FotoWare), Benny Holgaard (Shoptech.media) and Christoffer Bjørg Pedersen (Windjammer IT Services). Thank you to Jan Kold (NNIT) for making the connection to Epic.

I have been fortunate to have Melonie Dodaro, author of several books on how to use LinkedIn for marketing and sales purposes, review and make valuable comments to chapter eight.

Grit Neumann, senior online marketing consultant at the German company Ströer, gave me an introduction to SEO.

Gönül Kamali, Gregorio Navarro, Allan Martinson and Pamela Campagna have reviewed the manuscript and offered their pre-publishing comments. I am thankful for their input and endorsements.

A special thank you to Marylou Tyler for writing the foreword. I have been a big fan of Marylou ever since she published her first book, Predictable Revenue, in 2011. I was fortunate to join her for a breakfast-meeting in August 2018, when she did a project for a client in Copenhagen.

Emma Crabtree proofed the manuscript, and Jelena Galkina designed the cover and paginated the printed version. I have worked with Emma and Jelena for years and appreciate their excellent work.

ABOUT THE AUTHOR

Hans Peter Bech is a bestselling author and a frequent blogger on how to make information technology companies global market leaders. He has produced numerous books, papers, podcasts and videos on international business development in the IT industry. Hans Peter is also a keynote speaker, workshop facilitator, and an advisor for governments and companies. He holds a M.Sc. in macroeconomics and political science from the University of Copenhagen.